D0374789

The Closing of the Door

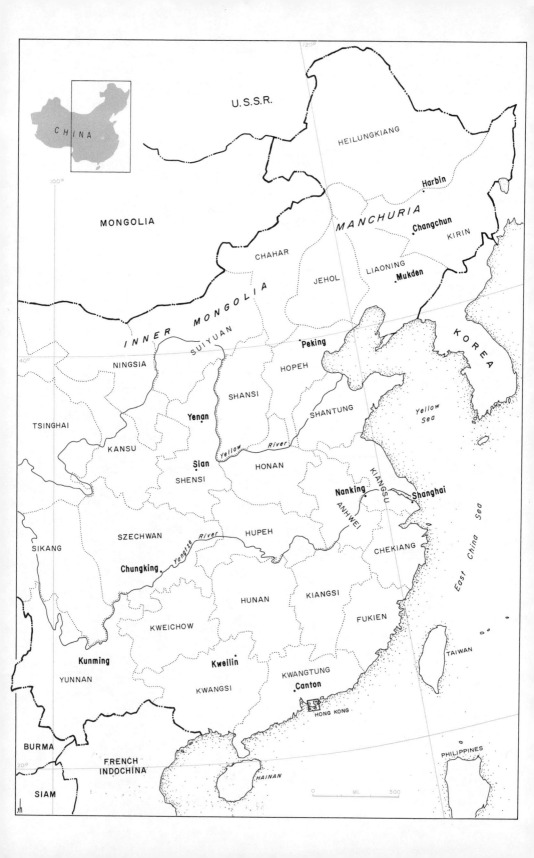

THE
Closing of the Door

SINO-AMERICAN RELATIONS
1936-1946

by
PAUL A. VARG

MICHIGAN STATE UNIVERSITY PRESS

1973

★
★
★
★
★

TO

Richard, Steven and Michael

Contents

Preface

In 1949, as the Communists achieved their victory in China and the government of Chiang Kai-shek fled to Taiwan, there were those who jested at the prospect of Taiwan occupying a position as a great power in the Security Council of the United Nations. The apparent absurdity of it did not prevent its taking place. For more than twenty years the myth of Chiang's Taiwan regime representing China was maintained, and the United States refused to enter into diplomatic relations with the mainland government. Both the United States and the People's Republic of China conjured up fears of each other. Only time proved adequate to restoring the light so that mutual rivalries and common interests could be seen realistically.

This volume seeks to analyze the developments during and after World War II, developments that led to the blackness of a long night. The American China policy created great controversy in the United States, arousing strong emotions that made the effort at objective analysis difficult and perhaps even hazardous. The question of the United States' position likewise became a political issue in China. Parties on both sides of the Pacific exploited it for political gain.

The American historian may reasonably hope to rise above the internal controversy but he confronts a more formidable intellectual task in seeking to understand the forces at work in the highly nationalistic and very fundamental social revolution that has taken place in China. The observer's own value system is likely to appear threatened and his response to be more emotional than rational. Yet to understand the other man's values is necessary if reason is to prevail in the complex world of international affairs. The author cannot presumptuously claim to have overcome his own parochialism. He, too, sees the world from his own vantage point, but he has sought desperately to be aware of this shortcoming.

The conflict between the United States and the Chinese Communists was cradled by differences in national interests, rival ambitions, and the perversity nourished by parochial moralism. Who was at fault is an irrelevant question, but a modest measure of understanding the reasons for the conflict is a requisite for improved relations in the future.

Only recently has the necessary source material become available to the public. Virtually all documents are now open to the scholar. These number in the thousands. The author is deeply indebted to the staff in the Contemporary Military Records branch of the National Archives; Thomas Hohmann gave generously of his time, and without his amazing knowledge of the records the author would soon have lost his way. The staffs at the Manuscript Room in the Library of Congress, the Franklin D. Roosevelt Memorial Library at Hyde Park, the library of the University of Oklahoma, where the papers of Patrick Hurley are deposited, and the Hoover War Memorial Library at Stanford University were more than generous in providing assistance.

The author is deeply indebted to Warren Cohen and Paul Sweet, his colleagues in the Department of History at Michigan State University, who read the final manuscript with meticulous care and who made many helpful suggestions. Harold Jacobson, a retired officer of the Department of State who served in China during the latter part of World War II and during the Marshall Mission, provided insights that only an observer of events could offer and he likewise took time to read the manuscript. Russell Buhite, Professor of History at the University of Oklahoma, who read parts of the manuscript, likewise was most helpful. The title of the book was suggested by my young friend, David Jones. Of course, the views expressed are the author's and they do not necessarily accord with those who provided valuable guidance.

The American Philosophical Society and Michigan State University contributed financial assistance which made possible the travel to the libraries throughout the country. Finally, Collen Heron, of the Asian Studies Center at Michigan State University, and the author's wife typed the manuscript. The author owes a very special debt to his wife, Helen, who not only typed many drafts before the final one, but also for her infinite patience in making sacrifices and for providing encouragement.

PAUL A. VARG
East Lansing, Michigan

The Closing of the Door

CHAPTER I

Prewar Relations
of the United States and China

In September 1935 Stanley Hornbeck, a veteran diplomat, observed that there was nothing peculiar about the United States' Open Door Policy in China. It was no more than a part of general foreign policy. "It is not," Hornbeck contended, "the policy of the American Government gratuitously or impertinently to inject itself into controversies which arise in or with regard to the Far East." He stated "The United States has certain rights, certain obligations, and certain legitimate interests in the Far East and in each country there, just as it has elsewhere." While it was the duty of the American government to look after "American rights, obligations and legitimate interests abroad," Hornbeck wanted it clearly understood that the United States "is committed by treaty not to the maintenance of the integrity of China, but to the creation of respect for the integrity of China."[1]

Hornbeck's statement reflected a period of great caution when the United States wished to avoid provocation of Japan. However, this position differed only in a minor degree from the underlying course the United States had pursued toward China since the writing of the Open Door Notes in 1899. Two basic reasons account for the policy pursued: first, China, in and by itself, was of limited importance to the United States; and, second, the balance of power in East Asia served to protect American interests so well that the United States did not find it necessary to be assertive. In the north, Russia and Japan, facing each other, provided a check on the ambitions of both, while in the south, England, France, and the Netherlands had created a stable order. Not until this established order in East Asia was threatened with an extensive reshuffling after the outbreak of World War II did the United States follow a bolder course.

This is not to minimize American concerns in Eastern Asia during the first four decades of the century nor is it to contend that Americans were indifferent to developments in China. Some Americans did take an interest in China's modernization, looking toward China as a future market. And a few Americans did believe that if the balance of power in East Asia were upset, American interests would be seriously endangered. Likewise, official policy did call for a zealous defense of the treaty rights Americans had acquired, and which were far from minor in nature; these included the right of extraterritoriality, the right to establish residence and do business in treaty ports, the right to pay no higher tariff duties than those prescribed by treaty, the right to navigate the Yangtze River, and the right to conduct missionary work. Because the United States was a party to the unequal treaties it was a party to Western imperialism.

At the same time the United States persistently protested new acquisitions of territory by foreign powers, enlargement of the treaty rights within the spheres of influence, and threats to China's independence and territorial and administrative integrity. These protests appealed to the public's sense of fair play. Consequently, they were magnified and came to be viewed as *the* American policy toward China. As a result, a myth arose that the United States was China's great defender as she suffered from foreign imperialism.

The American public's interest in China was threefold: religious and humanitarian, economic, and strategic. What each contributed to the making of government policy calls for analysis.

The myth of a philanthropic policy toward China thrived in the United States because at the nonpolitical level there were close and friendly relations. The work of hundreds of missionaries—preachers, teachers, and doctors—provided the chief tie. By the 1920s Chinese nationalism evoked strong feelings of antagonism to the educational and medical efforts of Americans, but transfer of control of schools and hospitals to the Chinese helped mitigate the hostility and by the 1930s Chinese nationalism was absorbed in countering the Japanese intrusions rather than the philanthropic efforts of Americans. In the overall development of Chinese modernization the missionaries made at most a modest contribution, but the thirteen American sponsored colleges and the scores of elementary and middle schools made firm friends for the United States.

On the other hand, however, the missionaries wielded great influence at home. The innumerable articles they contributed to the religious press and the thousands of accounts they gave to church audiences while they were on furlough did more to give form to the American image of China than all other factors combined. The industry of the Chinese, their ingenuity, their fatalism in the face of tragedy, and the prospect, however much an illusion, that they were turning to Christianity and would embrace western political and social ideals caused churchgoers to feel a responsibility for what happened in the Middle Kingdom. Only a few missionaries came to have more than a most superficial understanding of the drive of the Chinese for modernization and of the nationalistic fervor that caused the Chinese to look upon all foreigners as intruders, and these friends of China did not grasp the depth of the difficulties faced by the Chinese. These limitations, however, did not stand in the way of a feeling of sympathy for the Chinese as victims of others' imperialism, for their suffering in times of floods, droughts, and famines, and for the efforts of the Chinese to free themselves from a benighted past and their struggle to achieve modernization.

And American expectation that China was on the verge of modernizing furnished the strongest bond. That a modernized China would bear a striking similarity to America in terms of political, economic, and social ideals was assumed. Western intellectual imagination could scarcely be expected to foresee that a modernized China would, thanks to the felt needs arising out of her past and the unmitigated economic pressures confronting her, have a radically different orientation. Spared this fear, the missionary picture of great need, great human resources, and China's apparent looking to the West took hold of the American mind.

This particular stream of American thought flowed quite independently of that other stream of security and economic considerations that in the long run tended to be the real determinants of national policy. In spite of public goodwill and efforts of missionary boards to shape the government policy toward China, the missionaries were notably unsuccessful in doing so. The executive branch of the American government did exert itself to uphold the treaty rights of the missionaries but gave almost no weight to missionary opinion in making policy decisions.

Officers of the American government found it necessary to take into account national economic and strategic interests, and the dangerous opposition the United States would confront from Japan and Russia who had a much greater stake in China both economically and in terms of their own security. With very few exceptions, the course pursued was one of caution. Economic and security considerations were usually found not to warrant a bold course which would arouse the antagonism of the other powers in Asia.

In the late 1890s and the first several years of the new century the dream of a great China market for American goods thrived. A combination of New York merchants engaged in the China trade and of southern textile manufacturers who had recently discovered a demand for cheap cotton goods in northern China conjured up great dreams of a day when four hundred million Chinese would take care of the new surpluses produced by American industry. In 1898 these two groups came together to organize the American Asiatic Association for the purpose of promoting trade with the Chinese.[2] This association, in turn, gained ready entry into the editorial and news columns of the influential New York *Journal of Commerce.* Officers of the American Asiatic Association pushed their cause in Washington, where they readily gained a hearing from members of the Department of State whose special responsibility was American relations with the Orient.

The great China market proved to be a myth. The greatest barriers were in China. That country was virtually self-sufficient and had no great need to trade. Secondly, the limited transportation system reached only the people along the coast and in the lower reaches of the Yangtze. The lack of Chinese purchasing power provided another barrier. Moreover, the new American interest in China as a market coincided with two developments in China that discouraged trade. China, saddled with both indemnity payments and loans after the Boxer Revolt of 1900 had an unfavorable balance of international payments which, in turn, discouraged imports. In addition, especially in the years from the Russo-Japanese War to the Chinese revolution of 1912, the value of Chinese currency fluctuated widely with a consequent adverse effect on trade. The operation of these several forces withered away the earlier optimism, although from time to time there were manifestations of new hopes.

The apathy of American business and the absence of any aggressive government support contributed to the decline of earlier expectations. American business, at the turn of the century, failed to establish the banking facilities necessary to finance trade. Very few enterprises took the trouble to send their own representatives to push sales. Finally, American exporters were notably negligent in providing the kind of packaging of goods necessary to assure their good condition upon arrival and that would appeal to the Chinese trade. The government was equally lax. Prior to World War I, American consuls were poorly paid and shamefully housed. Several of those who served in China did so in a perfunctory fashion and brought no distinction to the consular service.[3]

Beyond the limitation of the American effort to capture the China market and that market's limitations, Americans faced the most severe kind of competition. Great Britain, Germany, France, Russia, and Japan exerted greater effort simply because they did not have the vast home market that American business enjoyed. Consequently, European and Japanese merchants were more aggressive. Their governments were likewise more supportive of their search for markets and in promoting trade.

American trade with China never amounted to more than three percent of the total of American foreign trade before 1930 and only slightly more after that date. American banking played a similar minor role. In the middle of the nineteenth century American shipping in China closely rivaled that of Great Britain, but from 1900 to 1920 American shipping accounted for an average of only 1.2 percent of all foreign shipping in China and of only 5 percent from 1920 to 1940.[4] Americans played almost no part in the financing of Chinese railroads. In the field of manufacturing, by 1936 British investments totaled more than $179 million, Japanese investments were some $134 million, while American investments totaled only $9.5 million.[5] This American manufacturing investment is especially interesting when compared with the 1940 estimated value of American missionary property in China of some $40 million or when compared with the $20 million American contributions to the Chinese famine relief in 1921.

In spite of the very limited economic interests, the American government never showed any reluctance to call upon China to protect American business enterprises. Nor did it hesitate to protest when other governments or their nationals interfered with American business. Yet Washington did no more than defend their rights under the treaty system. Moreover, the experience of previous decades did not create in the business community any great hope of a thriving trade if they did gain more active government support.

Security considerations entered into policy debates throughout the years 1900 to 1939, although the dangers appeared remote rather than imminent during most of this period. In the late 1890s Brooks Adams envisaged strong power-political reasons for developing close economic ties between the United States and China. The decline of England and the rise of Germany and especially the potential strength of Russia, given her great natural resources and favorable location, caused Adams to believe that the future of Western civilization would depend upon the United States. She must assume the role England had played. In this future struggle for power there lay great danger that China with her vast potential would serve as an ally of Russia. Therefore, Adams argued, American security depended upon countering Russian influence with strong commercial ties.[6]

The impact of Brooks Adams' thinking was limited, but security considerations received considerable attention after the acquisition of the Philippines at the close of the Spanish-American War. Acquisition brought with it the responsibility of protecting those remote islands. However, at no time in the next forty years did the United States achieve sufficient power to carry out the defense of the Philippines against a Japanese attack, but the responsibility remained and entered into calculations. Theodore Roosevelt described the islands as the American's Achilles' heel.[7] Japanese seizure of some of the German-held islands during the early months of World War I gave rise to wider concern. Woodrow Wilson, at the cabinet meeting where the decision was made to declare war on Germany, raised the question of Japan and went so far as to state that he would not call for war if it were clear that Japan would seize the opportunity to expand across the Pacific.[8] At the close of World War I Japan's strength as a naval power aroused widespread fears of future conflict.

American failure to pursue a firm policy of support for China's territorial and administrative integrity became even more pronounced in the years 1933 to 1938. The Manchurian Incident of September 1931 evoked public criticism of Japan and Secretary of State Henry Stimson cooperated with the League of Nations, but neither the League nor the Hoover administration chose to confront the Japanese with firm measures. The United States contented itself with refusing to recognize the Japanese puppet state of Manchuko and with participation in the Lytton Commission which conducted an on-the-scene investigation of the Manchurian development. These steps seemed to be aimed more at assuring the Chinese of American friendliness rather than support. In this respect they accurately reflected the long-established habit of bestowing a paternalistic sympathetic interest in China while at the same time deliberately eschewing meaningful opposition to Japan.

When the Roosevelt Administration came into power in March 1933, a further backing off from involvement took place. As Dorothy Borg has shown in her painstaking and scholarly study, avoidance of conflict with Japan became the major guideline of Roosevelt's policy from 1933 to 1938. Early in May 1933 China's premier, Wang Ching-wei, instructed his minister in Washington to explore with Stanley Hornbeck the possibility of the United States taking the lead in arranging mediation of the Sino-Japanese conflict. Hornbeck was led to believe that the Chinese entertained the hope "that the President of the United States might become seized with the idea of an offer on his part to assume the role of mediator or of taking the lead in organizing a movement among the major governments either toward united action calling upon Japan to halt or toward calling upon the disputants to call an armistice and proceed to negotiation." Hornbeck explained to the Chinese minister that the United States adhered to the position that it was more logical for the League or for Great Britain and France, whose interests were much greater in North China, to take the initiative. Hornbeck, in a separate section of the memorandum, clearly intended for the Secretary of State, maintained that negotiation could only result in China's capitulation and that it was better to have the situation remain fluid. Russia and Great Britain stood to lose much by further Japanese conquests, but the United States did not have much to lose. Hornbeck emphasized that in the area of Peking and Tientsin "there is nothing that is vital to us."[9]

Hornbeck, Director of the Far Eastern Division, continued to deplore China's losses, but, as we have noted, he also persisted in advocating a position of aloofness. Not until late in 1937 did Hornbeck begin to change his position. At that time he was asked for his views on a proposal by the Treasury Department. This involved a commercial transaction whereby the United States would finance the purchase by the recently formed Chinese trading company in New York of 180,000 tons of tung oil. The Chinese government was to receive either payment in full immediately or over the next three years, and it was estimated that the amount of the total payment would be $43,200,000. The purpose of the proposal was clearly to assist China in her war effort.

Hornbeck pointed out that Japan would view the transaction as a departure from neutrality. This did not disturb Hornbeck, but he argued that by itself this would not alter the course of events. The United States should, he contended, develop a full-scale program for assisting China in an effective degree and accept the fact that this would probably mean war and therefore the United States should prepare for this eventuality. In November 1938, and for the first time, Hornbeck called for a comprehensive general plan to halt Japanese "predatory imperialism."[10] But, while Hornbeck, was now prepared to chart a new course, Secretary of State Cordell Hull was not and he advised President Roosevelt accordingly. He argued that China had sufficient military supplies to continue resistance for another six to twelve months. Clearly, Hull believed it was wiser to delay the decision.[11]

Not until Japan moved into southern China was there significant apprehension about American security. Previously Japanese advances were restricted to Manchuria, North China, and Shanghai. While these moves aroused sympathy for China, they did not directly threaten the United States position in the Philippines nor her access to the important sources of strategic materials in Southeast Asia. Japan's New Order in Asia presented more nearly a direct challenge, and this loomed even more dangerous as it became apparent that the war threat in Europe was real. A conflict in Europe would diminish or even destroy the capacity of England and France to resist the Japanese in Southeast Asia. When the war in Europe did break out and the French succumbed, the danger became imminent. Only then did American security considerations in Asia become of vital importance.

Until then neither economic nor security interests had been of a magnitude to dictate a strong China policy. Consequently, there had been no confluence of these interests with the altruistic sentiments. But the joining of these considerations did not have long to wait. The world of international affairs in 1938 was already moving into a storm center where old habits of thought and traditional responses were outdated.

The overwhelming fact in China during the 1930s was the Japanese invasion. This was the most profound of all concerns of the Chinese. Americans, looking at China during the ten years from the Manchurian Incident of September 18, 1931, down to the Japanese attack on Pearl Harbor, also focused their attention on the Japanese conquests and they did so to the point where they were scarcely aware of internal developments in China. Serious American students of China, foreign service officers assigned to China, and a handful of professional experts on duty in Washington were better informed about Chinese internal problems. These individuals, like the public at large, sided with China against Japan, but their sympathies did not blot out serious reservations about the capacity of China's leadership nor inhibit them from perceiving that quite apart from the war with Japan there was an on-going revolution whose outcome was far from certain:

*   *   *   *

The northern expedition marking the triumph of the Nationalist revolution in 1926 was a united effort of Nationalists and Communists. The following year the Kuomintang ousted the Communists from the united front. The Kuomintang then sought to win the allegiance of powerful warlords who dominated the several provinces, at the same time trying to defeat the Communists, who, although greatly weakened, retained an uneasy control over large parts of the province of Kiangsi. In 1934 the Communists embarked on the now famous march reaching the remote regions of the northwest province of Shensi in 1935. During these years the Kuomintang arranged compromise agreements with provincial warlords and established a nominal control over the country at large. The regime—divided between extremely conservative elements who held the upper hand and liberal democratic elements who stood for reform and modernization—failed to move China toward the revolutionary ideals long advocated by the followers of Sun Yat-sen.

The American response to the Kuomintang prior to 1928 was one of fear of Communist and Soviet influence. Even after 1928, when the Communists were driven out, the Americans continued to be critical. In 1931 missionaries hailed the conversion of Chiang Kai-shek to Christianity, and favorable publicity was given to reports that he began each day with a session of prayer. The launching of the New Life Movement in the early thirties with its emphasis on self-discipline and clean living evoked approval and then came to be viewed as a poor excuse for postponing attack on the real problems. In the meantime the fighting between the Communists and the Kuomintang in Kiangsi led to sharp criticism of the behavior of both sides and more particularly of their hostility to foreigners. By 1934 and 1935 there was increasing American criticism of the Kuomintang, its conservative leaders, and likewise of the Soong family who appeared to be building the family fortune without regard to the national interests of the Chinese people. High rents and high interest rates extorted from the mass of peasants received increasing publicity.

Nelson T. Johnson, the American Ambassador, shared in the concern. The Kuomintang was not living up to its promises of social, political, and economic reform. In the spring of 1937, immediately prior to the outbreak of the war with Japan, Johnson was highly critical. After a lengthy conversation with the Reverend G. W. Shepherd, an adviser to the Generalissimo, Johnson wrote:

> I carried away from the conversation a conviction that Chiang Kai-shek, in wielding the power that has come to him, is apparently dependent for his moral encouragement upon foreigners like Shepherd

and Donald; that he lives like an oriental despot, isolated from his own people, who cooperate with him through fear and because they want the national unity for which he stands.[12]

The government of the Kuomintang had become the government of a small group who had no confidence in their fellow Chinese. Not only was the leadership lacking in vision but it persisted in placing major emphasis on liquidating the warlords at a time when the first demand of the people was for resistance against the Japanese.

Johnson informed one of his American correspondents that Chiang was unpopular and that he was accepted only grudgingly as the only one with ability to command obedience.[13] The menace of Japan was demeaning to the proud Chinese. "The relations," Johnson wrote to Ambassador Grew, "which exist between the Chinese and Japanese may be said to resemble somewhat the relations which would exist between a master and his slave."[14] To another friend Johnson wrote that the Chinese were bitterly ashamed that they had been unable to stop the Japanese, "a people whom they despise intellectually and physically."[15]

* * * *

In the two years preceding these observations of Nelson T. Johnson, popular discontent with Chiang's failure to resist Japan had led to a momentous change on China's political scene. By the autumn of 1935 the restlessness of the Chinese in the face of continuing Japanese aggression led to widespread student demonstrations demanding resistance. A surge of Chinese nationalism after December 1935 indicated that Chiang's campaigns against the Communists no longer had wide popular support. The first period came to a close with students and large parts of the population calling for an end to Chinese killing Chinese.

A new period, full of the most portentous developments for China's future, began in 1936. Chiang Kai-shek, still determined to concentrate on his domestic enemies before engaging the Japanese, ordered a new bandit suppression campaign against the Communists and placed the former Manchurian warlord, Chang Hseuh-liang in command. In December Chiang himself went to Sian to impress on Chang the importance of the new campaign, but winds of contrary opinion were now blowing in full force, and Chiang was soon forced to reverse his course.

Chang Hsueh-liang was already in communication with the Communists in northern Shensi; and his own troops, men evicted from their homes in Manchuria by the Japanese, were restless in the face of the prospect of having to fight fellow Chinese while the foreign invader was extending his control. Even more important, the Communists were now ready to embark on a new strategy. By June, Chang and the Communists had arrived at a common conclusion concerning the future.

From 1923 to 1927 the two protagonists had participated in a united front and they now moved in this direction again. The turnabout of the Communists from a policy of out-and-out class war to the united front strategy was not the result of a sudden decision. Beginning in 1934 the Communists in Europe had moved toward the popular front concept. At the World Congress of the Communist International in July 1935 the whole question of how to deal with recent developments, including the rise of the fascists, was thoroughly debated. The Chinese representative, Ch'en Shao-yu, led the way in arguing that the imperialists rather than opposing classes constituted the enemy.[16] The Congress adopted resolutions approving this position. In the next several months the Chinese Communist Party concentrated its propaganda on the Japanese imperialists and said less and less about the Kuomintang. At a meeting of the Chinese party in December 1935 a resolution was adopted accepting the strategy of the national front.[17] The new line called for cooperation with any and all parties who would oppose Japan and desist from attack on the Communists. The party, now ready to work with all others, would not, however, enter into compromises that weakened its own independence or sacrificed basic principles. Mao Tse-tung took the lead in this major shift. During the next several months the party continued to be critical of the Kuomintang but by the summer of 1936 it was saying that success in establishing a united front against Japan was dependent upon the leadership of Chiang Kai-shek.[18] The party was willing, subject to maintaining its own independence and freedom of action, to support his leadership.

This was the situation when Chiang Kai-shek went to Sian in December 1936 to demand of Chang Hsueh-liang that he carry out the bandit suppression campaign. There a group of picked men from Chang's staff invaded Chiang's headquarters with the aim of taking the Generalissimo captive. Alerted by gunfire, Chiang climbed out a window, dressed only in his night attire, scaled the wall of the compound, and fled. Within two hours he was taken by Chang Hsueh-liang's soldiers and held captive. It was not the intention of Chang to do away with Chiang but rather to persuade him to end the civil strife and resist the Japanese.

The first reports of Chiang's capture were received in Yenan with glee. On the other hand, in Moscow, his captors were denounced, and the Soviets called for his release. Whether Moscow's influence caused the Communists in Yenan to change their attitude or whether they altered their position for other reasons is still a matter of debate. The party divided sharply on what course to take but eventually concluded that it should seek an agreement. In reaching this decision they were undoubtedly influenced by consideration of their own limited strength at the time, the danger of rightist elements in Nanking launching a new campaign against them, and the fact that, although a prisoner, Chiang was not in their hands but in the hands of Chang Hsueh-liang, who was very much opposed to having the Generalissimo suffer bodily harm.[19] At any rate they entered into negotiations with Chiang while he was still a prisoner.

Two weeks after his capture the Generalissimo was released. He announced that he had entered into no commitments. His captors recognized that if it appeared that he had entered into agreements under duress those agreements would not have the binding effect of a freely negotiated understanding. During the next several months Chiang and the Communists hammered out a series of statements setting forth proposals for agreement. In the meantime, both sides exhibited restraint in their dealings. Not until the war with Japan had been in progress for two months was a formal and public agreement reached.

In August it was agreed that the Red Army should be designated the Eighth Route Army and it was placed under the nominal command of the Central Government. The manifesto on KMT-CCP Cooperation of September 22 provided that both parties would strive to achieve Sun Yat-sen's Three Principles, that: the Communists would cease to advocate armed revolt and sovietization, would bring an end to the existing Soviet government, and would place their army under the command of the Central Government. Chiang responded to this Communist declaration with a statement praising the Communists for subordinating their previous policies to the achievement of national interests.

The new united front was to have momentous consequences. The long-term aims of the Communists remained unchanged, but their strategy now was to cultivate all parties and all classes and pursue political and economic policies attractive to many and sufficiently mild to be offensive to only a few. This revolutionary turnabout, freeing the party to appeal to the aroused nationalistic feelings and for the time being to cater to the desire for moderate reforms, enabled the Communists to win widespread public support. The party leaders never compromised on their long-term aims and they were frank in their public statements to that effect. However, their long-range goals came to seem so remote that those who disagreed with those goals saw no reason to fear that they would ever be implemented.

The full consequences of the new united front policy of the Communists could scarcely be foreseen by anyone, Chinese or foreigner. The American ambassador, Nelson T. Johnson, was no exception. He and his associates wholly failed to recognize the importance of what had happened. Johnson saw what other untrained observers saw, namely the rise of a national spirit and the emergence of Chiang Kai-shek as a hero. Some months after the Sian coup he wrote to a friend that at first it had seemed strange that Chang Hsueh-liang had not emerged as the hero. Johnson ventured the opinion that the people had turned against the former Manchurian warlord because in seizing the person of Chiang Kai-shek he "suddenly made of Chiang Kai-shek a symbol of all that the Chinese people most wanted, namely unity." Johnson wrote, "Chang Hsueh-liang was guilty of an act of civil disturbance at the very moment he was calling for the abandonment of civil disturbance."[20] Ambassador Johnson, a man with long experience in China and with considerable understanding of the Chinese, stated that the Chinese were ashamed of the fact that they had not been able to stop the Japanese and they ascribed this to their failure "to act as a unit, to direct the force which the great population of China with its resources should be able to command at one point." While these observations were accurate, they failed to foresee the far-reaching consequences of the united front.

For more than two years the Kuomintang and the Communists worked together with considerable success. Unity was not the product of mutual understanding and trust but rather the result of the awareness of both that the public would be bitterly critical of any failure to support the war against Japan. The Communists adhered to the new policy with firmness. The Central Government did the same and showed its good faith by allocating supplies to the Eighth Route Army even though its own armies were in desperate need. It likewise provided the funds for paying the soldiers' allotments in three of the Communist divisions.

The Communists were playing a game of expediency. The outward display of cooperation with the Kuomintang in no way constituted a departure or yielding of Marxist-Leninist ideology. On September 14, 1939, shortly after the Nazi-Soviet Pact, Mao Tse-tung joined the Soviet leaders in denouncing both sides in the war in western Europe as imperialistic and demanded that it was necessary to fight all imperialist bandits, especially the British. He exhorted party leaders:

> Awaken the people and caution them against falling into the trap of imperialist bandits. Do propaganda among the people in order to convert the imperialist war into a revolutionary civil war within each country, and establish the people's united front against the imperialist war.[21]

Such views were scarcely conducive to continuation of the united front and they were matched by equally strident and hostile pronouncements by some elements in the Kuomintang.

By 1939 the first crack in the front appeared. In reality the Kuomintang and the Communists held diametrically opposed views on all issues expect on the question of the war. By 1940 serious disagreements arose over what areas each should control, over the Communist Fourth Army's operations south of the Yangtze, and over the question of supplies for the Communist armies. However, in spite of growing distrust in the next few years both sides continued to give at least nominal recognition to the united front.

*　*　*　*

On July 7, 1937, on the outskirts of Peking, near the Marco Polo bridge, the Japanese launched a military campaign that carried them to Shanghai and Nanking before the close of the year. Because Japan did not declare war, President Roosevelt was free not to apply the neutrality legislation, which provided severe limitations on trade with belligerents. His decision was based on the belief that China would have suffered more than Japan. However, the sale of oil and scrap iron to Japan at the time that she was engaged in making war on the Chinese aroused a storm of criticism. The American public was highly partisan toward China. A public opinion poll conducted in October 1937 asked; "In the present fight between Japan and China, are your sympathies with either side?" Forty percent answered that they had no sympathy with either side, 59 percent were sympathetic to China, and only one percent with Japan.[22] Another measure of American feeling was the effectiveness of Roosevelt's moral embargo. The President appealed to the manufacturers of aircraft and aircraft parts, engines, armaments, aerial bombs, and torpedoes not to sell these items where they might be used in bombing of civilian populations. His appeal met with strong support.[23]

Yet the Americans, although sympathetic with China, strongly opposed involvement in the war and they stubbornly resisted proposals which they thought led in that direction. In the same poll in which 59 percent expressed sympathy for the Chinese 64 percent said they were opposed to the shipment of arms and ammunition to China.[24]

It was during the first year of the war with Japan that Chiang emerged as a hero. In both China and the United States the Generalissimo came to symbolize Chinese unity and resistance. Whatever his strengths and weaknesses, it was generally believed that he alone could unify the country. This led the Soviet Union to support him and to direct valuable military supplies to the Central Government rather than to the Communists. Many Americans also held Chiang in high esteem. Evans Carlson, a retired Marine officer and a friend of Roosevelt who traveled widely in China and who was one of the first Americans to take a sympathetic view of the Chinese Communists, visited Nanking in November 1937 immediately prior to the Japanese capture of that city. In a letter to the President, Carlson wrote of Chiang's display of "marvelous fortitude and unswerving determination to continue to resist." He reported, "Madame Chiang is a human dynamo;" radiating energy and confidence. He found that Chiang and his wife shared the dangers of military operations. "They are true leaders, and a source of inspiration to the whole nation," Carlson wrote.[25]

Missionaries to China were outraged at the failure to distinguish between victim and aggressor. Some vented their feelings in letters to friends and to the press.[26] Three prominent missionaries returned to the United States in 1938 to present China's case—Dr. Walter Judd, later Congressman from Minnesota, Frank Price, who served as chairman of a committee established to win public support, and Searl Bates, missionary-educator. The Price committee unquestionably influenced public opinion to a significant degree, although some of its effectiveness was nullified by the reluctance of mission boards to make the position of their missionaries in Japan even more difficult than it already was. The missionaries likewise encountered in the churches a strong peace movement which resisted the taking of sides.

The first cautious crossing over onto a new and less ambiguous path came in July 1939 when Secretary of State Cordell Hull announced that the trade treaty with Japan would be terminated at the close of six months. Termination of the treaty would leave the United States free to impose trade restrictions. His purpose was to inform the Japanese that the United States strongly objected to their course of action and would not content itself with making diplomatic protests nor would it gradually and calmly adapt to Japanese domination of Asia. The warning served its purpose. The Japanese were deeply aware of their dependence on the United States for oil and for iron and steel, and they probed for signs of what the United States would do once the treaty expired.

Japan suffered another shock in late August of 1939 when Germany and the Soviet Union signed their pact. In 1936 Japan had entered the Anti-Commintern Pact with Germany. The public part of that pact said no more than that the parties would resist the activities of Communist parties engaged in extending the Communist revolution, but a secret clause was directed at the Soviet Union. This specified that the parties would not give aid to the Soviet Union if that nation launched an unprovoked attack against one of them and that neither country would enter into a political accord with the Soviet Union, contrary to the intentions of the pact without first consulting the other party. Now, three years later, Japan learned that Nazi Germany had betrayed her.[27] Its primary purpose in entering into the agreement with Germany had been to protect its northern flank from possible Soviet attack. Now it appeared that the Soviet Union was to be free to confront it without fear of what might take place in Europe. In the negotiations between Germany and the Soviet Union the Russians had, as a matter of fact, placed major emphasis on gaining assurance that Germany would not support Japanese aggression.

As full of portents as these developments in the summer of 1939 were, the United States and Japan were not yet locked into a collision course. Secretary Hull, in the months following his announcement that the trade treaty would be terminated, carefully avoided steps that might lead Japan to take even more aggressive measures. In taking this position Hull was supported by Ambassador Grew in Tokyo, who did his best to convince his superiors in Washington that there was still reason to hope for some mitigating change in Japan's policy. Grew was deeply aware of the uneasiness in the Japanese government and the anxiety of many civilians as they perceived that war might result. "Shidehara diplomacy," noted Grew, "has existed." He wrote to Hull, "It can exist again."[28]

In the United States public opinion expressed ever stronger disapproval of the course the Japanese were pursuing in China, and there was strong sentiment in favor of putting a stop to the sale of the sinews of war to Japan. Yet the public was decidedly opposed to direct involvement in the war. Among the few who favored a strong course even if this led to war was Henry Stimson. In a letter to the *New York Times* in January 1940 he charged that the United States had been furnishing the supplies which had enabled Japan to pursue war in China.[29] The last thing the Japanese desired was a war with the United States and therefore, if the supplies were cut off, she would be forced to accept the fact that the action of the United States made it necessary for her to make peace.

*   *   *   *

The fall of the continent of Europe to Hitler in the late spring of 1940 immediately confronted the United States with the very real prospect of Japan successfully establishing her long-proclaimed new order in Asia. With the French and the Dutch prostrate under the heel of Hitler and the British reduced to a defense of the home island, the old barriers to Japanese expansion in Southeast Asia were no more.

The change had two other major impacts on American thinking. First, if the Japanese gained control of Singapore and the sea lanes of the South Pacific, they would in all probability cut off the shipment of important supplies to British forces in the Near East and Middle East and thereby reduce England to fighting a war that would no longer include an offensive threat. Reduced to only defending the home islands, it appeared doubtful that England could survive. This analysis was placed before President Roosevelt in December 1940. The second impact was that whatever action the United States took would markedly affect the will of those who were continuing to resist Germany and Japan. Any sign of compromising with Japan would contribute toward weakening resistance and might even lead to withdrawal from the war of both China and England. The United States would be left alone to face the consequences of a new world order in which in all probability she would be forced to fight without allies.[30]

Japan was now in the mood of optimistic contemplation of the golden opportunities spread out before her. The United States, on the other hand, found it necessary to exert all possible influence on the British, French, and Dutch to resist Japanese demands. The first of Japan's demands called on the British to close the Burma Road, a supply line to beleaguered China. She based her demand on the necessity of terminating the China incident. At the same time she demanded that the British close the border between Hong Kong and the mainland. The reasons given were the same. The British, after close consultation with the Americans, procrastinated. At this season of the year, said Great Britain, little was transported between Hong Kong and the mainland and the amount of goods transported over the Burma Road amounted to only 5,000 tons per month. Moreover, said the British, the road from Burma was a legitimate artery of traffic and many of the goods passing over it were not war supplies. Moreover, to close it would work a hardship on Burma and India. Japan's charge that the British, in permitting the traffic, were guilty of an unneutral act was returned with the reply that if she were to close it, China would be justified in demanding that the British cut off trade with Japan on the grounds that the trade was unneutral. Given the desperation of the moment, Great Britain knew that it could not refuse; it could only delay its assent in the hope that some new development might strengthen its hand. It looked to the United States for support, received a friendly hearing and encouragement but no promise of assistance if the Japanese should decide on war as it was rumored they would. Finally, the British agreed to close the road for three months.

In late June Japan presented France with a set of demands. Again Japan claimed that it could bring the China incident to a close if it could prevent the shipment of supplies to China. The French procrastinated, seeking to bargain over every minor point in order to delay. In late September there was no more to debate and the Japanese moved into Indo China. The United States protested to France, who replied that it had sought the support of the United States but the United States had refused all assistance.

During the same tense weeks the Japanese sought to drive the Dutch into agreeing to furnish Japan with the supply of aviation gasoline it needed. The Dutch, too, consulted the United States. Again there was no promise of assistance, but the Dutch were strongly encouraged by the United States to hold out. In each case, as the Japanese well knew, the United States strongly opposed yielding to the demands, and that opposition served as the only encouragement the imperial powers of Europe received.

In the midst of the crisis the Roosevelt administration carefully avoided every action that could be interpreted as compromise. It extended a new loan to China and questioned the Japanese as to the legality of their actions while cautiously suggesting that the United States would gladly consider Japanese grievances but could not give approval to Japan's adventure in China.

During the June crisis Congress had passed the National Defense Act granting the President the authority to limit or prohibit exports of materials necessary to national security. Members of the administration then entered into a sharp debate as to how far to go in cutting off exports to Japan. Representatives of the Treasury argued in favor of a complete embargo on oil and iron and steel. The Department of State opposed so sweeping a ban on the grounds that it would cause Japan to resort to war. Sumner Welles succeeded in limiting the order, which was announced on July 26, to aviation gasoline and the highest grade of melting iron and steel scrap.[31]

The granting of a $25 million loan to China served not only to encourage China to stay in the war but gave notice to Japan that while the United States was not yet prepared to involve itself in the military hostilities it was not to be sidetracked into taking any step that could be viewed as appeasement. The policy was clearly to encourage those who were still fighting Germany and Japan and to make it equally clear to these two powers that the United States was firmly resolved to stand solidly opposed to the Germans and Japanese achieving their ambitious aims.

To carry out foreign policy in a nation where the public was on the one hand horrified by the havoc wrought by governments dominated by a predatory spirit and equally horrified by the danger that some show of opposition would lead to military involvement was no easy task. On September 30 Hull recorded his conversation with the British ambassador who had queried him as to what the United States would do if British reopening of the Burma Road led the Japanese to declare war. Hull's answer was in one respect evasive but it did not lack a note of firmness. He cited the record of United States opposition to Japanese aggression—"these acts and utterances have comprised repeated aid to China, successive moral embargoes, abandonment of the commercial treaty, actual embargoes under law, the sending of our Navy to Hawaii, together with appropriate statements and notes of strong remonstrance against Japanese steps of aggression and constant repetition of the basic principles of world order under law."[32]

On the other hand, throughout the crisis of the summer of 1940, in spite of strong convictions that the future of the United States depended in large part on the survival and victory of the British and the Chinese, domestic political considerations caused the Roosevelt administration to adhere to the time-honored tradition of noninvolvement and no alliances. Consequently, close cooperation continued to be on an "exchange of information" basis. So scrupulously was this adhered to that in November when it appeared that Japan might resort to force in the Netherlands East Indies, Admiral Hart, Commander of the Asiatic Fleet, did not feel free to enter into discussions as to what joint operations by the British and Americans might be launched. Hart set forth the argument that, while he did not know what the United States would do, given the possibility of joint American-British action, perhaps there should be discussions. These, he thought, might be based on the hypothetical assumption that the United States would become actively engaged if the British chose to resist a Japanese attack on the East Indies. Yet, Hart also pointed out that discussions on the basis of this assumption could scarcely be carried out even though every precaution was taken not to commit the United States in advance. He noted, "It is realized, however, that in practice there lies danger of certain implications of actually having made political commitments by the very fact of accepting such an assumption as having elements of possibility." He wrote, "Thus if they came to be known, such conversations might have domestic complications sufficient to deter our statesmen; but from a military viewpoint the necessity for them is obvious."[33]

The necessity of excrutiatingly painful reflection on the requirement of giving careful thought to the constitutional provisions concerning the executive's responsibility and the Congressional responsibility in the conduct of foreign affairs provided one of the perplexing problems. Defense of national interests had somehow to be met without violating the Constitutional mandate that only Congress could declare war. Steps taken in defense of national interests must not nullify the right of the people through their elected legislative representatives the freedom to decide between peace and war. And at the same time an inchoate public opinion must not be set emotionally aflame in opposition to firmness, thereby narrowing future freedom of action.

The precarious search for steps that looked to the defense of national interests without striking alarm that the United States would become directly involved was tortuous to decision makers. However, at the close of the year Joseph Grew wrote to the President addressing him as Frank, expressing satisfaction with the course that had been followed. Diplomacy, he sadly observed, "has been defeated by trends and forces utterly beyond its control . . ." Grew observed, "Japan has become openly and unashamedly one of the predatory nations and part of a system which aims to wreck about everything that the United States stands for." He praised the "policy of unhurried but inexorable determination in meeting every Japanese step with some step of our own."[34] The policy had made a deep impression on the Japanese people.

In the process of resisting Japan, relations with China changed. Whereas China had formerly been the object of philanthropic or altruistic concern but not a country upon which the future welfare of the United States depended, it was now one of the few remaining bulwarks against the revolution of predators. Hull was later to be charged with having offered Japan nothing but legalistic formulas and endless recitations from the sacred scripture of the Nine Power Treaty and the Kellogg-Briand Pact; and, indeed, Hull did base his hopes for the future on a system of international relations based on law. However, to read his notes simply as legal opinions is to take them out of context and to remove the blood and flesh from the body he sought to save. Independence and territorial and administrative integrity may be said to have been theoretical concepts, but the reiteration of these encouraged those resisting to believe that the United States would eventually become involved. In reality, these legalistic pronouncements were not that to the Chinese nor to Hull. To the Chinese these terms involved the right to have their own nation and to enjoy the fruits of their own labor.

The Chinese interest jibed with the American interest in an orderly system of international relations. The more immediate Chinese interest of resisting the Japanese militarists likewise corresponded with American opposition to the threats of Hitler. So what happened to China was inextricably tied to what would happen on the other side of the Atlantic. During those crucial days of 1940 before the Soviet Union's involvement in the war and the redressing of the balance of might, China assumed a new importance.

In his letter to Roosevelt, Joseph Grew acknowledged that there was another path open but he carefully pointed out that this meant the complete domination by Japan of all Southeast Asia. During the previous summer he had retained some ray of hope that a conflict between the two nations could be avoided. Japan had then been teetering uneasily over the basic question of whether or not to cast her lot with the Axis. In September Japan entered the Tri-Partite Pact, making itself the future sharer of the spoils of victory with Germany and Italy and gaining, in turn, a commitment of German and Italian support if a power not then involved in the war should become engaged in war with Japan. Grew continued to believe that there was a large and important body of opinion in Japan that favored friendly relations with the United States but he also had concluded that it was inarticulate and ineffectual. Moreover, even among the moderates there was a near unanimity of opinion on the China incident.[35] No one favored a complete about face, but most important was the fact that Japan was under a military dictatorship and no opposition was tolerated.

On the China question the United States was not free to agree to the kind of terms with regard to China that would have satisfied the Japanese after their years of struggle. It was not certain that China would collapse if the United States made itself a party to such a settlement but the danger of China so doing was real. Moreover, to have shifted courses would have had serious effects on the will to resist in Europe.

The lengthy negotiations, the efforts of both sides to maneuver for advantage, and the futile efforts to find some *modus vivendi* that occupied the statesmen of both countries during the next eighteen months bear only incidentally on this narrative. Only three of the steps taken by the United States are relevant to understanding the new relationship to China that emerged.

On July 25, 1941, President Roosevelt issued an order freezing all Japanese assets in the United States. As the President interpreted the order it meant that there would be no more trade with Japan. The danger of immediate Japanese retaliation had entered heavily into the debates preceding the action, but Roosevelt and Churchill chose to gamble on their intuitive feeling that Japan would delay in the hope of British defeat.

Half-peace and half-war already prevailed, for the United States had taken actions that clearly went beyond neutrality. Almost a year before the Roosevelt administration had sanctioned the establishment of the American Volunteer Group, known as the Flying Tigers, under Claire Chennault. By the summer of 1941 the Flying Tigers were already engaged in air combat. However justifiable in terms of national interests this action was inconsistent with neutrality. China, too, was the recipient of aid under the Lend-Lease Act from the early part of 1941, shortly after the law had been enacted. In July 1941

Roosevelt allotted $600 million of lend-lease aid to China.[36] Planes had already been shipped to China for the use of the Flying Tigers. After the enactment of Lend-Lease, China received spare parts for the planes and large supplies of gasoline. Months before Pearl Harbor the Lend-Lease Administration entered into an agreement with China committing itself to supplying thirty new army divisions, and large quantities of goods for this purpose were landed in Burma during 1941.[37] While in the status of a nonbelligerent, the United States had entered into partnership with China for the purpose of stiffening Chinese resistance against Japan. In those final months of 1941 as the statesmen of the United States and Japan continued the search for a *modus vivendi,* Japan made the cutting off of aid to China a major condition. The United States did not comply.

China had become an ally in fact before becoming an ally by official agreement. It achieved its new status by means of maintaining a bloody and brutal war against Japan. To those Americans who had befriended China in an altruistic spirit nothing could have been more rewarding than the sight of their "ward" heroically standing up against the prospective enemy of the United States. However, Japan's challenge to national interests and not altruism as regards China had dictated the policy now in force.

Stanley Hornbeck, Chief of the Far Eastern Division in the Department of State, clearly expressed the reasons for the measures taken to stop Japan. In a memo written on September 12, he warned that "there can be no compromise with the Japanese Nazis; if and in so far as we deal with the German Nazis in firm words and in terms of force."[38] Japan, as Hornbeck saw it, was weak and quite unlikely to make war on the United States if the latter made clear its position and determination. Japan, he wrote, "is economically wearied and weak, has overextended herself, has hostile neighbors in all directions, possesses a good but not a superior navy, and has little or nothing in the way of liquid resources with which to support that navy . . ." Only a few days before Pearl Harbor, Hornbeck predicted that if war came the United States Navy within a year would clash in a major battle with the Japanese Navy, destroy it, and force Japan out of the war.[39] These miscalculations are less important than the fervency with which he believed that the United States must take a stand.

Hornbeck sympathized with China but what gave his argument force was something else. On November 26, 1941, he wrote, "Our foremost practical objective in relation with the Far East at this time is (or should be) to make sure that Japan not succeed in achieving her objective of establishing what her leaders envisage as the 'new order'." She faced only two barriers to achieving her objectives, namely continued resistance by China or resistance "by Russia and/or Great Britain and/or the Netherlands and/or the United States." Hornbeck observed, "There is little chance that the resistance which may stop Japan will be Russian and/or British and/or Dutch."[40] He warned that it was altogether possible that if sufficient assistance did not reach China and reach it in time Chinese resistance would come to an end. These observations led him to conclude:

> It is for this Government to choose, for our agencies of production and our agencies to choose, whether (a) we shall speedily augment the flow of military materials from this country and delivery thereof to China or (b) take the chance (there being a real risk) of China's dropping out and its being this country that has to fight (and fight pretty much by itself—for, once the fight in the Far East is on we cannot count on having major assistance there from any other country) toward preventing Japan from attaining her major objective—which it is our major objective to prevent her from attaining.[41]

Clearly the United States adherence to a firm policy which, in turn, led Japan to declare war, grew out of the conviction that if Japan succeeded in establishing its New Order in Asia so complete would be its control of East Asia that the United States would be reduced to the status of a supplicant. Permitted to persist in the course it had chosen, Japan would quickly augment its present power by the control and exploitation of the vast resources of the area. Given the dominance of the military in Japan and the aggressive attitude that had been demonstrated, it was almost inevitable that Japan would pursue so aggressive a course that the United States would have no choice but to resist even in the face of great odds. Viewed thus, the dangers to the United States appeared intolerable.

China entered into the calculations of the American government in an important degree. The Chinese alone were actively engaged in fighting Japan and should they find it necessary to make peace with Japan the United States would be left to fighting Japan alone. The traditional American friendship for China was not an important factor in the reaching of decisions on policy. However, decision makers found it easier to make those decisions because important groups of the American public, motivated in considerable part by friendship for China, had prepared the public at large to side with China and oppose Japan.

The sequence of events and developments that ended with the Japanese attack on Pearl Harbor marked the final collapse of the old order of relations between nations in the far reaches of the Pacific. The United States had opposed the change in the status quo without giving deep thought to what was to replace it. Given the nature of past relations between the United States and China and the configuration of political relations in that part of the world as well as Chinese resistance over the past four and one-half years, it was inevitable that the United States should take the lead in proposing that a new and more powerful China should be the dominant power and that it would serve as the stabilizing force in the Far East. It was assumed, of course, that China would be friendly and peace loving, the kind of a modernized version of the Middle Kingdom that Americans had so long cherished.

Notes to Chapter I

1. Stanley K. Hornbeck, Chief of the Far Eastern Division, Department of State, "Brief Statement of Policy of the United States in and with Regard to the Far East," Hornbeck Papers, Box 20, Hoover Library, Stanford University.

2. Charles S. Campbell, Jr., *Special Business Interests and the Open Door Policy* (New Haven: Yale University Press, 1951), pp. 42–44.

3. Paul A. Varg, *The Making of a Myth The United States and China* (East Lansing: Michigan State University Press, 1968), pp. 46–47.

4. Chi-ming Hau, *Foreign Investment and Economic Development in China 1840–1937* (Cambridge: Harvard University Press, 1965), p. 61.

5. Ibid., p. 81.

6. Brooks Adams, *America's Economic Supremacy* (New York: The Macmillan Co, 1900).This is a brief summary of the argument of the book as a whole.

7. A. Whitney Griswold, *Far Eastern Policy of the United States* (New York: Harcourt, Brace and Co., 1938), p. 123.

8. Cutten Jones Clinard, *Japan's Influence on American Naval Power 1897–1917* (Berkeley: University of California Press, 1947), p. 165.

9. Stanley Hornbeck, "Manchuria Situation Tientsin-Peiping Area China's Tentative Appeal to the Powers," May 9, 1933. PSF - China, Roosevelt Papers, Roosevelt Memorial Library, Hyde Park, N. Y. November 14, 1938.

10. Ibid., "The Tung Oil Project and American Policy in General in Regard to the Far East," PSF - China, Roosevelt Papers.

11. Memo by Cordell Hull, November 14, 1938, PSF - China, Roosevelt Papers.

12. Memorandum of Conversation with the Rev. G. W. Sheperd, May 17, 1937, Nelson T. Johnson Papers, Library of Congress.

13. Nelson T. Johnson to Thomas Lamont, May 11, 1937, Johnson Papers.

14. Nelson T. Johnson to Joseph Grew, June 4, 1937, Johnson Papers.

15. Nelson T. Johnson to Thomas Lamont, May 11, 1937, Johnson Papers.

16. Lyman P. Van Slyke, *Enemies and Friends: The United Front in Chinese Communist History* (Stanford, California: Stanford University Press, 1967), p. 53.

17. Ibid., p. 59.

18. Ibid., p. 64.

19. Ibid., p. 83.

20. Nelson T. Johnson to Thomas Lamont, May 11, 1937, Johnson Papers.

21. Lin Yutang, "Conflict in China Analyzed," *Far Eastern Survey*, July 18, 1945.

22. George Gallup and Claude Robinson, "American Institute of Public Opinion Surveys, 1935–38," *The Public Opinion Quarterly*, Vol. 2, 1938, p. 289.

23. Herbert Feis, *The Road to Pearl Harbor: The Coming of the War Between the United States and Japan* (Princeton: Princeton University Press, 1950), p. 40.

24. Gallup and Robinson, op. cit., p. 289.

25. Evans Carlson to Miss Le Hand, Nov. 29, 1937. PSF Roosevelt Papers.

26. Paul A. Varg, *Missionaries, Chinese and Diplomats: The American Protestant Missionary Movement in China, 1890–1952* (Princeton: Princeton University Press, 1958), pp. 259–60.

27. Feis, op. cit., p. 34.

28. Ibid., p. 42.

29. Ibid., p. 49.

30. Ibid., pp. 90–93.

31. Ibid., p. 92.

32. *Foreign Relations of the United States Diplomatic Papers* (Washington, D.C.: Government Printing Office, 1955) Vol. IV *The Far East*, Memorandum of Conversation, by the Secretary of State, September 30, 1940, pp. 159–60.

33. Ibid., The Commander in Chief, United States Asiatic Fleet (Hart) to the Chief of Naval Operations (Stark), Nov. 13, 1940, pp. 208–11.

34. Ibid., The Ambassador in Japan (Grew) to President Roosevelt, Dec. 14, 1940, pp. 469–71.

35. Ibid.

36. J. Franklin Ray, "Getting the Goods to China" *Far Eastern Survey*, March 8, 1943, pp. 51–54.

37. Ibid.

38.   Memorandum of September 12, 1941, sent to Adolf Berle, October 21, 1941, Hornbeck Papers.

39.   Hornbeck Memo, December 1, 1941, Hornbeck Papers.

40.   Hornbeck Memo, November 26, 1941, Hornbeck Papers.

41.   Ibid.

CHAPTER II

The Breach Between the United States and China Opens

The myth of the United States serving as the defender of China rested on a false assumption. The fact that American public opinion was friendly toward China had at no time in the preceding four decades caused the American government to shoulder responsibility for China's security from hostile powers. This reality had been obscured from public view by government pronouncements in respect to the Open Door and China's independence and territorial and administrative integrity. After the Manchurian Incident of 1931 and during the course of the undeclared war beginning in 1937 this orientation also made it easy to believe that the Chinese were setting an example of heroic resistance. The Chinese Nationalists did their best to nourish this view and they were ably assisted by their American friends. This made it easier for the Roosevelt administration to pursue a tough policy with Japan. However, the government policy had its origins in considerations of national interest rather than the friendly public attitudes toward China. Only after Pearl Harbor, when the realities of war had to be faced, did the wide differences between China and the United States come into full view. Each of the two nations insisted on the accountablity of the other. Each found the other wanting.

Relations between China and the United States foundered on the shoals of false expectations, differences in priorities, and misunderstanding during the first year of American involvement in the war. The rapid deterioration in mutual confidence followed upon anticipation that all differences would be swallowed up by the common interest in defeating Japan.

Americans, seeing the war in Asia from their own perspective, missed a basic fact. The Nationalist Government in China saw the Communists as the primary enemy with which it must deal. Japan would eventually be defeated by the Western allies and therefore did not receive major consideration in military decision making. The Communists posed the great threat and this fact dominated the thinking of the Chungking government. Americans, on the other hand, persisted in giving the highest priority to defeating Japan and viewed the Nationalist concern with the Communists as a barrier to taking effective military action against the Japanese. This difference, never bridged, led to disastrous disagreements and eventually to mutual disillusionment and acerbating judgments of each other.

The Chinese Communists viewed the war with Japan as the great opportunity to carry out a revolution eventuating in their governing China. The Communists aligned themselves with nationalistic feelings aroused by Japan's harsh occupation of their country and assumed the role of the zealous defender of China against the foreign invader. Their primary concern was, no less than in the case of the Kuomintang, to rule China in the future.

Allies often differ in their war aims and yet manage to reconcile their conflicting interests. No such reconciliation took place between the United States and Nationalist China. Instead, the differences not only persisted but grew in importance.

This unbridgeable gulf widened as Americans came to China and confronted a society extremely different from their own. Not only was China strange to them, but like others of their fellow countrymen uprooted by the war from familiar surroundings, their new places of sojourn became the scapegoat for their frustrations. They suffered a double cultural shock which often turned their observations askew.

Nevertheless, their reports concerning the Kuomintang reveal much about wartorn China, the nature of its government, what war did to Chinese society, and the tensions to which it gave rise. Sometimes their observations and their efforts to analyze made little allowance for differences and suffered from attitudes that bordered on snobbery, but if given to making harsh judgments, the realities of China were scarcely less harsh and evoked equally severe criticism from Chinese.

Even during the long winter of 1941–42, while the enemy pushed relentlessly forward, Americans in China expressed deep concern that the extravagant propaganda in China's behalf in the United States might lead to miscalculation and disillusionment. After several Americans in Chungking deplored the unwarranted portrayal of a China vigorously fighting Japan, Ambassador Gauss cabled the Secretary of State stating that he agreed that the American press "has unwisely accepted and exaggerated Chinese propaganda reports of alleged military successes . . . and it is true that American and other radio commentators and editorial writers are overemphasizing the military potentialities of China's great manpower, I have confidence that this propaganda will not be permitted to affect American military planning to our future detriment."[1] Gauss was not unique in perceiving that China did not have the capacity to wage a modern war against a first-rate military power such as Japan. While many members of the American government also recognized this, the American public did not. The realities of China were far beyond the range of their vision.

Before Pearl Harbor, the public viewed China through the sympathetic eyes of foreign correspondents, and friends of China sought to convey the justice of the Chinese cause rather than the labyrinth of her political divisions and the weaknesses of her social and economic system. The Chinese were, according to this sympathetic view, the first nation to fight the Axis. They fought under great hardship, having to move industries, schools, and factories hundreds of miles inland as the Japanese army occupied the coastal plain. The bombings of Chinese cities evoked sympathy for the Chinese and condemnation of the Japanese. The Japanese campaign against Nanking, for years afterward headlined as "The Rape of Nanking," came to symbolize the ruthlessness of the conqueror and the heroic and stubborn resistance of the Chinese. Newsreels, books, periodical articles, and press reports emphasized the unity and determination of the Chinese to resist. Even the line between the Kuomintang and the Communists had long been blurred so that the Communists were viewed as another in the long link of contending forces in the warlord conflict.

Few people were inclined to take a more sober look at the realities in China. Friendly correspondents and former missionaries at home generally preferred to drive home the differences between the invader and the invaded. Few sought to write about the divisions within China. Fewer still chose to give publicity to the seamier side of Chinese politics or the fact that the war had come to a standstill: the Japanese controlled what they needed to control, and the Chinese only moved forward when the Japanese chose to pull back their lines. Disturbed by this situation, the head of the American military mission in China warned the War Department in Washington that the reports of the marvelous achievements and abilities of the Chinese Army "are absolutely without foundation." He thought the American public "usually so sane and well informed" had been deceived. He attributed this to Chinese propangandists in America and to the sponsorship of the propaganda by outstanding individuals, "including missionaries as well as adherents to radical and liberal points of view" and then noted the "emotional appeal . . . which China has always held for a great many Americans, many of them veterans in things Chinese."[2] However, the chief of the Chinese military mission to the contrary, old China hands saw that even the inadequate forces of Chiang were a great improvement over the traditional Chinese forces.

Those few who knew China firsthand expected little and were therefore less disillusioned. They recognized that China's economy and its wobbly political structure rendered it incapable of fighting a first-class modern and militarized nation. Almost wholly lacking the industrial base to provide the sinews of war, a nation that produced no artillery, no aircraft, and almost no oil, China's only strength lay in its manpower and the fact that it possessed a vast hinterland to which its government could retreat. Nor could its government mobilize the few resources it possessed. At best that government, led by Chiang Kai-shek, could only manipulate the centrifugal forces to prevent their retreating to their original orbits of regional warlord autonomy. Lacking a modern integrated economy and an industrial base and handicapped by the weakness of the political structure, China had no choice but to adopt a strategy of grudging concession to the enemy rather than aggressive warfare. Others would eventually take on the burden of aggressiveness. Americans, viewing it from the American perspective, called it a lack of will to fight. The concept was strange to Americans and unpardonable. In a letter to Major General Leonard Gerow, written only some five weeks after Pearl Harbor, Colonel John R. Francis, stationed in Chungking, wrote of the weaknesses of the Chinese army and closed with a warning: "Will it fight offensively? No. Why? There is a lack of what it takes to make men fight an offensive action." He reported that many Chinese officers had expressed the opinion "that they can win this war by never again firing a shot." He wrote, "In other words they expect us to win it for them." The tone was that of moral indignation. Viewed from Chungking, Chiang showed shrewdness in not seeking to achieve what others would do for him.

News reports from occupied China occasionally referred to the ineptitude of Chinese generals, to the hasty retreats of Chinese armies, and to the political failings of the Central Government. However, the predominant view of China was highly favorable. China had resisted beyond expectation. Friendly observers said that Japan went to war simply because China, by 1937, was clearly on the way to achieving the strength necessary to becoming master of its own household.

The deterioration in wartime China led to a further decline of public confidence in the Central Government. Eighty percent of the Chinese people were peasants and their interests received no attention. The government, tied to the landed gentry, closed its eyes to the exorbitant rents and high interest rates paid by the peasantry. In 1941 the average interest rate on farm loans was 20 percent. A year later the interest rate was up to 36 percent on private loans. Interest rates on government loans were 12 percent, but most of the farm loans came from private creditors who borrowed from the government and then loaned the same money to the debt-ridden peasants.[3] This extortion was only one of the peasants' many reasons for viewing the government with hostility.

The brutalities of the war were real and so was the suffering of millions of Chinese, but the troubled and distressing scene of disunity, apathy, and economic deterioration was equally so. To those on the spot this had long been apparent. As early as January 9, 1940, the Consul General of the United States at Hankow, Clarence J. Spiker, observed that the various Chinese factions continued to struggle for power and not one of them was ready to take determined individual action against the Japanese "so long as there exists the likelihood of civil war following a hypothetical Chinese victory."[4] Experienced observers during the next few years continued to stress that the Central Government was a congeries. Chiang, intent on achieving national unity, sought to diminish the autonomy of regional factions and in several cases to shift sources of supplies and to so employ regional armies in the war that the strength of those factions would be diminished while he appeased others. The strategy of war was determined less by considerations of how best to defeat the Japanese and more by the politics of eliminating dangerous rivals and rewarding those who were either loyal or whose strength made them too dangerous to offend. Because survival for both the Central Government and the regional factions hinged more on how the war was to be fought than it did on success against the Japanese, plans were made accordingly.

Even more destructive in terms of the war effort was the rivalry of the Kuomintang and the Communists. Both were committed to defeating Japan, but each set as its first war aim, not the defeat of Japan, which the United States and allies could be relied upon to achieve, but its own emergence in the domestic struggle. Cooperation between the two came dangerously close to complete collapse by 1940. Early that year occurred the first clash between the Communist Eighth Route Army and an army under the Central Government. A year later, in January 1941, Central Government troops, numbering an estimated 80,000, surrounded and attacked the new Communist Fourth Army. The Central Government justified the action on the ground that Communist commanders during 1940 had violated government orders. The Communists had built an army of 500,000 which acted independently of Chungking, moved south of the Yangtze contrary to the commander of the Central Government, and had established independent governments in areas behind the Japanese lines.

In the summer of 1941 Ernest Hemingway spent three months in

China. Prior to Hemingway's leaving, Henry Dexter White of the Treasury Department asked him to gather information on the conflict between the Kuomintang and the Communists. The distinguished novelist did so and then reported his observations with great forthrightness. Hemingway presented a gloomy picture. He believed that there would be "no permanent settlement of the Communist problem in China until an agreement between the Generalissimo's Government and the Soviet Union settles definite limits to the territories the Communist forces are to occupy." He forecast what later developments proved to be true, namely that the Communists would extend their sphere of influence and seek a defensible frontier. He noted also that the bitterness between the Communists and most of the Kuomintang leaders could hardly be exaggerated. One Kuomintang official told Hemingway that Communism was the "Heart Disease" while the Japanese invasion was only a "Skin Disease."[5]

The American novelist was deeply impressed with Chou En-lai, whom he met in Chungking. He wrote of his "ability, brilliance and charm" and how he did "a fine job of selling the Communist standpoint on anything that comes up to almost everyone in Chungking who comes into contact with him." While Hemingway was there, Chou and his wife were entertained at dinner by Chiang and Madame Chiang. Communists in Chungking were tolerated as a matter of window dressing, but elsewhere they were hunted down.[6]

The degree of repression and the activity of the secret police shocked Hemingway. "Students suspected of liberal views, and by this I do not mean Communist but merely those who are left of political views of the gentry or landholding class," he reported, "are liable to arrest and imprisonment in concentration camps."[7]

Civil war, he thought, could be delayed, but a Soviet-supported boundary settlement and a refusal on the part of the United States to finance a civil war would be necessary. He likewise warned that "we should also not accept completely the value the Communists put on their own war effort." America, thought Hemingway, had "an exaggerated idea of the part they have played in the war against Japan." He observed, "Their part has been very considerable but that of the Central Government troops has been a hundred times greater."[8]

The breakdown of the cooperation that had prevailed during the first two and a half years of the war had its origins in conflicting interpretations of the united front and sharp differences in social ideals. Ambassador Gauss, who had replaced Nelson T. Johnson in 1941, in one of his first reports stated that ever since the fighting against Japan had come to a standstill in 1940, there had been "a recurring and increasing evidence of the fictional character of the united front." The leaders of the Kuomintang, according to Gauss, conceived of the united front "as subordination to one party." He wrote, "Opposed to this conception of unification and uniformity is the Communist Party concept of collaboration by distinct entities as the basic objective of a united front."[9] The Communists, by far the smaller of the two parties, feared that acceptance of the Kuomintang's formula could only end in a loss of their own identity and future political influence. Personal animosities among the leaders was enough to prevent a real united front. Four months prior to Pearl Harbor, Gauss warned that after the war with Japan there would be civil war in China.

The internal disunity had its parallel in serious economic difficulties, but in 1941 the Central Government continued to demonstrate considerable energy and ability. An economist representing the Treasury Department, after a visit of some length during the fall of 1941, gave the Central Government credit for many achievements. Among the more notable of these was the nationalization of the assessment and collection of taxes, the introduction of a system of government collection of rice and the payment of soldiers and officeholders in rice, the regulation of the price of rice, and finally significant improvements in banking. Both industrial and agricultural production had increased somewhat during the year.[10]

However, by 1941 inflation threatened to bring economic ruin. The problem was so serious that a highly respected Chinese economist, Dr. Franklin Ho, in an interview with a member of the American Embassy, warned that China was in far more danger of defeat due to economic stress than to military weakness. Ho estimated the monthly expenditures of the government at U.S. $60,000,000. Only one-tenth of this sum was being collected in revenue. The resulting inflation, Ho said, led to some factories closing down early in July when the price of rice, in which a large proportion of wages were paid, reached a new high. Some measures had been taken in the way of increasing revenue but not enough had been done, and the government would also have to reduce expenditures.[11]

Others, including the American ambassador, charged that inflation was in large part a result of the hoarding of goods and speculation. Ambassador Gauss thought the solution lay in "the drastic taxation of those most able to pay, namely speculators, hoarders, and landlords, together with measures to compel these classes to buy Government bonds and saving certificates in large amounts." Such measures, said Gauss, "might have the effect of forcing these classes to disgorge hoarded goods." But, added Gauss, it was "doubtful that the Government, which is itself closely allied to banking and landholding interests, will undertake to place sufficiently severe pressure upon those elements to induce any marked release of commodities and diversion of capital to the uses of the Government."[12]

Inflation, it turned out, continued to haunt the Kuomintang regime in the years ahead. By late 1942, Arthur Young, American adviser to the Ministry of Finance, estimated the average price level at 35 times the 1937 level.[13] The basic causes were the costs of war and the shortage of goods due to China's being cut off from the outside world. In December 1942 Chiang ordered the establishment of a system of price control. Prices and wages were to be fixed at their level on November 30. All shops were to post the legal prices. Black marketing was subject to heavy penalties. The effort was launched with an enthusiastic publicity campaign. Within a month of its going into effect, price control was undermined by widespread evasion. The major newspaper in Chungking reported that "every purchaser and seller are violators" and inquired of the government whether there was a sufficient number of prison cells to hold the violators.[14]

In an effort to curb inflation the government, beginning in 1942, created new taxes on capital, profits, and turnover. The effort had important political implications, since the revised land tax of 1941 was highly unpopular in rural areas. It meant that the business and propertied classes of the cities were not contributing proportionately to the financing of the war effort. The government's effort to correct this imbalance met with little success. Arthur Young attributed the failure to reliance "upon self-assessment, despite the inadequacy of accounting practices and of business records." Consequently, there was widespread evasion of these taxes.[15]

The inflation was likewise due to the failure to curb expenditures. Because of the political influence of army generals, the armies were much too large. Generals were paid, in part, on the basis of the number of troops they had. Contributing further to excessive military spending was the practice of paying army generals a lump sum for the support and equipping of their forces. No accounting of how funds were used was required. At the same time the government indulged in employing far more personnel than necessary.[16] This practice, although common to bureaucracies around the world, the Chinese could ill afford from a fiscal point of view.

Another of the realities not well understood by the American public was the nature of Kuomintang rule. At the same time that Americans were rallying to the Four Freedoms and denouncing Fascism and predatory militarism in Japan, they were assuming that Chinese rule approximated the ideals of democracy. The fact that the ruling factions in the Kuomintang did not share these views escaped the attention of most Americans.

The political order in China was far different from what they believed it to be. In 1941 Chiang Kai-shek was not a dictator, and the Kuomintang did not set totalitarian goals for itself. China, however, was far from democratic although it was not Fascist. The political system was built on the premise that one-party tutelage was necessary for a time. Minority parties existed and did have a token voice in purely advisory bodies. The Kuomintang party membership equaled less than one percent of the total population and yet it claimed the authority to govern. Within the Kuomintang were liberal groups who favored representative government and social reform, but these groups had almost no influence in the party. Along with one-party rule there existed a vast gendarmerie and a large organization of secret police who ferreted out opposition. Like the Fascists in Europe the Kuomintang likewise sponsored a semimilitary youth corps whose members were indoctrinated in a highly prescriptive nationalism. The government also maintained a strict censorship of the press and foreign correspondents complained that their stories were screened before transmittal abroad.

In the United States at the time of Pearl Harbor little awareness of these aspects of the Chinese political order existed. Almost two years passed before the realities became known to the public, but

Americans in China, present in increasing numbers, suffered early disillusionment. Glorification of the Chinese cause consequently gave way to distrust.

Disillusion made equally rapid headway among the Chinese and for equally understandable reasons. On both sides the great expectations of 1941 began to wither almost at once.

The Chinese had placed their hopes on United States involvement in the war against Japan. The stereotyped picture of American wealth and the vast industrial machine caused the Chinese to be fully confident that American entry would turn the tide almost at once and the enemy would be rolled back. Instead, the dreary news reports for months after Pearl Harbor told only of Japanese victories in the Philippines, in Hong Kong, in Singapore, and in the islands of Southeast Asia. The disastrous Burma campaign swept away the last fading wisps of confidence.

The tide of battle was soon to turn, but by then Chinese goodwill had given way to the realization that the United States was first committed to the defeat of Hitler. The strategy rested on adequate grounds. Once Germany had been defeated the fall of Japan would soon follow, but a victory over Japan after a long delay in attacking the Germans might well mean that the war would still end in disaster for the United States.

The decision to give priority to the European theater had as a corollary giving to the European allies a high priority in the furnishing of lend-lease aid. The soundness of the strategy in no way mitigated the shock to the Chinese. Their response was one of indignation. Their own needs could not have been more desperate and the long years of war with Japan gave them the conviction that they had earned support. The president of China's Legislative Yuan, Sun Fo, announced that if the Allies were going to remain on the defensive in the Pacific then China must either negotiate with Japan or simply sit by and let the war follow its own course. Ambassador Gauss considered Sun's statement a veiled threat and contended that it did not represent Chinese public opinion. Yet he also acknowledged that the fact that Chinese censorship had cleared it gave the statement semi-official blessing.[17] Rumors of a settlement with Japan persisted. Opinions expressed by high-ranking members of the government seemed to justify serious concern. In the early summer of 1942 General

Stilwell told Gauss that Madame Chiang had said in his presence that unless planes were forthcoming from the United States, China would have "to consider another course, implying making peace with Japan."[18]

The critical internal situation in late 1941 led Chiang Kai-shek to look to the United States for a solution. Pearl Harbor and American entry into the Pacific war set the stage for an unprecedented request. On December 30 Chiang spoke to Ambassador Gauss and appealed for a loan of $500,000,000. He based his plea on the need to prevent further economic deterioration but even more on the necessity of counteracting Japanese propaganda, the rising ascendancy of defeatism and the danger that the puppet regime in Nanking would be able to take over.[19] The argument that China might withdraw from the war at the very time that the United States was facing disaster in the Pacific was well timed. The request set off a controversy between the United States and China and a major debate within the American government.

The proposed loan was clearly political. China had ample funds in the United States to draw upon, a $50 million stabilization fund which had not been touched plus lend-lease. The amount asked for was roughly equivalent to the gap between estimated revenues and expenditures in the proposed Chinese budget for 1942. Chiang advanced the idea that his government would sell savings certificates backed up by the American credit thereby removing Chinese yuan from circulation. This mopping up of the excessive amounts of Chinese currency would, it was argued, curb inflation. However, the effectiveness of this device—and there was no assurance that the credits would be put to this use—appeared questionable. During the long and querulous discussions that took place in the Treasury, State, and War Departments, the proposed loan was frankly accepted as political. China was to be kept in the war; Chiang was to be supported against the Wang Ching-wei's puppet government in Nanking, and faith in eventual victory was to be bolstered.

The proposal caused an almost interminable series of meetings in the Treasury Department which was charged with handling foreign loans; there it evoked the most ambiguous kind of discussion. Secretary Morgenthau consistently supported the loan, probably because if he opposed it and China withdrew from the war he would become the scapegoat. He was particularly distrustful of the State Department and feared that officials there aimed at trapping him in a position of opposition to the loan. Morgenthau expressed his real opinion of China's request to the Ambassador of Russia, Maxim Litvinov who, when told about it, termed it "blackmail." Morgenthau not only agreed but voiced disgust with the Chinese for taking advantage of the United States when she had her back to the wall.[20]

Morgenthau, while never opposing the loan, sought to elicit from T. V. Soong how the credits would be used. Soong confessed to being at a loss for an explanation considering the credits already available to China.[21] In the course of the lengthy discussions Morgenthau's advisers made the highly dubious proposal that one way out was to specify that the credits be used to pay the soldiers in the Chinese army.[22] Soong approved with enthusiasm. The Treasury officials saw in the proposal a means of extending the credits under lend-lease and thereby avoiding the difficult task of selling the proposal on Capitol Hill. President Roosevelt likewise approved. However, Chiang Kai-shek quite rightly rejected the idea on the grounds that it would create a cleavage between the Chinese soldiers and the general economic structure.[23]

The State Department was slow to respond to the loan proposal, but Hornbeck gave it his personal support and so did Adolf Berle. Cordell Hull, ill at the time, hedged but delivered a lengthy soliloquy to Morgenthau on how much he had done for China since 1937. This prompted Morgenthau to comment to his own associates, "Well, being an historian doesn't make history."[24] In the meantime Sumner Welles came into the act, and the State Department aligned itself in support of the proposal and did so with some firmness after Congress readily approved by passing a resolution.

Finally, the time arrived for writing a draft of the proposed agreement. All were agreed that the wisest course was to assume a stance of generosity by minimizing conditions to be met by China and by leaving the question of repayment for later discussion. It was generally agreed that the loan would never be repaid. This was war, the United States confronted a dangerous struggle, and the "loan" was a subsidy to a military ally. However, Article II read: "China desires to keep the Secretary of the Treasury of the United States informed as to the use of the funds herein provided and to consult with him from time to time as to such uses."[25]

On March 1 Ambassador Gauss cabled that he had received reports that the Chinese resented the provisions for control.[26] "The Ministry," Gauss reported, "has been disappointed to find that the loan is not granted, as the Press has stated, as an absolute gift in recognition of China's contribution to the war effort in general." He added that he thought the United States should firmly insist on retaining the provisions for consultation.

Then a battle ensued between the State and Treasury departments. Treasury officials favored omitting Article II. State Department officials supported the Article and, if not it, an exchange of letters providing for consultation. At a meeting in the Treasury Department, Hornbeck explained the position of the State Department. To yield to the Chinese request, he said, would lead to future trouble between the two governments. It would set a precedent for China to lay down the terms in future negotiations. Then, in a peevish manner that betrayed his resentment against the Treasury Department for involving itself in foreign affairs quite as much as it did his distrust of China, Hornbeck reviewed relations with China since 1937 and informed the Treasury group that the war with Japan was a war entered into by Chinese choice. He said:

> The Chinese were not fighting for civilization, but for themselves and the United States had steadily supported China. Not until 1939, when we told them so, did the Chinese begin to say that they were fighting for civilization. Although we had common enemies our wars were different. We happened to be on the same side, fighting against the same enemy. China was trying to make out that we owed her something. We do not owe her anything. In December they asked us for a loan, and the money had been voted as such, and not for a gift. . . .[27]

Hornbeck's vituperative challenge did not meet with a friendly response. Jacob Viner, eminent economist, then working in the Department of Treasury, immediately countered Hornbeck by saying that, by insisting on the contents of Article II, the United States was telling China that it was a second-rate government, "and that we could not trust them [the Chinese] with the intelligent use of the funds."[28]

The State Department adhered to its position but was willing to settle for a letter agreeing to consultation. Two days later T. V. Soong forwarded the letter and on that day, March 21, 1942, the agreement was signed. It specified little other than that China was to have available $500,000,000 in credits. It included no provisions as to security, rate of interest, the uses of the loan, or repayment.

The loan set a precedent whereby the Central Government of China dictated how most of the issues arising in the next several years were to be resolved. The precedent was not to be reversed until the spring of 1944. The letter written by T. V. Soong agreeing to consultation on how the loan was to be used was ignored. By April 11 Secretary Morgenthau confronted the fact that China meant to do as she saw fit. In a meeting on that day Henry Dexter White outlined the contents of a cable from H. H. Kung. China had already publicly announced the issue of bonds and savings certificates to be backed by $200,000,000 from the $500,000,000 credit. The United States had not been informed of these steps until they had been taken. In addition, Kung requested that $200,000,000 be transferred immediately to two accounts in the Federal Reserve and that $200,000,000 be invested in United States Treasury obligations.[29] Reports were already in that the response to the sale of savings certificates was poor, and this did not change in the months ahead. Ambassador Gauss attributed the failure to fear on the part of prospective buyers that the Central Government would eventually pay off in depreciated yuan.

In April 1942, at a time when a Japanese invasion of India appeared imminent, General Bissell informed the Chinese that it had become necessary to divert pursuit planes scheduled for China to the United States Tenth Air Force for protection of India and the British Eastern fleet. The Generalissimo protested vehemently. China had been waiting for additional planes for more than a year and the Army, when it learned of this, would "feel themselves robbed of a widow's mite" and Chiang warned "will certainly resent not being treated as a worthy ally who has unstintedly given all to common cause."[30]

China's demands for further support continued. In the late summer of 1942 the Combined Chiefs of Staff discussed a new set of requests from Chungking. The British questioned whether supplies should be diverted to China. They argued that the Chinese had shown no fighting spirit and expressed the view that China could hold out for another year without further assistance. After an incon-

clusive debate, the government in London asked its ambassador in
Chunking to report on the situation. He, in turn, consulted with
Ambassador Gauss, who acknowledged that not only had there been
no effective resistance but American intelligence "even indicated
that the Chinese forces were under orders not to attempt any determined resistance, but gradually to withdraw. . . ." However, the
American Ambassador then called attention to the reasons for this
situation. He argued that the Chinese will to resist had not declined
but, given the extremely limited reserves of munitions the Chinese
had no choice but to avoid fighting "until they should feel that it can
be used effectively for permanent gains—or unelss they definitely
have the backs to the wall and are making a last stand."[31]

The average tonnage flown in over the Hump in 1942 ranged from
300 to 700 tons a month, and even during the second half of 1943
was only about 7,500 monthly. Seventy-five percent went to the
American 14th Air Force.[32] Priorities of other allies accounted for
the very limited supplies sent to China. In the meantime, the Chinese countinued to press for further support. There were those in the
United States who supported the Chinese requests. Among these was
Admiral Leahy who feared that if the war in the Pacific were definitely postponed the Japanese would be so deeply entrenched that
they could not be dislodged.[33] Former Ambassador Bullitt went further and argued that additional supplies must be sent to China even
over the protests of the European allies.[34]

The Chinese made endless appeals, and both T. V. Soong and
Madame Chiang went over President Roosevelt's head seeking the
support of his political opponents.[35] As early as April 1942, after
Senator Warren Austin of Vermont called for a doubling of efforts to
supply China, the Office of the Chief of Naval Operations sent a
memorandum to the State Department declaring that there was no
way to get supplies to China and that given the lack of an offensive
spirit in China the sending of supplies would have little or no result.
The memorandum ended with the thumping judgment, "The simple
truth is that we will be well on our way toward defeating Japan by
the time lines can be opened for delivery in real quantity."[36]

The decision which had been made early was adhered to, although
from time to time the Chinese were offered hope of more planes and
munitions. In several instances major shipments scheduled for China

were diverted to other theaters because failure to do so would in all probability end in disaster. Admiral Leahy continued to be concerned. As late as May 9, 1943, he noted in his diary:

> I recommended to the President that he grant the request of Chiang Kai-shek to use all available transport for the next three months to send aviation material from India to China but I got no support from the other Chiefs of Staff.[37]

Leahy was not alone in pleading China's case. Hornbeck, who had been critical of the Chinese in their loan negotiations early in 1942, also took the same stand. In April 1943 he urged that there was only one way to change Chinese thought with regard to the war and that was by increasing the delivery of all kinds of needed supplies. He concluded his memo with words that well expressed the feelings of the Chinese:

> The Chinese are thinking with their eyes, their hands, their feet, their tired bodies and their empty pocket books, rather than with their ears.[38]

Neither arguments of strategy nor words of assurance that China was now to become a member of the select group of four major powers could erase Chinese bitterness. During late 1942 and 1943 they clung to the hope of a second Burma campaign that would open the door to assistance.

The twin questions of priorities in fighting the war and providing China with desperately needed supplies would have more than sufficed to bring about a lack of confidence and mutual distrust. However, there were other major sources of conflict and misunderstanding.

Ever increasing numbers of Americans went to China in the early years of the war, and most of them were wholly unprepared for what awaited them. Complaints of smuggling, theft, and graft honeycombed the original goodwill of these observers. The black market prospered, and American currency brought many times the official exchange rate. Goods intended for the Chinese Army disappeared. Experienced China hands explained it as the desperate and inevitable by-product of low salaries of Army officers.

As early as 1941, Ernest Hemingway had warned of the consequences of low pay for Army officers. A lieutenant-colonel, after ten
years of military service of a most rigorous kind, earned 126 Chinese
dollars per month, 43 dollars less than he had received in 1937. Given
the inflation—in 1937, one dollar bought fourteen pounds of rice and
in 1941 only two pounds—Hemingway had ventured the opinion
"that in the present wage scale of officers in the Kuomintang Army
there is a greater threat to Chinese continuance of the war—not this
year, but for next year—than in any other single destructive possibility."[39]

John Davies of the American Embassy told the grim story which
was making the rounds in Chungking. A major general, wishing to
take a local beauty as his bride, approached her mother to gain her
consent. The mother, according to the story, replied, "Why I even
told a truck driver that he couldn't have her, do you think I would
marry her to a Major General."[40] The story was probably apocryphal
but the conditions it suggested were real. In fact the life of many a
soldier and of even lower rank officers posed a question of survival.
Consequently, it was easy to justify less than honorable transactions.
However, this did not prevent erosion of confidence.

The traffic between Free China and the occupied areas gave rise
to American criticism. Trade thrived and sometimes enjoyed official
encouragement. A member of the American Embassy made as careful a study of the situation as conditions permitted and concluded
that the business had reached grand proportions. Information concerning a single transaction in the southwestern provinces showed
that 1,000 horse loads of goods had been shipped across the lines. In
North China the volume of business was so great that the banks in
Sian, handling the financial side, established relations with banks in
Shanghai and Tientsin for taking care of remittances. To encourage
this illegal trade, authorities in some parts of China waived the collection of duties. Japan, controlling the trade, permitted the sending of
consumer goods to the occupied areas and received in return valuable strategic materials such as tungsten. George Atcheson, who
wrote the report, concluded that the illicit trade constituted a serious
danger to the war effort and exposed Chinese commanders to the
temptation to profit personally. He cited what he termed a reliable
report of a Chinese commander interfering with a British sabotage

project "because it would have interfered with the peaceful commercial intercourse which had been established between his area and the area beyond the Japanese lines facing him."[41]

Probably more damaging in the long run, as far as effect on American public opinion is concerned, was the frustrating experience of foreign correspondents in Chungking. Their special professional grievance lay in the strict censorship of the stories they proposed to transmit. The grounds for deletion appear not to have been well defined, but criticisms of the Kuomintang and references to the Kuomintang-Communist controversy were censored. On occasion when they protested it was explained that internal difficulties were not properly the concern of foreigners. On occasion they met arbitrary treatment bordering on contempt. Twice, in May and in June 1943, they were summoned to the offices of the Ministry of Information in the middle of the night to receive allegedly important news releases. Later investigation of the factual bases for the releases led them to conclude that the stories were false and that they had been summoned late at night to prevent them from verifying the stories before transmitting them.[42]

In spite of the efforts of the Central Government to have only the most flattering side of the Chinese war effort presented, by 1943 the American press began to carry highly critical accounts of the situation in China. T. A. Bisson, in an article in the *Far Eastern Survey*, described the Kuomintang as antidemocratic and feudal and the Communists as democratic and modern. The article created a furor in government circles in Chungking, and the right to transmit stories was promptly withdrawn for any correspondent who had any affiliation with the Institute of Pacific Relations because that organization published the journal in which the Bisson article appeared.[43] During the same period Hanson Baldwin published two articles, one in the *New York Times* and one in *Reader's Digest*, both of them critical of the Kuomintang. A more moderate article, but one with a critical note, by Pearl Buck appeared shortly after Baldwin's pieces. Chinese officialdom, accustomed to expect only praise in the American press, reacted with alarm.[44] A member of the American Embassy learned from a Chinese who was present at a special meeting called to consider the problem, that the Minister of Information, in discussing a Baldwin article, "was virtually hysterical and his usual fluent English

became unintelligible gibberish." Continued criticism, predicted the
Embassy, would probably "increase the present anti-foreign bias
which the Generalissimo, Madame Chiang . . . and others seem to
have and will turn that bias more and more in our direction."[45]

The antiforeign bias of the Chinese was not new. Criticism from
abroad helped give it new life, but it began to vent itself before
American critics and stirred the ashes of old resentments. Faced with
economic deterioration, mounting inflation, and ever-increasing
hardships both among the civilians and in the army, it was almost
inevitable that the foreigner should become the scapegoat. Legitimate criticisms of government policies by the Chinese press were
ruled out by the tight censorship. With this outlet for their frustrations cut off, the Chinese journalists concentrated increasingly on the
faults of their Western allies.

And alongside of this, the presence of Westerners in China assured
that criticism of China would thrive as naturally as pigweed in a
garden. Visitors to a land utterly strange made their usual critical
observations. Practices rooted in Chinese life but alien to a foreigner
evoked censure. Widespread criticism of the government by the
Chinese reinforced the inclination to be critical.

Shortly, the presence and reports of American soldiers stationed in
China became a source of concern. Madame Chiang, while in the
United States giving speeches in behalf of the Chinese cause, received scores of letters from families whose sons were in China protesting that what she said did not jibe with the bitter charges American soldiers were sending home.[46] By July 1943 the American
Embassy received reports that the government had issued rules limiting contacts with foreigners.[47] The first reports led the Embassy to
inquire of its representative at Kweilin, where many American
troops were quartered, as to the truth of the charge. Ringwalt, the
American representative, forwarded a copy of the instructions that
had been issued by the Chinese government. He stated that the local
Chinese professed to be convinced "that the Chinese have fears
above all that the American public may become aware of the true
state of affairs in China, and that American public opinion in respect
of China may undergo a severe reaction from whole hearted and
uncritical admiration and sympathy to apathy and cynicism."[48] Ambassador Gauss reported that the regulations concerning association

with foreigners were not being enforced but he commented, "It remains a fact that the vast majority of Chinese officials at Chungking are still reluctant to discuss freely with foreigners any questions which might imply criticism of government policy."[49]

Critics of the Kuomintang outside of the government were more than willing to convey to representatives of the United States their grievances against their own government. This was particularly true of those who belonged to minority parties or who pinned their hopes for the future on the overthrow of the Kuomintang and the rise to power of some combination of regional military leaders. They looked to the United States, hoping for support in the event of an overthrow of the government. However, movements to establish some new coalition of groups waited upon further deterioration of the situation and also looked forward to the day when American forces would supposedly land on the coast. This might present an opportunity to draw upon American supplies in return for commitments to assist in the defeat of the Japanese.

Behind the shifting tides of China's internal struggle existed the potential for both hostility and goodwill toward the United States. American soldiers generally received a friendly reception. Fliers downed in Japanese occupied territory told stories of villagers endangering their own security in seeking to assist them in returning to Free China. Yet the war had not erased the unhappy memories of a hundred years of dealing with the Westerners. It is doubtful that either the Americans or the Chinese accepted each other as equals, and the Chinese were keenly sensitive to the inferior position allotted them in the past. The unequal treaties compromising Chinese sovereignty had long been a source of humiliation. In January 1943 the two countries signed a treaty whereby the United States relinquished extraterritoriality and the right to station American troops in various places in China. The yielding of these privileges, heralding a relationship of equals, came too late. The immigration policy excluding the Chinese from coming to the United States and the ill treatment many of them encountered were not canceled out by the extensive and genuine philanthropic efforts of Americans. Had China achieved strength and a sense of security in the years since the national revolution of the 1920s, the readiness to feel slighted might have been dulled, but this was not the case. Americans sometimes

found it difficult to acknowledge that the goodwill of their countrymen toward China was not reciprocated. For instance, as early as
1935 Gauss had written to Willys Peck:

> I have been impressed by the fact that, notwithstanding the exceed-
> ingly friendly and helpful attitude of the United States toward China,
> both in the past and in recent years, there has been no reflection of any
> real appreciation of that attitude in the position of the Chinese Gov-
> ernment toward American interests in this country. I do not advocate
> a modification of the American attitude, but feel that it merits a much
> more satisfactory response from China.[50]

One hundred and fifty years earlier a tough-minded American,
Alexander Hamilton, had warned his fellow countrymen that grati-
tude among nations is a weak reed to lean upon. Whatever goodwill
Americans had acquired in China could not compete with the dedi-
cation of Chinese to their own interests. In 1942 the self-interests of
Chinese were obvious and clear, and their appreciation could be
counted on only to the degree that these interests were met.

In August 1943, T. V. Soong, then Chinese Minister for Foreign
Affairs, sent a lengthy message to the Secretary of State reciting the
many occasions when the United States had declared that China was
an equal among the four major allies. Then he went on to cite the
numerous allied agencies established to carry on the war and plan
the peace, pointing to the fact that the Chinese were not represented
on a single one. Soong charged that the Chinese had not even been
called upon to present their own programs. Nor was China represented on the Combined Chiefs of Staff, and when Chinese had been
invited to appear they were treated as witnesses rather than as participants in a common war effort. Nor had any Chinese been invited
to sit in the several wartime conferences of the leaders of state.[51]
China, in spite of Franklin Roosevelt's statements assuring her of
great power status, had been bypassed.

Only a few weeks before T.V. Soong sent this prickly message, the
American Embassy in Chungking reported that General Hsiung
Shih-hui, recently head of the military mission to the United States,
had returned to China "with a strong anti-American attitude, . . . and
with an inclination to align himself with members of the so-called
'Peace Party' which favored making peace with Japan. Upon reading

this report a member of the Department of State wrote that the American military services had treated him with scant courtesy and consideration. . . ."[52] The fact that the Chinese general was in reality not a military man, that he was a reactionary, and that he did not speak English undoubtedly explained in part the reception he had received, but this did not excuse his treatment. The incident did not justify any charge of race prejudice; China had clearly made a poor choice of representatives, but given the past history of anti-Chinese feelings in the United States, it was probably viewed in that light.

These several strains upon mutual confidence and goodwill would have been no more than temporary and minor irritations if the course of military events had not been so disastrous. While this book does not presume to be a study of the military aspects, successes and failures of military efforts were of paramount importance in determining the state of relations between the United States and China. Because military developments were dogged by failure, other conflicts loomed larger. The most important aspect of the war from a Chinese point of view was Burma.[53] Only that border state offered promise of a reopening of the lanes of supply, and the disaster threatening China had its origins in the shortage of both military materiel and civilian goods.

In January 1942 General Joseph Stilwell was appointed Chief of Staff to the Generalissimo. The precise relationship of Stilwell to Chiang Kai-shek was ill defined and subject to differences of interpretation, but the real difficulty had its source, not in the vagueness of the instructions, but in the personalities of the two men and the problems confronting them. In March 1942 the British and Chinese lost Burma and, almost as damaging, lost confidence in each other. Chiang Kai-shek had called for an overall plan of operations and offered the services of two divisions. General Wavell contended that, given the fluid situation and the many unknowns, the determination of strategy would have to await further developments. At the same time he turned down the offer of Chinese troops. Stilwell arrived when the operation was underway. In the fashion which gave him the name "Vinegar Joe," Stilwell gave way to acerbity and indulged himself in making hasty and harsh judgments of both Wavell and Chiang.

The loss of Burma reduced China to dependence on supplies that could be flown in from India. These were meager, and the Chinese were eager for their American and British allies to retake the area. Chiang called for a new campaign but made the commitment of Chinese troops contingent upon the assignment of adequate British ground forces and insisted above all that victory in Burma would require large scale British amphibious operations. Given the many demands on the far flung battlefront, the British delayed.

In the meantime Stilwell was left with the task of doing what he could to strengthen the Chinese armies. This entailed the training of Chinese troops, and the distribution of lend-lease supplies, and dealing with Chiang Kai-shek. As early as July, 1942 Lauchlin Currie, assistant to President Roosevelt, after a visit in China, concluded that Stilwell was an unfortunate choice.[54] Stilwell was most certainly the hero of his troops, a man who trudged along their side through the jungles in the retreat from Burma, and a man who was determined to take whatever steps were necessary to create a military force capable of driving back the Japanese. He had one war to win; Chiang had several. Therefore, as Stilwell made decisions on the basis of preparing a military effort against the common enemy, he ran counter to Chiang who faced the necessity of coordinating the effort against the Japanese with his own aim of strengthening national unity. The latter called for the recognition of political aims, that is, so distributing supplies and so mapping strategy that the various regional generals, many of whom were ready to resist Chiang's program of centralization, could be kept in line. Stilwell had no patience with this juggling act because it repeatedly stood in the way of taking what were, given his one goal, the necessary steps. Stilwell fully understood the problem, but he was equally determined not to play the game of politics, believing that if he entered that arena he would be bested and his usefulness destroyed.

His efforts to steer this course were compromised by the presence of General Claire Chennault and the 14th Air Force. Chennault readily accumulated capital in the form of the goodwill and confidence of Chiang by carrying out an efficient air defense against the Japanese. He shared Stilwell's contempt and distrust for many leading Chinese officers but his own operation was much less dependent on their cooperation than Stilwell's. Chiang found it easy to work with Chennault and nourished this tie to his rich American ally, thereby gaining greater freedom to deal in a spirit of independence with Stilwell. The latter was left to rely on the argument that unless there came into being well-trained and well-equipped ground troops to defend the air bases the Japanese would destroy them as soon as Chennault's air campaign became effective.[55]

The friction between Chiang and Stilwell caused concern in Washington. In the face of criticism, General George Marshall defended Stilwell as the most able man available for the China post. In April 1943 Lauchlin Currie forwarded a memorandum to Marshall dealing with conditions in China and the difficulties encountered by Stilwell. The memorandum, probably called into being by Roosevelt's increasing concern over the feud between Chiang and Stilwell, was the work of John Davies of the American Embassy, who had worked closely with the American commander.

Davies provided a graphic and realistic description of the China scene. The Chinese were conserving their strength and to a considerable degree leaving it up to the United States to do the fighting. This attitude on their part was the product of sheer military exhaustion. Davies likewise accepted simply as facts of life the venality that permeated the Chinese Army, the trade between the Chinese and the Japanese and the nature of Chinese domestic politics. He wrote of the Generalissimo that he "maintains his paramount position as he attained it—through political manipulation." Davies wrote, "He is not a dictator. He has no absolute overall command. He manipulates a delicate and shifting balance of power." As a result, Davies explained, "there is no one with whom Stilwell can deal."[56]

Davies then described the nature of the Chinese Army. He wrote:

> The Chinese Army is not an army in the sense that we use the word army. Rather it is an agglomerate of feudalistic military forces held more or less together by personal loyalties, endowments, grants in aid, threats of superior weight and indifferent toleration. The Generalissimo's relation to this armed mass is variable. A few divisions he can count upon to obey his orders fairly faithfully, within the limits of their ability. Others, no. He wisely does not attempt to issue to some of the more independent commanders orders which he has reason to believe they would be unwilling to obey. Many orders are issued only after negotiation with the commander of his Chungking representative.[57]

Given these facts, Stilwell found it extremely difficult to carry out his directives. Davies acknowledged that "Vinegar Joe" had "not

concealed his thoughts on Chinese incompetence and corruption."
On the other hand, Davies observed, Stilwell has been "wise enough
not to try to play their game for if he had done so they would have
bested him at every turn."[58]

The Stilwell issue remained in the background during 1943 in
large part because Marshall remained loyal to him. By early 1943
Roosevelt was disturbed by the reports of Stilwell's hostility to
Chiang. During that gloomy year conditions in China deteriorated to
the extent that the continued rule by the Kuomintang came into
question. It had been assumed earlier that China could hang on, but
the regime was increasingly subject to charges of incompetence, of
corruption, of lacking the will to fight, and of callousness toward the
sufferings of its own people.

These conditions emphasized the importance of recapturing
Burma. Chiang pressed for a large-scale campaign and promised to
provide twenty divisions provided the British agreed to an amphibious operation and the Americans supplied a division. At the Casa-
blanca Conference in January 1943, opinions among the military
men were divided. General Marshall and Admiral Ernest King supported a Burma campaign with firmness. General Henry Arnold, of
the Air Force, prompted by Chennault, who viewed it as both costly
and unnecessary, opposed it.[59] Roosevelt strongly supported it;
Churchill did not oppose it. The decision reached called for a campaign in November 1943.

Then came a landslide of other demands. Chiang and Chennault
insisted on a major strengthening of the air forces in China; the
shipments seriously interfered with preparations for the recapture of
Burma. MacArthur and the commanders in the South Pacific and
Central Pacific argued that the time had arrived for a series of island
hopping campaigns.[60] From Moscow came impatient demands for a
second front in Europe.[61] From England came Churchill with questions concerning the difficulties of jungle warfare and the danger of
exaggerating the importance of the China theater and being lured
into minor projects that promised no significant gains.[62] By May 17
Chiang threatened to make peace with Japan unless Roosevelt made
a firm commitment to increase Chennault's air force and unless the
tonnage over the hump was increased.

The plan to retake Burma was not yet revoked but it was no longer on the main line under construction. Preparations went forward. Stilwell worked with his usual ardor in preparing the way. Yet, many pieces remained to be put into place, and the pieces had not been committed by each of the various players. Most problematical was the amphibious force to go forth to recapture Rangoon from the sea.

In August at the Quebec Conference it was decided that the great invasion of Europe was to take place in May 1944. In the meantime, the Burma operation had slipped into postponement. Its future now depended upon the decisions to be reached at the forthcoming conferences of the leaders at Cairo and Teheran.

The first plenary session at Teheran opened on November 28. Roosevelt reviewed the plans for the Pacific including the proposed Burma operation.[63] At this same session Joseph Stalin announced that once Germany had been defeated the Soviet Union would join the war against Japan.[64] The earlier strategy of attacking Japan from air bases in China was already assuming less urgency because of the American success in the Pacific island hopping campaign and now, with the prospect of the Soviet Union driving toward Japan from its Pacific maritime provinces that strategy appeared even less important.

At the meeting in Cairo, Chiang had shifted grounds several times on the question regarding plans for the Burma campaign. However, he remained firm on the necessity of an amphibious operation to take the Andaman Islands. Then, after the Teheran meeting, Roosevelt and Churchill met again at Cairo. It was there that Churchill gave a full explanation of his views. Now that the Soviet Union was committed to entering the war against Japan, he explained, "this would give us better bases than we would ever find in China, and [this] made it all the more important that we should concentrate on making Overlord [invasion of Europe] a success." The Prime Minister went on to question the importance of the Burma operation, by now scheduled for March, and pointed to the fact that the Allies were being asked to commit 50,000 troops to dislodging 5,000 Japanese from the Andaman Islands.[65] Roosevelt and his staff sought in vain to commit the British to the amphibious operation. The point at which the long-delayed operation came to a crunching halt was the availability of sufficient landing craft for both the English Channel crossing and the Andaman Islands operation. Roosevelt was left with the unenviable task of informing Chiang Kai-shek of the decision.[66]

On December 23, 1943, Chiang sent his reply protesting the relegation of the China theater to the background and reminding President Roosevelt that the decision had given rise to misgivings on all sides. He could not, he explained, send his troops where they would be exposed to being outflanked by the Japanese in Burma.[67] Chiang had already, at Cairo, asked for a new billion dollar loan. The tragedy in China, however, was already taking a new direction for, by the close of 1943, behind the curtain of occupation, military failure, economic deterioration, and the collapse of administration, domestic forces had assumed a new alignment. The Communists had emerged as a second China, powerful, dynamic, and heralding a new order.

NOTES TO CHAPTER II

1. Clarence E. Gauss to the Secretary of State, February 21, 1942, *Foreign Relations of the United States 1942 China*, p. 25.

2. John A. Magruder, United States Military Mission, to Department of War, February 10, 1942. *Foreign Relations of the United States 1942 China*, p. 15.

3. Report by Carl F. Remer and R. D. Wolcott, January 23, 1943. CAD 014 Military Records, National Archives.

4. Spiker to Secretary of State, January 9, 1940, ibid, 1940, p. 261.

5. *Morgenthau Diary (China)*, Prepared by the Subcommittee to Investigate the Administration of the Internal Security Act and other Internal Security Laws of the Committee on the Judiciary, United States Senate, February 5, 1965 (Washington: Government Printing Office, 1965), Vol. I, pp. 458–62.

6. Ibid.

7. Ibid.

8. Ibid

9. Gauss to Secretary of State, August 20, 1941, *Foreign Relations of the United States The Far East, 1941*, pp. 534–35.

10. Treasury Department Inter-Office Communication, February 17, 1942, Digest of Report by Mr. Fox to the Secretary of the Treasury on China's financial and economic conditions, *Morgenthau Diary*, Vol. I, pp. 730–31.

11. Memorandum of John J. Macdonald, Second Secretary of the Embassy, of Interview with Dr. Franklin Ho, Nankai Institute of Economics, *Morgenthau Diary*, pp. 497–98.

12. Gauss to the Secretary of State, May 5, 1942, quoted in *Morgenthau Diary*, Vol. I, pp. 824–29.

13. Arthur N. Young, *China's Wartime Finance and Inflation, 1937–1945* (Cambridge, Mass.: Harvard University Press, 1965), p. 147.

14. Ibid., pp. 33–34.

15. Ibid., p. 63.

16. Gauss to the Secretary of State, November 16, 1942, *Foreign Relations of the United States 1942 China*, pp. 545–46.

17. Ibid., Memorandum of Conversation of Gauss with General Joseph Stilwell on July 11, 1942, p. 112.

18. Memorandum of Conversation with Stilwell, July 11, 1942, Gauss to

Secretary of State, *Foreign Relations of the United States 1942 China*, p. 112.

19.   Gauss to the Secretary of State, December 30, 1941, cited in *Morgenthau Diary*, Vol. I, pp. 547–48.

20.   Entry for January 29, 1942, *Morgenthau Diary*, Vol. I, pp. 634–35.

21.   Entry for February 2, 1942, *ibid.*, p. 635.

22.   Entry for January 13, 1942, "Financial Assistance to China," ibid., p. 610.

23.   Ibid., p. 610.

24.   Ibid., p. 660.

25.   Ibid., p. 746.

26.   Paraphrase of cable from Gauss, March 1, 1942, ibid., p. 763.

27.   Meeting in Mr. Bell's Office, March 19, 1942, 2:30 P.M., ibid., p. 781.

28.   Ibid., pp. 781–82.

29.   Meeting in the Secretary's Office, 11:00 A.M., April 11, 1942, ibid., pp. 810–12.

30.   SEGAC to Currie, April 19, 1942, Roosevelt Papers.

31.   Gauss to the Secretary of State, September 4, 1942, "Memorandum of Conversation with British Ambassador," *Foreign Relations of the United States 1942 China*, pp. 148–49.

32.   According to Arthur N. Young, financial adviser to the National Government, China received only about 1 ½ percent of Lend-Lease aid in 1941–1942; in 1943 and 1944 only about half of one percent; and in 1945, up to the end of the war, about 4 percent. Arthur N. Young, *China and the Helping Hand 1937–1945* (Cambridge: Harvard University Press, 1963), p. 402.

33.   Papers of Admiral William Leahy, Library of Congress, Entry in Diary, April 14, 1943.

34.   Ibid.

35.   Leahy Papers, *Diary*, Entry for April 7, 1943.

36.   Office of the Chief of Naval Operations to the Department of State, April 16, 1942, *Foreign Relations of the United States 1942 China*, p. 31.

37.   Leahy Papers, *Diary*, Entry for May 9, 1943.

38.   Memorandum of Stanley Hornbeck, April 3, 1943, *Foreign Relations of the United States 1943 China*, p. 44.

39.   *Morgenthau Diary, China*, p. 462.

40.   Memorandum by John Davies, Jr. Gauss to the Secretary of State, July 14, 1942, *Foreign Relations of the United States: 1942 China*, pp. 210–11.

41. Memorandum by the Assistant Chief of the Division of Far Eastern Affairs (George Atcheson), April 7, 1943, *Foreign Relations of the United States: 1943 China*, pp. 45–46.

42. Atcheson to the Secretary of State, June 23, 1943, *ibid.*, p. 65.

43. Ibid., July 24, 1943, p. 79.

44. Ibid., August 13, 1943, p. 87.

45. Ibid., pp. 87–88.

46. Memorandum of Conversation with the Reverend Charles L. Mecus and the Reverend Leo J. Ferrary, Atcheson to Secretary of State, September 17, 1943, ibid., p. 120.

47. Atcheson to the Secretary of State, July 20, 1943, ibid., pp. 76–77.

48. Gauss to the Secretary of State, September 18, 1943, p. 125.

49. Ibid., pp. 125–26.

50. Gauss to the Secretary of State, February 19, 1935, Enclosure Gauss to Willys Peck, February 18, 1935, Department of State Archives, 893.00/12976.

51. T. V. Soong, Minister for Foreign Affairs, to the Secretary of State, August 18, 1943, *Foreign Relations of the United States: 1943 China*, pp. 94–95.

52. Memorandum by the Assistant Chief of the Division of Far Eastern Affairs (Carter Vincent), September 21, 1943, ibid., p. 127.

53. The proposed Burma campaign was a topic of almost constant discussion between the Chinese and Americans in Chungking throughout 1942 and 1943. In September 1943 George Atcheson warned once again that failure to recapture Burma would be a disaster to Chinese morale of first magnitude. Atcheson to the Secretary of State, September 11, 1943, ibid., p. 117.

54. Leahy Papers, *Diary*, entry for September 10, 1942.

55. General George Marshall urged that a campaign be undertaken in Burma and warned that unless material reached the Chinese, the air fields used by the Americans would be taken by the Japanese. Memorandum for the President, March 16, 1943, by General George C. Marshall, Department of the Army, National Archives.

56. Lauchlin Currie to General Marshall, April 22, 1943, Executive #10, Item #57, Records of O P D, National Archives.

57. Ibid.

58. Ibid.

59. For a detailed account of the negotiations and the positions taken by each of the several leaders, see Herbert Feis, *The China Tangle* (Princeton, N.J.: Princeton University Press, 1953), p. 67.

60. Ibid., p. 65.

61.   Ibid.

62.   Ibid., p. 66.

63.   *Foreign Relations of the United States: The Conferences at Cairo and Teheran 1943*, p. 488.

64.   Ibid., p. 489.

65.   Ibid., pp. 675–76.

66.   Ibid., p. 725.

67.   Ibid., p. 856.

CHAPTER III

American Disillusion with the Kuomintang

China, at the outbreak of the war, had only recently entered upon the slow and painful process of economic and political modernization. While statistics on China were not wholly reliable, a Chinese economist, D. K. Lieu, placed the railway mileage at approximately 12,500, with most of them in Manchuria and along the coast, and the highway mileage at 50,000. Lieu estimated the number of factories to be 2,435 and their total capitalization at about $30 million in American dollars. The factory labor force was less than half a million and three-fifths of these were women and children. The country's resources in iron, coal, and especially fuel oil were developed only to a very limited extent, of fuel oil almost not at all.[1] On the side of assets was the recently established new and stable currency and a banking system adequate to peacetime needs.

The war placed demands on this economy that could not be met. Most of the limited productive facilities were located in what quickly became occupied territory. The Chinese labored heroically to transport machinery and other productive assets by boat, rail, truck, and by sheer carrying to the interior. Production in Free China during the early war years even surpassed prewar production in some few categories related to the war effort. The localized character of the economy also proved to be an asset insofar as the great majority of the population made their living by tilling the soil and were to a degree self-sufficient, and therefore less victimized by the crippling effects of the war on the economy.

This provided slight consolation when the gap between wartime needs and the capacity to produce widened into a vast gulf. D. K. Lieu, the Chinese economist, likened the effect to strangulation. "Less and less supply of essential goods," he wrote, "reached China from the outside world and the coastal provinces, just as the breath of a strangled man, becomes shorter and shorter," As the rope tightened around the country's neck, the power to resist declined and economic chaos ensued. "It is one thing to fight," Lieu noted sadly, "but it is another and an entirely different matter to be suffocated to death."[2] This was a much too simple explanation of China's difficulties, but the cutting off of access to foreign supplies during the war was certainly a factor of considerable importance.

Free China, consisting of approximately the same area as the mountain states of the western United States, but much less developed in terms of both production and transportation, was cut off from the rest of the country and from the outside world. Yet it sought to support an army of almost three million and a population equivalent to that of the United States. There were only 28 blast furnaces in Free China and the output of steel declined. In 1943 only 10,000 metric tons of steel were produced. There were only 1,300 miles of railways in Free China. There were almost no roads built to accommodate automobiles and trucks. Herein lay one of the causes of the frightful tragedies that beset the Chinese people and reduced the government to becoming, it seemed, the enemy of its own people.

Inflation appeared after the first months of hostilities as the shortage of goods began to make itself felt. As the gap between revenue and expenditures widened and the government printed money to make up the difference with only limited reserves to support the new issue, prices rose and by 1943 spiraled.

The government, fully aware of the danger, moved to meet the problem, but given the nature of the economy neither price controls nor rationing were effective. The teeth of government controls simply failed to take hold in the economy. Attempts at price control proved to be like vain flailings against the wind. Transportation, much of it by the most primitive means, constituted a major element in determining costs, so that costs varied greatly according to the location of the market. In the major centers, such as Chungking, it was not too difficult, but to set the prices for each of the hundred of markets in China's ten thousand villages proved to be impossible. Policing price control proved to be even more difficult, for there were few major spouts of production and hundreds of minor ones, just as there were few large channels of distribution but an infinite number of small ones.

Efforts at rationing failed in general and for much the same reason. The government succeeded to some degree in those lines of production, such as cotton textiles, where there was a limited number of distributors and manufacturers. It could not police the myriad petty manufacturers tucked away in the back stalls of the narrow little passageways that constituted the arteries of China's towns and cities.

A streak of inflation ensued. Using the price level of July 1937, when war with Japan began, as an index equal to 100, wholesale prices mounted to 1,121 by January 1941, to 7,930 by January 1943, to 14,850 by July 1943, to 26,402 in January 1944, and to 44,789 in June 1944.[3] The political and social results of this spiraling rise in prices added up to the survival of the most venal and the erosion of reasonable self-restraints on the part of those whose skill, position, or resources enabled them to guide their individual skiffs through the monetary rapids. Not all suffered alike. Living costs ranged like wild geese flying from Chungking and Kunming down to the largely self-sufficient village whose self-sufficient peasants were to a degree immune. But no one wholly escaped. Communist-controlled areas also suffered the same virulent inflation, making everyday economic transactions a desperate game of survival.

In the ensuing maelstrom the government at Chungking became the target of all criticism, justified and unjustified. The rougher the water of the surrounding social sea the more government leaders succumbed to a loss of faith in their constituency and the more they yielded to seeking solutions by repression. Prior to the war years the Kuomintang's major aim was the achievement of national unity by shrewd manipulation and bargaining with regional military bosses who, in turn, used their wits and their troops to elude the noose of threatened centralization.

The painful process went on its weary way during the war years. Neither the presence of the foreign invader nor the desperate plight of the masses interrupted the jockeying for position. Moreover, unification, in itself a desirable goal, in the hands of the increasingly reactionary Kuomintang and the increasingly dominant military element in the government, became no more than an excuse for perpetuating their own power. The leaders succeeded in some measure in extending their control; but the regional regimes of Szechwan and Yunnan continued to exercise a great degree of autonomy, and some other provinces also retained considerable independence. Because significant political and social reforms implied unification, the local leaders usually had no greater interest in progressive measures than the leaders of the central government.

The man at the top of the pyramid, Chiang Kai-shek, succeeded in managing the uneasy coalition of forces by making compromises when necessary and by ruthless destruction of rivals whenever the opportunity presented itself. The KMT controlled approximately two-thirds of the central forces; the other units of the large army were only nominally under his control. To a considerable degree he negotiated with generals rather than commanded them. Some warlords deserted him and joined the puppet forces.

The Kuomintang Party was similarly an uneasy political congeries held together by the Generalissimo. Its members' views ranged over a wide spectrum, including some on the left, conservative business types who wished to modernize the country but to limit control to a few, reactionaries who viewed Nazi Germany as their model, and liberals who firmly believed in representative government, Western legal institutions, and economic and social reforms. The total party membership equaled only one percent of the total population, and the party, in turn, was controlled by a handful of powerful conservatives and the military. As early as 1927 Chiang had lost most of his revolutionary fervor and had thereby lost touch with the masses and their felt needs and aspirations. In the words of a United States Army intelligence report the Communists were closer to the principles of Sun Yat-sen than was the Central Government.

Support of the party rested on the bureaucracy's and the army's dependence upon it for their positions. Given the precarious position of the petty official in a society offering few economic opportunities, he faithfully served the party in return for his own security. In the lower ranks the party's patronage remained loyal because it was the only way to survive. At these lower levels, in the local army garrison, the city, the province and the village, the rewards were not power but petty jobs in the bureaucracy, small rewards in the way of privilege, and access to compensation for favors. At the top of the structure the rival groups remained within the party seeking to use it. The leaders in the National Government did not think in terms of the desirability of building a broad political base. The C-C Clique considered powers based on the traditional power—centered gentry and industrialists soundest. The peasants—more than eighty percent of the population, illiterate, ill-informed, and absorbed in their daily routine tasks—did not matter.

Outside this political structure, Chinese society resembled a huge iceberg. Only small segments of those who enjoyed some modest wealth, comfort, and education protruded through the social strata of the great masses. They were isolated phenomena in a society whose chief characteristic was the struggle for survival. They, too, knew the precariousness of their position. Like the high walls which rendered their homes secure from vandals, the modestly privileged found psychological security from the surrounding scene of brutality in their sense of superiority nourished by their education, their urbanity, and their superior drive and ability. The world beneath them was too much to cope with. They feared the illiterate masses as potentially volatile. They could support or tolerate the Nationalist Government as long as it maintained the system that allowed them to function as professionals, subprofessionals, or small entrepreneurs.

This was the society over which the Kuomintang presided. Within that structure the government had few options to extend its control or to meet the problems created by the war. Chiang was a prisoner of the cliques and factions surrounding him. These cliques could quietly and even unobtrusively, by not cooperating in those areas in which their cooperation was necessary for the government to function, control policy.

The system inspired a minimum of loyalty among the masses and grudging cooperation among the petty tyrants of officialdom, those who enjoyed the advantages of local influence, and the few organized political groupings. The patchwork system might have survived had the government found it possible to manage the problems of inflation, conscription, and mobilization. The magnitude of these problems would have defied the most able men even if they had been free to move as national interest dictated, for the problems were almost beyond solution. As it was, circumscribed by the political necessities of retaining the support of a variety of centers of powers, the government was reduced to measures of token military resistance, meeting the costs of war by use of the printing press, trading with the enemy to meet in some small part the demand for consumer goods, and bargaining with a wealthy American ally whose priorities were elsewhere. In the meantime, the individual parts, seeking to survive, grasped at the meager opportunities available, thereby contributing to the complete breakdown of public morale.

The avalanche of tragedies sufficed to overwhelm a people renowned for fatalism in the face of tragedy.

The weaknesses and failures of an entire political and social system became personalized. After 1937, Chiang Kai-shek symbolized the regime. His private strengths and weaknesses provided an easy and simple way of explaining readily what was intricate, not easily perceived, and beyond the realms of the ordinary observer's domain of both information and understanding. This was true in China and in the United States. The result was an exaggeration of Chiang's importance although the Generalissimo was more than a mere puppet pulled thither and yon by a variety of elements involved in a power struggle. In spite of his limitations in the face of one of the twentieth century's kaleidoscopic transformations, Chiang came to represent Chinese resistance and nationalism to such a degree that not even the Communists, who despised him, nor the leaders in the Soviet Union, chose to defy him openly. Both professed a willingness to recognize his leadership. At the same time, the myth surrounding him and the individual reality differed sharply.

Those who had occasion to meet him personally did not find him a charismatic figure. An American residing in Chungking looked upon him as an enigma but viewed his love of power as his dominant trait. The total report made clear that the author was highly conversant with the situation in Chungking, that he was critical of United States Army Headquarters for the friendly association with the Communists, and that he viewed the Burma campaign as a mistake. The American wrote:

He is an immense complex personality, full of contradictions. His ruthlessness is only equalled by his addiction to high-sounding generalities
and copy-book mottoes. He is deeply cunning in all things Chinese, but
thoroughly inexperienced and inept in dealings with the outer world.[4]

Others cited qualities of stubbornness and an inability to trust anyone
who did not wholly agree with him or pretended to agree. These
were qualities he displayed during the crucial years. They were in
part a product of his narrow military education, but they were also
undoubtedly nurtured by the nature of the society in which he ruled.
He presided over a delicate balance of forces and he survived not
because of popularity or great social vision that inspired confidence
but because he was adroit in playing one group against another.
While he more often obstructed liberal reforms, as an ardent nationalist with an antiforeign bias, he promised the Chinese equality in the
family of nations and repudiated foreign domination. His party repeatedly committed itself to reforms, but Chiang gave these efforts
no support. At a time when Chinese society suffered from gross forms
of exploitation and the masses bitterly nursed their grievances, he
turned his back on them. In the end, in turn, he received their backs.

Criticism of Chiang and his regime overreached the facts, but the
desultory performance led to disillusion. Family ties, connections
with those who had influence, and ability and willingness to pay for
the privilege of office determined appointments. As a result, the
bureaucracy fell into ways of indifference and incompetence. At the
upper levels, loyalty to the Generalissimo rather than competence
constituted the basis for appointment. His extreme distrust ruled out
many able people. Consequently, the government slid into a state of
mere time serving.

The working class had failed to benefit by Kuomintang rule even
before the war. No factory worker received sufficient wages to support a wife and children. The war and the accompanying inflation
gradually reduced their real income to twenty-seven percent of what
it had been in 1937.[5] Craftsmen and rural workers suffered less from
inflation but did not escape the extortion of tax collectors, the terrors
of military conscription, and the suffering wrought by the war.

China's peasants, although less subject to the hardships imposed by
inflation, suffered other ills. In March 1944 Everett Drumright, Sec-

ond Secretary of the Embassy, traveled through parts of Shensi. North of Sian, in a valley known for its fertile soil and fine crops of cotton and wheat, he found that the relations between the peasants on the one hand and the army and government officials on the other were severely strained. He attributed the tension "to imposition of onerous grain and fuel taxes, miscellaneous exactions and the ever-increasing corruption and graft of the officials." The farmers, he said, were being pressed to such a point of desperation that uprisings could be expected. Drumright, who was concluding a two month trip through several provinces, observed that the situation was "typical of conditions in many other areas of Shensi, Honan, Anhwei and other provinces."[6]

Reports from American representatives had not lauded the Nationalist Government or its leadership at any time since it had come to power in 1928. The reports became gloomier as the economy and the spirit of the people withered in the heat of war. By the late summer and autumn of 1943 the accounts reaching Washington were scarcely less than appalling and that was to be the tone through December 1944, at which time the Methodist missionary, Olin Stockwell, was to write to his board in New York that it was "difficult to write in anything but a lugubrious tone." He wrote, "One feels about China these days that she has reached bottom," going on to say:

> Several facts are clear. China has no more fight in her, and the Chinese army is utterly undependable as a force of resistance against the Japanese. The central government has completely lost the confidence of the educated in China, and continued fascist methods cannot compel a revival of that confidence. Local military warlords are impatiently awaiting the collapse of the central authorities so that they can step in and take over.[7]

Not all missionaries took so bleak a view, but the hundreds of reports that reached Washington from Embassy officials, representatives of the Office of Strategic Services, military men, and news correspondents uniformly expressed deep dismay. Even the great admirer of Chiang, Dr. Walter Judd, formerly a medical missionary, in reporting to John Carter Vincent of the State Department after a visit in Chungking, appeared pessimistic. A Chinese friend had told Judd that the Kuomintang government "had reached a point where it was too weak to rule but that it was too strong to be overthrown, and that it would therefore continue in power." Vincent, in a memo for Joseph Grew, noted, "Dr. Judd seemed to think that it was a very apt description of the situation."[8]

A judicious and not unfriendly assessment by American military intelligence in December 1943 concluded that China could contribute almost not at all to the carrying on of the planned offensives against Japan. With the exception of a few divisions, the army was underfed, poorly trained, poorly led, and even more poorly equipped. The population was war weary and also demoralized by the widespread corruption of officials. Nothing then should be expected for improved conditions, and an efficient army could not be developed in the time that the war was likely to last. These conclusions were accepted in high places, but so also were other observations in the report. China must be kept in the war in spite of her inability to contribute to the offensive against Japan because should she make peace the shock to the American people would be devastating. In addition, in spite of the weakness of the Chinese armies if China left the war now, then a million men of the Kwangtung army would be available for redeployment to the South Pacific.

Sympathetic understanding of China's predicament could have bridged the gulf in part, but this was ruled out by the shock of Americans as they learned of the corruption, brutality, human suffering, and mismanagement. These were to a considerable degree the by-products of the weak economy which had scarcely entered upon modernization but political blundering was certainly also a major contributing factor. An ally unable to carry its weight in the war would have generated a degree of contempt in any case. Given the focus of attention on the moral and human shortcomings that were the result rather than the cause of China's weakness, Americans added a sense of moral outrage to their contempt. However askew their analysis of the causes, they gradually came to see the facts.

The most shocking accounts were those of the famine in Honan in 1942 and early 1943. Two correspondents visited the province early in 1944. The report of one of these observers, Theodore White, reached Washington through the Office of Strategic Services. The graphic account told of dogs eating human bodies by the road, peasants seeking human flesh under the cover of darkness, endless deserted villages, stinking beggars swarming around every city gate, babies abandoned to cry and die on every highway. Peasants were eating elm bark, peanut shells, pond weed. The correspondent saw people "stuffed into boxcars, flatcars, old coaches, layer upon layer deep." They were "crowded upon the roofs of these cars—children, old men and women clinging to any possible finger grip" as the train hurtled along. "Sometimes," he wrote, "their fingers get so numb from the cold that they [the Chinese] fall off rushing trains and are killed, but the trains never halt." He continued, "It is always the same where refugees gather aboard special trains—stench of filth, crying babies, doomed wrinkled faces swathed in dirty towels against the cold, and acres of blue-gray clad humanity, spotted here and there with red-clothed babies and an occasional peasant woman wearing a dirt smeared red remnant of her bridal costume."

It was China at its lowest point. The report continued:

> They were just people walking in the cold in repetitions of familiar patterns: again and again we saw a father pushing a wheelbarrow, the mother hauling in front with a rope, a baby lying on padding in the barrow crying and more often silent. . . . There were men who had collapsed with wives helping them along or mothers who had collapsed with children gazing at them and crying. The children were astounding—some leaned on staffs like old men, others carried bundles bigger than themselves, others seemed to be dreamwalking with unseeing eyes. The trek went past us westward, hour after hour, as it had been going for months and would continue for many days. The wind blew hard from the east and dust chased after them as they drifted along.[9]

The famines in Honan resulted from crop failures, but the hardships endured could be attributed in part to the government. Peasants, in spite of a very poor crop in 1942, paid taxes in grain. In some cases, the American correspondent reported, "they paid out more grain than they raised, selling land, goods, and animals in order to buy grain to meet the government needs." The army in the area collected as usual what it needed. Government officials received their regular allotments. The government was sharply criticized for taking an indifferent attitude until late in the day. The fact that transportation difficulties made it extremely difficult to send relief did not assauge the local population's bitterness. When the Japanese invaded the province in the spring of 1944, the peasants of Honan rose up against the Chinese troops, captured 50,000 rifles, and fought on the side of the Japanese.[10] The Honan tragedy left a permanent mark. Nowhere else in China was there such mass suffering.

However, deep distress was not limited to Honan. American reports told of abuse, tragedy, corruption, and the breakdown of government everywhere. The Central Government issued military conscription quotas for each province and then local officials, acting in the manner of press gangs, went from village to village presenting their demands. Because entry into the army was viewed as an almost certain death sentence, every effort was made to elude military service. The press gangs often seized anyone who happened to be on the streets, tied them together with ropes, and marched them off at gun point.

This practice continued in spite of an order by the Ministry of War forbidding press gangs. Conscription also became a device for extorting money from a village. How general the practice became cannot be determined. William R. Langdon, Consul General at Kunming, reported that the local mayor had openly announced that unwilling conscripts could contribute mules or horses to take their place. The local Chinese newspaper reported that 120 had applied for permission to do so. The candidate for conscription was asked to contribute CN $100,000 for the purchase of the animals, an amount of money many times as great as the actual cost.[11]

Drumright of the Embassy, a man given to caution in reaching conclusions, after his trip through Shensi early in 1944 cited the case of the village of Fuyintsun. The village was asked to provide eighteen military conscripts, but the military authorities "do not wish to receive these recruits and should they be sent to the military authorities for induction they would be horribly mistreated, beaten and forced to flee for their lives, following which a further demand would be made for recruits from the village." Drumright observed, "The military authorities do not wish recruits, they wish *money* in lieu of the recruits."[12]

Conditions in the army likewise led Americans to write highly unfavorable reports. As early as June 1943 George Atcheson of the American Embassy provided a picture of the general deterioration and commented on the decline of the army's quality and morale. He quoted a Chinese newspaperman as stating that the army was "ineffective either for resistance to Japanese attack or for quelling these agrarian disturbances." Many troops, said this newspapermen, "are half starved," and increasing numbers were deserting. More recently, several generals along with their troops had gone over to the puppet regime in Nanking.[13]

In April 1943 Stilwell reported on the malnutrition and the corruption in the army. According to "Vinegar Joe" one division, during the previous year, had lost 1,500 through malnutrition. As a sample of the rackets in the Chinese army, Stilwell cited the case of a division commander who had set up a fund for soldiers who died of sickness. Stilwell reported that the allowance for burial was $15.00, that the commander took out $7.00 and passed $8.00 to the hospital superintendent who then took $4.00 and passed on $4.00 to his assistant. The negotiation ended with the assistant pocketing $2.00 and paying the carpenter $2.00.

A clerk in the American Embassy reported that of the troops he had seen passing on one road only one company, numbering about 300, was equipped with a rifle for each man. Of the remainder there were about eight rifles for a company.

In September 1944 Ambassador Gauss forwarded a copy of a letter written by a prominent scholar and educator, Chiang Mon-lin, Chairman of the Chinese Red Cross and President of the University of Peking. After a personal investigation he had concluded that soldiers and recruits were in a deplorable physical condition and he had so informed the Generalissimo. As a result, Chiang had made his own personal investigation and found conditions in a Chungking training camp so deplorable he had discharged the official. Dr. Chiang Mon-lin stated that out of every one hundred men drafted, only ten were physically fit and that only twenty-two out of every hundred were physically able to fight after they had been fed and trained.[14]

The same educator charged that officers provided for their own families first and troops did not receive the food to which they were entitled. He concluded that China's first need was food, secondly, medical attention, thirdly, able commanders, and lastly modern arms.[15] These observations were made by one who had been close to the Generalissimo.

William Langdon, Consul General at Kunming, forwarded a gruesome account of the treatment of Chinese soldiers. Soldiers were dying every day due to lack of food and shelter. Half-starved soldiers roamed the streets collecting decayed vegetables from which they made a gruel. This, in turn, had caused dysentery among a majority of the soldiers in the city, resulting in a daily average of four or five deaths.[16]

The lack of proper provisioning led to troops confiscating the goods of the peasantry. In July 1944 the hostility to the troops of the Central Government was the cause of open fighting between these troops and soldiers under the command of General Liu Wen-hui in Szechwan. In October 1944 Langdon reported on the number of newspaper editorials in the Chinese press in Kunming criticizing the government. One editorial stated that "soldiers who were strong and vigorous at the time of their conscription can now be seen on the streets of Kunming thin and pale and often barely able to walk." The municipal health department reported that 138 dead Chinese soldiers had been picked up during the month of August and an additional 69 in September.[17]

These conditions appeared to prevail in widely scattered districts. A Chinese intelligence officer who had been stationed in the area confided to the Second Secretary of the American Embassy that the system of conscription and of training and the treatment of soldiers in the Shantung-Kiangsu-Honan-Anhwei border area was miserable. Officers, he said, spent their time in smuggling goods from and to the Japanese and were also involved in the sale of narcotics. The soldiers lived off the people and were hated.[18]

Everett Drumright reported seeing thousands of troops from Szechwan marching to the Communist border area. He described them "as the most tattered, torn, tired and famished group of soldiers he had ever seen, many of whom were literally skin and bones and some of whom would perhaps die before reaching Paoki—troops who are not now and probably never will be in a condition to fight either the Japanese or the Communists."[19]

In June 1944 an Embassy official in an interview with two Chinese attributed the military debacle in Hunan to the low quality of Chinese officers. At the front, these officers, according to the Embassy official, had carried on a flourishing trade with the Japanese, thus lowering the morale of the troops. The officers were growing rich. At the same time, rank-and-file soldiers were suffering from undernourishment. A second Chinese source stated that the troops were infected by the knowledge that rival generals would not cooperate in fighting the enemy because they were more interested in avoiding losses that would weaken their position in the competition among rival factions.[20] The same observation was made by Sun Fo, the son of Sun Yat-sen and President of the Legislative Yuan, regarding the lack of cooperation among generals in the fighting at Hengyang.[21] But not all Chinese failed to put up effective resistance in Hunan. In fact, the troops under General Hseuh Yueh fought heroically. Ironically, Hseuh occupied semiautonomous status and was denied all support by Chiang.[22] Those who were critical of the conditions prevailing in the army had their views confirmed during the course of a long line of defeats by the Japanese in 1944.

The widespread criticism and series of military losses caused the Generalissimo to meet with a group of high-ranking officers for a two-week period in August 1944. Chiang called for reorganization and reform. It was decided that the soldiers should receive better care and better training. Officers who failed to carry out their duties were to be punished. According to one unconfirmed report the Generalissimo charged General Ho Ying-chin with misinforming him of the miserable conditions, of mishandling conscription, and with profiting from schemes he carried out on the side.[23]

A few weeks later the Peoples Political Council delved into the alleged scandals. Criticism centered on Hsu Kan, the Minister of Food, and Ho Ying-ch'in, Minister of War. After a review of the mishandling of food supplies, according to an informant the Embassy considered reliable, Hsu was asked why he tolerated such abuses. Hsu replied, "You must all know that no honest man seeks to enter the service of my Ministry." Ho faced at least an equally bristling inquiry from Council members, several of whom had carried out their own private investigations. They demanded to know why troops at the front were poorly equipped and why many of them were starving. Apparently he could provide no satisfactory answer.[24]

It was at this time that the Generalissimo dismissed Ho and made efforts to carry out reforms. No one questioned his sincerity, but several American and Chinese observers doubted that he would be able to accomplish much because too many officials would circumvent his orders. They could do so with some degree of impunity.

The primary interest of most Americans in China lay in the effectiveness of the Chinese army, the very weakest point in the regime. One American observer stated that only about half the soldiers were equipped with rifles.[25] Another military observer described the Chinese army as having "an almost negligible combat effectiveness."[26] Still another estimated that half a Japanese division was equal to a full Chinese division.[27]

The difficulty rested in part on the political considerations facing Chiang when he made what overtly appeared to be military decisions. Failure to provide supplies might lead to revolt, strengthening of one unit might be militarily advantageous but pose the danger of building up a rival. Each army, in turn, gave first thought to preserving its strength.

The situation was succinctly described in a paper prepared by General Stilwell's staff. "Political considerations," said the report, "enter into military considerations which have direct bearings on where troops will fight, which armies will receive equipment and how control is exercised." The American command, it was said, had to take into consideration the domestic side of every move. "Supplies," said the report, "must be so distributed so as not to unbalance one local set of half independent commanders as against another." The report continued, "Training must be offered so that the Generalissimo's own command will get the most benefit from it. Even strategy must be planned with an eye on political and personal considerations."[28]

Yet Chiang extended his control over areas that before the war were wholly under the rule of warlords. In the Szechwan province, the location of Chungking, General Liu Hsiang had reigned supreme, but a change began when he pledged support to the Central Government at the outbreak of war. After Liu's death the Kuomintang was gradually able to take over control of the province. Sinkiang, in the far northwest, constituted almost an independent satrapy under General Sheng Shih-tsai, who worked closely with the Soviet Union; however, in 1942, as the Soviet Union concentrated all its attention on turning back the German armies, Sinkiang came under the control of Chungking. Yunnan, directly south of Szechwan, preserved its autonomy in part, but the National Government also made some headway in this province.

These gains were paralleled by efforts to mobilize social groups under the control of the regime. Labor unions were controlled by the government and used to further its own aims. Youth was organized into the semimilitary *San Min Chu I* Youth Corps for the purpose of nationalistic indoctrination. Sun Fo described the highly regimented corps as developing its members into "heel-clicking puppets."[29]

The Kuomintang itself included groups of varying political shades, but as an American student friendly to the Nationalists put it in 1943 the hierarchy was "at best a collection of cliques among which Chiang Kai-shek acts as a moderator and preserves his own interests by the immemorial practice of playing one group off against another."[30] The cliques did not represent diverse approaches to problems of society. They were held together by mutual interest in preserving their own position at or near the top of the hierarchy. The three major groupings were the organizational party headed by the Ch'en brothers, the Whampoa military party, and the Political Science group. Chiang owed much to the Ch'en brothers; at the same time, as a military man and former head of the Whampoa Military Academy, he was tied to this second group. Both groups maintained their own secret service and kept a close check on each other.[31] Chiang played one against the other but he was not free to dictate to either, although it is true that he dismissed General Ho. By 1944 observers in China generally agreed that the C-C Clique held the upper hand. In any case neither group looked to the public for support, both adhered to one-party rule and viewed suppression of dissent as a legitimate function of government. In addition, both were intensely nationalistic, distrusted all foreign powers, and were prepared to use them when they could.

Neither the sharply limited political vision of these groups nor their primary concern with their own immediate political position was conducive to an imaginative meeting of the wartime economic, social, and military problems. By late 1943 and early 1944 the surrounding sea roared with anger and disgust. Strict censorship and the large organization of secret police served as dikes, but enough public criticims seeped through to suggest the scope of unrest.

Public criticism of the Nationalist Government did not appear in the United States until 1943. Official Chinese reaction to the unfriendly stories appearing in the American press in the spring of 1943, already discussed in an earlier chapter, was one of great alarm.

The response of Chinese critics of the Nationalist Government, was quite the opposite. They welcomed criticism on the ground that under pressure from the United States the government would have to face realities. In April 1944 Ambassador Gauss told of a high-level conference called by the Generalissimo at which he ordered them to prepare a plan for meeting the criticisms. The session, reportedly made up of reactionaries, took no action, but Gauss stated "we may safely say that we feel, and many liberal-minded Chinese also feel, that in the long run constructive criticism will be productive of benefit to China and to Sino-American relations, especially as such criticism furnishes sincere and objective Chinese critics of the present reactionary control of the party and Government with support in their quiet efforts of beneficial influence."[32] Gauss believed that American liberal criticism "impels at least an outward change in Chinese Government tendencies."[33]

John Service, serving on General Stilwell's staff, had an interview with the leaders of two minority parties, the Youth Party and the National Salvation Association. Both men continued to have faith in Chiang, believing that he demonstrated flexibility in the past and would do so again under pressure. American criticism, they said, "had been extremely beneficial" and was welcomed by liberal Chinese."[34] The two parties continued to support Chiang.

In spite of suppression of critical views, some Chinese were so well-known and enjoyed so much prestige that they could voice dissent. A distinguished scholar, Chang Lan, who represented genuine opposition to the existing regime, wrote a pamphlet entitled "China Needs Democracy", which appeared in September 1943. According to Chang, neither the Party nor the Government could any longer arouse the people to the needs of the nation. The public was much too disillusioned to listen to appeals because of "the corruption of the bureaucracy and the commercialization of officials." His judgment rang with severity:

Law and decree have both become scraps of paper. . . . Economically, the organs of monopoly and taxation have proliferated and have become burdensome and complicated. The result is that the government is hated on every side, the people are harassed, and the major gain flows into the pockets of the middlemen. As for the food policy, people who have no grain are made to pay grain. As for conscription, the homes who have no men must still provide men. These circumstances appear everywhere.[35]

In February, Arthur Ringwalt, Consul General at Kunming, reported to the Embassy that a member of the faculty at National Southwestern Associated University had sharply criticized the government in a public lecture. Recent proposals by the Generalissimo calling for a new constitution, he charged, were merely an effort to delude foreigners. In an interview with Ringwalt the professor, Chang Hsi-jou, said "there is no rule of law, there is no freedom of speech, no freedom of the press, no freedom of association; there is no guarantee against arrest and punishment without due process of law."[36] Eventually the professor went over to the Communists and in 1972 he was President of the Chinese People's Institute of Foreign Affairs in Peking.

Criticism also emerged within government circles. Early in 1944 Sun Fo took the lead in calling for democracy and constitutional reform. On February 23 he spoke before the Central Training Corps on the topic "Democratization of the Government and Planned Economy." The Kuomintang, Sun charged, had "forgotten the very substance and method of democracy," and "has unfortunately assumed the attitude and habits of ruling a ruling cast."[37] The American Embassy, in reporting the speech to Washington, stated that it was the first instance that had come to its attention "of outspoken semi-public criticism by a Kuomintang and Government leader of the fascist tendencies. . . ."[38]

Again, on April 3 Sun spoke in Chungking on "The Challenge to the San Min Chu I Youth Corps." The speech stressed the importance of freedom of speech and the need to think for oneself.[39] In another speech, before the Legislative Yuan, according to a report received by Gauss, Sun stated that China was a Fascist state and the Generalissimo a dictator.[40]

In May representatives of cultural circles in Chungking presented the Central Executive Committee with a statement protesting the suppression of freedom of speech and press. They charged that articles and books had been barred even though they in no way contravened any law. Action had been based on the vague assumption that they "did not accord with national policy or national characteristics or the demands of the war of resistance." In forwarding a copy of the protest, Ambassador Gauss informed the Secretary of State that it seemed unlikely that it would have been presented a year before. During the past year, he observed, "there has been an increasingly vocal critical attitude toward Kuomintang policies."[41]

In June, in anticipation of the arrival of Vice President Henry Wallace, the students of National Southwest Associated University placed posters on walls welcoming him as coming from a democracy and expressing regret that China was not a democracy. The students announced that they were opposed to Fascism and denounced the secret police and the treatment of soldiers.[42] Of course, in a truly Fascist state the students would not have been free to protest.

These first signs of revolt within areas controlled by the Nationalists coincided with the eruption of hostility in the corps of foreign correspondents. In February, at a government press conference, the representatives of the press asked about the blockade of the Communists. Theodore White refused to accept the official denial of a blockade and he was joined by others in pressing questions that evidenced hostility.[43]

Beginning in March the Japanese launched a series of successful military campaigns in Honan, badly defeating the Chinese forces although the Chinese greatly outnumbered them. By June the Japanese offensive had moved south into Hunan, and on June 18 Changsha fell to the Japanese. Only at Hengyang did the Nationalist forces show firm resistance. By November the Japanese had carried their offensive into Kweichow and by November 10 they occupied Kweilin and Liuchow.

These developments, in turn, awakened a desire to resist further centralization and gave rise to an important movement in the southwest to set up an independent government. Another development got underway in the southeast. Marshal Li Chi-sen of the Kwangsi military clique led a movement to bring together dissidents and to gain a position of influence in the Central Government. Li's efforts gained strength thanks to the consideration being given by a variety of groups to the establishment of a united front. Among the proponents were members of dissatisfied provincial groups, of the smaller parties who advocated democracy, liberals in the Kuomintang, and some military people. Li had not yet achieved any significant strength, but Joseph Grew in Washington thought it called for careful watching.[44]

In July there was a popular revolt against the Central Government in the Suifu area of the province. In August a movement took place to establish a provincial government to be known as the Southwestern Government of Joint Defense.[45] Dissident military leaders were involved.

There was considerable restlessness and threats of an uprising in the Chengtu area of Szechwan. J. K. Penfield, Second Secretary of the American Embassy, believed "that it was based primarily on a feeling that Szechwan and the Szechwanese are not being given a voice in national affairs commensurate with their contribution and importance." A more immediate issue was the repayment by the Central Government of rice loans negotiated in 1941 and 1942. There were other complaints, failure to appoint Szechwanese to positions, use of Szechwanese troops in the most dangerous positions, and failure to get American lend-lease military equipment.[46]

By October the rapid advances of the Japanese armies in Honan and Kwangsi aroused fear in Yunnan that the province was next on the list of enemy targets. The press in Kunming published urgent appeals for American military aid and support. General Lung Yun, Chairman of the Yunnan Provisional Government, formerly an "illiterate tribesman and now an unscrupulous despot," in the words of the American Consul at Kweilin, approached the United States directly.[47] He was supported by a local newspaper. The Kuomintang denounced his move as "provincialism." In turn, representatives of the Provincial government came forth with cries of slander and denunciations of the Central Government. The American Consul General professed that he did not know what would happen but he thought the Central Government did not trust General Lung and had no wish to see the Yunnanese armies strengthened, for they were already among the best. The distrust of Lung led to his being kidnapped in the middle of the night in October 1945 by officers of the Central Government.

The rising criticism of the Central Government and the succession of military defeats led some Chinese to hope that the Generalissimo would take the lead in bringing about reform. Liberals based their views in large part on China's dependence on the United States and felt certain that he would find it necessary to respond to American pressure. Miss Yang Kang, literary editor of the most important newspaper in Free China, wrote to John Service, calling for a total mobilization and said this could only be achieved through a coalition of all parties. The United States, she said, should promote this. It would be most disillusioning if the United States continued to support the present government.[48]

At the meeting of the Central Executive Committee in May those hoping for reform met disappointment. Chiang dismissed the charge that China was not a democracy as evidence of lack of understanding. Democracy, he said, was the goal. He advised that China should welcome sincere and friendly criticism, but much of the criticism constituted interference in China's internal affairs. Much of the foreign criticism should not be taken seriously. In the summary forwarded to Washington, the Embassy stated, "There is no indication in any reported versions of the Generalissimo's speeches that the vital military, political and economic problems with which China is now confronted were given the exhaustive and thoughtful consideration warranted by existing conditions."[49]

In a message to the Secretary of State on July 11 Ambassador Gauss reported that T. V. Soong thought Chiang was deeply worried but that he showed no signs of being prepared to meet the emergency. Gauss added that in his estimate the situation could only be met by a radical measure to achieve a united front of the representatives of all parties. This, he noted, would require a complete about- face on the part of the Generalissimo.[50] It was soon to become clear that Chiang was prepared to pursue bold measures, but these were measures to perpetuate the regime and not to bring about the reforms advocated by his critics.

The adamancy of Chiang in suppressing opposition and the recent awakening of the American public to the realities in China widened the gulf between the two countries. In April 1944 Raymond Gram Swing, one of the most widely listened to news commentators, expressed fear that the shock of suddenly finding that China was under totalitarian rule would prejudice the American public and the public's basic sympathy would be weakened. He called on the State Department "to give the fullest assurance to the leaders in Chung-

king that their own future, and the future relationship with this
country, depend on the earliest extension of democracy in China,
and staunch resistance in the meantime to extreme one-party des-
potism." This quite meaningless prescription for the solution of a
profound and complex problem far beyond the commentator's ex-
pertise symbolized the readiness of the mass media to make the
Chiang regime the target of self-righteous indignation.

By September 1944 General Chennault looked at the situation in
a different light and, while acknowledging that the Central Government had been the target of much criticism, saw as a major factor in
its gradual decline the defeats suffered by its armies at the hands of
the Japanese. He attributed these losses to the concentration of the
strongest Chinese forces in Burma. Now China's military strength
was reduced almost to the vanishing point. This, he believed, would
have far-reaching political repercussions. Yenan would benefit as
Chungking grew weaker. In his letter to President Roosevelt, Chennault stated, "There is only one way out now, as I see it. That is for
us to sponsor thorough political reconstruction at Chungking, followed by true unification between Chungking and Yenan."[51]

NOTES TO CHAPTER III

1. D. K. Lieu, *China's Economic Stabilization and Reconstruction* (New Brunswick, N. J.: Rutgers University Press, 1948), pp. 11–15.

2. Ibid., p. 66.

3. Ibid., p. 89.

4. "The Political-Military Situation in China," p. 5. Hurley Papers, University of Oklahoma.

5. Arthur Young, "By the end of 1943 at Chungking the money income of teachers . . . had risen only about a fifth as much as the cost of living, and of government officials only about a tenth, . . ." Young, *China's Wartime Finance and Inflation, 1937–1945*, p. 320.

6. Gauss to Secretary of State, March 27, 1944, *Foreign Relations of the United States Diplomatic Papers 1944*, Vol. VI, *China*, p. 384. Hereafter cited as *U.S. Foreign Relations 1944.*

7. Olin Stockwell to Frank T. Cartwright, December 28, 1944, Archives of the Board of United Methodist Missions.

8. Memorandum by the Chief of the Division of Chinese Affairs (Vincent) to the Director of the Office of Far Eastern Affairs (Grew), October 17, 1944, *U.S. Foreign Relations 1944*, p. 174.

9. Report to Office of Strategic Services, March, 1943, File 379.5, National Archives.

10. Ibid., September 4, 1944, File 94582, National Archives.

11. William R. Langdon, Consul General at Kunming, to Secretary of State, July 1, 1944, File 86741, National Archives.

12. Gauss to Secretary of State, March 27, 1944, Enclosure: Drumright to Gauss, March 16, 1944, File 893.00/15339, National Archives.

13. Atcheson to Secretary of State, June 9, 1943, Enclosure: Subject: Chinese Newspaperman's Concern Regarding Present Situation in China, File 40362, National Archives.

14. Gauss to Secretary of State, September 21, 1944, Enclosure: Copy of a letter setting forth remarks of Chiang Mon-lin, National Archives.

15. Ibid.

16. William R. Langdon to Secretary of State, July 1, 1944, File 86741, National Archives.

17. Ibid., October 13, 1944; *U.S. Foreign Relations 1944*, p. 173.

18. Edward E. Rice, Second Secretary of Embassy to Hurley, December 18, 1944, ibid., pp. 210–11.

19.   Gauss to Secretary of State, February 1, 1944, ibid., p. 316.

20.   Ibid., June 29, 1944, pp. 110–11.

21.   Ibid., July 27, 1944, p. 135.

22.   Warren I. Cohen, "Who Fought the Japanese in Hunan? Some Views of China's War Effort," *The Journal of Asian Studies*, Vol. XXVII, November 1967, pp. 111–15.

23.   Gauss to Secretary of State, August 19, 1944, *U.S. Foreign Relations 1944*, pp. 147–48.

24.   Ibid., September 22, 1944, pp. 160–61.

25.   "Notes on Problems Connected with Our Mission in China," p. 2, memorandum prepared for Hurley by G2 in Stilwell's headquarters, Hurley Papers, University of Oklahoma.

26.   Ibid., p. 2.

27.   Ibid., p. 6 (a).

28.   Ibid., see section entitled "China Situation."

29.   Gauss to Secretary of State, June 7, 1944, *U.S. Foreign Relations 1944*, pp. 447–448.

30.   David N. Rowe, "Balance of Power in China," *The Far Eastern Survey*, November 29, 1944, p. 232.

31.   Ch'ien, Tuan-sheng, *The Government and Politics of China* (Cambridge: Harvard University Press, 1950), pp. 129–31.

32.   Gauss to Secretary of State, April 18, 1944, *U.S. Foreign Relations 1944*, pp. 56–57.

33.   Ibid., April 3, 1944, pp. 392–93.

34.   Ibid., April 21, 1944, pp. 397–98.

35.   Ibid., February 21, 1944, File 893.00/15287, National Archives.

36.   Ibid., February 17, 1944, File 893.00/15292, National Archives.

37.   Ibid., March 27, 1944, *U.S. Foreign Relations 1944*, p. 385.

38.   Ibid.

39.   Ibid., April 25, 1944, File 74335, National Archives.

40.   Ibid.

41.   Ibid., June 15, 1944, *U.S. Foreign Relations 1944*, pp. 457–58.

42.   William R. Langdon to Gauss, July 11, 1944, File 893.00/7–1144.

43.   Gauss to Secretary of State, February 23, 1944, *U.S. Foreign Relations 1944*, pp. 349–51.

44.   Memorandum by the Director of the Office of Far Eastern Affairs (Grew) to the Under Secretary of State (Stettinius) May 31, 1944, ibid., p. 445.

45. Arthur R. Ringwalt, Consul at Kunming, to Gauss, August 28, 1944, File 893.00/8–2844, National Archives.

46. J. K. Penfield, Second Secretary of the Embassy, to the Secretary of State, September 13, 1944, *U.S. Foreign Relations 1944*, pp. 569–71.

47. William R. Langdon to Gauss, August 18, 1944, pp. 144–47 and Langdon to Secretary of State, October 19, 1944, *U.S. Foreign Relations 1944*, pp. 175–76.

48. Gauss to Secretary of State, July 20, 1944. Enclosure: John Service "Hope of Chinese Liberals that America Can Save China by Forcing Democratic Reform," July 11, 1944, File 893.00/7–2044, National Archives.

49. Gauss to Secretary of State, June 8, 1944, *U.S. Foreign Relations 1944*, pp. 448–52.

50. Gauss to Secretary of State, July 11, 1944, File 893.00/7/1244.

51. Major General Claire L. Chennault to President Roosevelt, September 21, 1944, *U.S. Foreign Relations 1944*, pp. 158–60.

CHAPTER IV

The Turning Point
in Sino-American Relations

Long before 1944 the disintegration of the Chinese Central Government and its failure to fight effectively caused deep concern in the Roosevelt administration and among the Joint Chiefs of Staff. However, during those World War II years neither the President nor the American military could afford to do more than exercise patience. China was simply too important in their future wartime plans. At that time it appeared that only from air bases in China would it be possible to bomb Japan. In addition, although China failed to take the offensive against Japan, its participation in the war kept large numbers of Japanese troops occupied in China at a time when they might have been deployed against the United States in the Pacific. The importance of these considerations enhanced China's bargaining power.

China's advantage in negotiations remained largely intact until the close of 1943. The United States had been heavily committed to operations in the Pacific even during the first year of the war in spite of the first priority given to defeating Germany. This heavy involvement caused concern to the British; at a meeting of the Combined Chiefs of Staff on January 18, 1943, they expressed fear that the United States was changing the priority. Admiral Ernest King denied it saying that the United States simply wished to go forward with the war in the Pacific so that as soon as Germany was defeated the main attack could be launched against the Japanese.[1] Marshall went further, contending that the United States, to avoid a sudden and disastrous reverse, must continue to maintain the initiative in the Pacific. The overall operations in that area, Marshall argued, hinged upon providing air support to China for operations against Japan and Japanese shipping. This, in turn, depended upon the reconquest of Burma. Marshall warned that unless that operation took place "a situation might arise in the Pacific at any time that would necessitate the United States regretfully withdrawing from the commitments in the European theater."[2]

During the course of 1943 this gradually became the American position. At first Roosevelt questioned the necessity of a Burma operation, expressing the view that Stilwell was too preoccupied with reconquering the territory that had been lost. The President sided with Chennault who contended that it was only necessary to create a strong air force in China, but he never overruled the Chiefs of Staff.[3] Chiang sided with Chennault, who argued that air power alone could defeat the Japanese, but he also favored the reopening of Burma subject to the launching of a large-scale amphibious operation against Rangoon prior to the opening of a land campaign. At the conference of the British and the Americans in Washington in May 1943, T. V. Soong argued that the reopening of Burma was absolutely necessary.[4] Churchill immediately took a strong stand in opposition, but did not rule out a limited operation in the north of Burma. This did not deter the Joint Chiefs from proceeding with their plans, and when Roosevelt met with Chiang at Cairo in November 1943 he too supported the plan. Stilwell, who was in attendance at the sessions of the Joint Chiefs at Cairo, stated that the opening of Burma was an essential first step toward China launching an aggressive campaign against the Japanese in the Hong Kong area.[5]

At Cairo, Roosevelt and the Joint Chiefs assumed that the British had changed their position. They were well aware of Wavell's earlier opposition to an amphibious operation on the ground that surface vessels could not carry out an operation in the face of shore-based aircraft unless they had the protection of their own shore-based aircraft. They were likewise aware that Churchill had strongly opposed the proposal, contending that it would be a major strategic error to disperse Allied strength and that the Burma jungle was no place to fight.[6] However, by November 1943 the British commander in the theater, Admiral Mountbatten, was prepared to launch a campaign in Upper Burma. Tensions between the British and the Americans over this issue had declined, and General Wedemeyer praised Mountbatten for his aggressiveness and cooperation.[7]

At the Cairo Conference other questions arose. The Generalissimo, whose Yunnan troops were to bear the brunt of the campaign, wanted it understood that their participation was contingent upon the continued shipment of 10,000 tons of supplies per month to China and that the demands of the Burma campaign must not be permitted to interfere.[8] At the November 25th meeting of the Joint Chiefs of Staff at Cairo the seriousness of the supply problem became apparent. The supplies requested for the Yunnan force, General Somervell reported, were far less than for the numerically smaller British force. The Chinese faced starvation rations. Marshall questioned Somervell further, and the latter revealed "that the comparison between the British forces and the Yunnan force with respect to supplies was at ten to one." Marshall asserted that he would pursue this matter, but Admiral Leahy thought the Chinese "should be presented with the alternative of accepting the Mountbatten plan or giving up the Burma campaign."[9]

Further complications arose when the Generalissimo once more stipulated that his troops would participate only if the British agreed to a large scale amphibious invasion of the Andaman Islands and Rangoon.[10] Roosevelt and his staff agreed to this demand.

The high priority Americans gave to China was further attested to by Roosevelt's request two weeks earlier for agreement to build the Chengtu airfields for the operation of B-29 bombers against Japan.[11] Marshall, too, was determined to work with China. In one of the early meetings of the Joint Chiefs at Cairo he raised the question of what demands Chiang would make on President Roosevelt. He wanted to protect the President against unreasonable pressure, but he also recognized that it was highly important for Chiang to show that he could get what China needed.[12]

This cooperative spirit on the part of the Americans was generated by the belief that China must be kept in the war so that the United

States could get air bases and look forward to Chinese support in attacking the Japanese forces on the mainland. The hard pressed Chiang regime used its bargaining power to advantage. Chiang desperately needed to bolster his political support. The regional warlords were becoming ever more resentful of his encroachment. By late 1943 they were sparring for every advantage and threatening Chiang's position. One way the Generalissimo could retain some measure of their allegiance was to buy their support with American funds.

The days following the Cairo Conference marked the beginning of a downward swing of the Generalissimo's American assets. At the Teheran Conference some days later Stalin promised he would enter the war against Japan after the defeat of Germany.[13] This made it less important to strengthen China and likewise, along with the successful American island-hopping campaign in the Pacific, reduced the value of air bases in China from which to attack Japan. Teheran changed the situation in another major respect. The cross-channel invasion of the European continent was set for the following May. Roosevelt and his military advisers continued to give a high priority to the recapture of Burma, but when they met Churchill in Cairo after the Teheran Conference, the Prime Minister resolutely opposed an amphibious operation against the Andaman Islands and Rangoon. He clinched the argument by pointing out that all Allied landing craft would be needed for the Overlord invasion of Europe. Roosevelt was left with the unpleasant assignment of informing Chiang Kai-shek that there would be no amphibious operation.[14]

Chiang replied that the "strategy of relegating the China War Theater to the background has given rise to serious misgivings on all sides." The opening of Burma, he said, "is a matter of life and death for China."[15] His complaint was based on the pitifully little aid China had received. Shipments by plane over the Hump averaged less than 10,000 tons a month and seventy-five percent went to the support of the American forces in China.

China faced a desperate situation. Inflation was severe, the army suffered from malnutrition and lack of equipment, graft existed everywhere—in part because army officers, government officials, and those on fixed incomes could not support their families.

Disappointed by the dropping of the plans for the Burma operation, Chiang, in December, turned to strengthening his position by asking for a billion dollar loan. China, given the shortage of transportation facilities, would not be able to use the money to relieve present stresses but money in the bank in New York would improve the political position of the regime.

Americans reacted strongly to the request for a loan. Confidence in the good faith of the Chinese had been undermined by controversy over the rate of exchange between the dollar and the yuan. The Chinese yuan, valued at 30 cents in 1937, had gradually fallen to five cents at the official rate, but even this did not reflect its real decline. Due to the extreme inflation in China, the yuan had fallen on the open market by 1943 to half a cent.

The breakdown of the economy and the political failures resulting from the war, horrible in their impact on the Chinese people, need no retelling. Inflation reflected the degree of economic and social dislocation that took place. The National Government made honest efforts at price control and rationing, but those efforts came to naught because there was no way to police either price control or rationing in a highly localized economy.

This economic decline reduced China to a most ineffective and disillusioning ally. The differences in culture and tradition added to the distrust. The alliance suffered, too, because of a difference in priorities. However, these probably would have been bridged if China's economy had permitted her to be an effective fighting force.

China's insistence on adhering to the artificially high official exchange rate meant that whenever the American government exchanged dollars for yuan it received far less than was given. Throughout the fall of 1943 American officials pressed for scaling down the exchange rate. They saw no reason why the United States should pay five times as much or more for Chinese goods and services.

But many Chinese were no less convinced that their miseries were in large part due to heavy American army expenditures in China. The *Ta-kung-pao*, a leading Chinese newspaper, expressed disappointment in the way the United States handled its military program. The terrible inflation, charged the editor, was due to American soldiers exchanging their American currency for Chinese currency on the black market.[16] This Chinese complaint was not without basis. The disbursing officer of the Treasury Department in China and various American agencies purchased yuan in the black market, thereby contributing to the inflation.[17]

An American missionary at Chengtu, F. Olin Stockwell, asked: "But why blame it on the U.S.A.? Quite evidently the army and all the rest of us would rather work through the banks in the regular way." The difficulty, Stockwell observed, was a result of the Chinese setting the exchange rate "at such an unreasonably low figure that it is apparent to all that it did not mean anything."[18] Stockwell, confronted by the fantastic rise in prices, met his personal crisis by turning back his salary because it would buy next to nothing and resorted to selling his private belongings at inflated prices so as to meet his daily living costs.

The Generalissimo and his brother-in-law H. H. Kung, the Minister of Finance, adamantly opposed any change in the exchange rate. To change it, they said, would further undermine confidence in the Chinese currency and increase the pace of inflation.

In the ensuing crisis the request for a loan and China's refusal to change the exchange rate became inextricably tied together. Both caused deep resentment. Ambassador Gauss saw no reason for granting a loan.[19] Secretary of the Treasury Henry Morgenthau likewise objected and cited the fact that China still had 460 million dollars left over from the loan granted in 1942.[20] At a meeting on January 1 with his advisers, Morgenthau expressed disgust. How long, he asked, "will the Kuomintang group or any other group stand for this grafting family at the head of the Government?"[21] The State Department took a similar view, but strongly opposed a blunt rejection of China's request. Its opposition was overruled.

On January 5, 1944, Hull sent Roosevelt's message to be delivered by Ambassador Gauss. He cautioned the ambassador that it would be well to deliver it in person with the aim of moderating the hostility it was likely to arouse. The message rejected the loan request, called for modification of the exchange rate, and stated that the past sales of gold had been misused by speculators for the purpose of profit.[22] Because it appeared that Chiang's purpose in wanting a loan was to provide for postwar reconstruction, the message also added that it was too soon to determine what kind of postwar aid should be granted. There was only one modest concession, and this was not without strings. The United States would be willing to ship U.S. $12 million in gold a month.[23] This, said the note, could be sold in the open market and would enable the Chinese government to provide the American Army with the currency it needed.

On January 11 Ambassador Gauss delivered Roosevelt's message to Chiang, who was accompanied by Madame Chiang and H. H. Kung. Five days later Gauss returned to receive the Generalissimo's reply. "The proposals of the Treasury Department are, to my mind," said Chiang, "not those of one Allied nation to another, but savor of a commercial transaction."[24]

Chiang firmly held that the economic situation in China made it impossible to pay the costs of the American military presence. The cost had risen to the point that if China carried the burden without adequate assistance her economy would collapse. In recent weeks, Chiang noted, he had been faced with demands that China undertake to build airfields that would cost $13,000,000,000 in Chinese currency. This had reference to the huge new air base for B-29s at Chengtu.

This project was only part of the problem but dramatically illustrated the basic difficulty. The American Joint Chiefs debated its feasibility at length, then shelved it, and finally, after the postponement of the Burma operation, approved it in the expectation that it would redress the deep disappointment Chiang had experienced in the dropping of the amphibious invasion. Chiang, probably not aware at first of the tremendous cost of the project, gave his approval. By mid-January, when he received Roosevelt's message turning down the loan, the magnitude of the project and its frightening dimensions in terms of cost were an immediate reality. Three hundred thousand conscript laborers and another seventy-five thousand contract laborers were already at work. Without any machinery whatsoever they were to carry the dirt, sand, and rocks for the runways and to pound those runways into an even surface by hand. In the next three months Chinese laborers hauled by hand some 16,000 tons of rock and sand.[25]

But the cost of the new air base was only one of the burdens placed on the weary Chinese. In addition to the cost of several other air bases, China provided the currency to pay for the lodgings and food of the American soldiers. During the course of Ambassador Gauss' conference with the Generalissimo and Madame Chiang, she had observed that there was a wide difference between the diets of American and Chinese soldiers. The cost of feeding the individual American was CNC $300 a day whereas this would suffice to feed a Chinese soldier for a month.[26]

It was Chiang's solution, however, that shook Washington officials. After March 1, only six weeks away, he bluntly announced, the American Army in China would have to depend on itself. "China," he said, "cannot be of material or financial assistance in any projects the United States Army may have in mind."[27]

The Ambassador, stunned by this ultimatum, defended the position of his government. "I stated my impression that view of American economists is to effect that no amount of American money in the United States to the credit of China would remedy China's financial and economic situation any more than if the whole of our machine gun output were hypothecated to China and remained in the United States."[28] To this Chiang replied that American economists had no knowledge of the Chinese economy or Chinese psychology and it was the psychological aspect of the situation which mattered most.[29]

Ambassador Gauss advised Washington that Chiang was neither a petty thief nor a robber baron but he recommended firmness. He had, he said, met no Chinese who thought an additional loan would help them. Nor, in his own view, was there any sound basis for Chiang's refusal to alter the exchange rate. He fully recognized the burdens imposed on China by the American Army and the United States should pay the cost, but he saw no reason for increasing "those heavy expenditures another five times because of the unrealistic attitude on the exchange rate. . . ."[30]

It remained for Washington to decide, and there a sharp division took place. To members of the State Department too much was at stake in maintaining good relations with China to permit a petulant response and they took the long view.[31] But representatives of the Treasury and War Departments exhibited more wrath than patience. Henry Morgenthau was "mad as hell."[32] The War Department also favored a tough line and drafted a message to be sent to Chiang. When State Department representatives questioned the blunt nature of the message, General Lucius Clay, Assistant Chief of Staff for Materiel Service of Supply, said it had been fully discussed with General Marshall and Secretary Stimson and both realized its implications "including the possibility that it might result in the American Army's pulling out of China complete."[33] Clay added that "the War Department has serious question as to whether its efforts in China are worthwhile." Chiang was bluffing, Clay thought, and moreover "if the United States Army were to stop shipping supplies to China Chiang Kai-shek would immediately fall." Clay further explained that the dignity of the American Army was at stake and in particular the prestige of General Stilwell.[34]

At a second meeting on the afternoon of January 19 General Brehon B. Somervell, Chief of Army Services of Supply, explained the arrangements the Army was to make with China. He informed those present that Marshall and Stimson were determined to be tough. They were dissatisfied with the cooperation they were getting in China and with China's failure to fight. Somervell minimized the Chinese protest that the inflation was due to American soldiers converting their American currency into Chinese *fapi* in the black market. There had been, to be sure, trouble with the black market and the last day he was there he saw "a half dozen or so Chinese shot for black market operations in Kunming." Morgenthau then said he was not going to stand in the way for political or financial reasons if the military considerations made it necessary to meet the Chinese demands. How far was the Army prepared to go in resisting the Chinese, he asked. Somervell answered "that they were willing to go to the limit if necessary." They were, he said, prepared to stop building airports in China and were ready to approach Japan from another direction. Finally, Somervell observed, they "could break Chiang Kai-shek by withdrawing American support if they wanted to with an expenditure of $100 million by 'buying one of his competitors.' "[35] Toward the close of this session Morgenthau phoned Roosevelt, read the proposed message, and the President approved it. Roosevelt flatly rejected a billion dollar loan to China.[36]

After a conference of the three departments, Alger Hiss, an officer in the State Department, reported that he and his colleagues strongly opposed sending the message drafted in the War Department and approved by the President. They favored pursuit of a course offering some promise of agreement. Both Dean Acheson, Assistant Secretary of State, and Hiss favored a loan, although they thought it should be less than a billion dollars. They admitted that Chinese cooperation was far from adequate but they also held that the situation of American military forces in China "would become radically worse and indeed impossible were the Chinese to launch upon a program of conscious obstructionism."[37]

The representatives of the Treasury and War Departments agreed to postpone sending the message for one day. The following day Emilio Collada of the State Department stated that the army's rigid opposition to concessions to Chiang rested on the fear of Congressional criticism. He likewise observed that while complete information was not at hand, if the army agreed to Chiang's demands, the cost of carrying on the war in China might go as high as 100 million a month. Collada cited the considerations presented by the Treasury; mainly that a loan would provide no immediate help to China. Chiang, he stated, in all likelihood was primarily interested in getting "his hands on a large dollar credit which would lie virtually idle until after the war . . ." He acknowledged that from a political viewpoint a loan would be helpful to Chiang in that it would provide evidence of continued American support and assure Chiang that he could acquire the capital goods China would need in the immediate postwar period.[38]

Dean Acheson, unlike the representatives of the Army and Treasury, had no desire to force a showdown. In an effort to gain a compromise he proposed that a decision be postponed until cool heads could work out a solution. He argued that consideration should be given to offering China an immediate loan of a limited amount and assurance of a loan after the war. If War and Treasury insisted on an immediate answer, Acheson and the State Department suggested an agreement whereby ten percent of the expenditures in China be met at the existing official rate of exchange and the other ninety percent at the rate prevailing in the open market. In addition, the United States should commit itself to a postwar loan.[39]

The lengthy debate in Washington came to a close late in the evening of January 20. The message decided upon was essentially the one originally drafted in the War Department. The United States was to meet all costs of its own war effort in China, but China was again urged to alter the exchange rate. The currency provided by China would be credited toward her account and taken into consideration when the time arrived for a final postwar settlement.[40] On receiving this message Kung made a counterproposal whereby the exchange rate would remain unchanged but China would add an additional CN $10 to each dollar exchange transaction of the Army and for this would receive credit as reverse lend-lease. This did not meet the expectations of the United States, and the proposal was rejected. In the course of the two-hour presentation by Kung, he asked what would happen if China made peace with Japan and observed that the Japanese had been making "some very good offers."[41]

After this conference with Kung in Chungking, Ambassador Gauss cabled the Secretary of State that he and his American colleagues had reached the conclusion that the "Chinese government has no intention whatsoever, if it can be avoided, of cooperating with us in seeking and finding a realistic way for us to avoid continuing exploitation and to obtain something like our money's worth in connection with our military expenditures." Then Gauss posed a key question: How important were the Army's plan of operations? Were they vital to the attack on Japan? If not, then the United States could retrench and thereby bring pressure on China. On the other hand, if they were vital, then the United States had no choice but to face the fact that it was at the mercy of China.[42]

At this point, in late February, the Embassy finally received from the Army figures on the cost of proposed operations. The Army estimated that costs from March 1 through June would be about twenty-four billion Chinese dollars.[43] The economic impact of these expenditures on the Chinese economy would be great. The sum was more, thought Gauss, than the total revenue the Chinese government would collect in 1944. The Chinese would have to issue huge amounts of additional paper currency, thereby promoting further disastrous inflation. The Army operations would also increase American costs in China, assuming continuation of the twenty to one exchange rate, to approximately $300 million a month. If this tendency continued and the exchange rate was not changed, Gauss warned, "the China theater will ultimately become the most expensive theater of the war."[44]

There appeared no way to circumvent the impasse reached in late February 1944. Yet neither side could look with equanimity on the prospective American withdrawal or the possible collapse of China. The United States staked its hopes for Asia on the existence of a strong and friendly China serving as a stabilizing force in that part of the world. These hopes were now in danger. China had even more to lose. If the United States were to withdraw, the Chinese Nationalists could no longer expect to receive American assistance for postwar reconstruction, and even the prospect of this might lead to overthrow of the Chiang regime.

Edward Acheson, financial advisor to the American Army in China, put the question bluntly when he wrote:

> This question should be examined in the light of the circumstances and conditions peculiar to China and the Chinese. It must be studied against the background of an economy which has never thoroughly integrated and the loose structure of which has been badly mauled by 6 years of war; and of the background of the inflationary spiral caused by China's war time commercial isolation from rest of world; lack of adequate means of transportation and distribution of food and supplies; of the almost complete lack of governmental control over prices, material and wages; of the venal character of merchants, contractors and many officials whose cooperation is essential to construction and supply.[45]

To this Acheson added that if we drove the Chinese economy to the point of collapse the United States would probably have to build it up again.

The actions of the two governments confirmed the fact that neither was prepared to face the ultimate consequences of a break. In January China continued to furnish the American Army with the currency it needed. In turn, in March, the United States deposited $25 million to China's account in the Chase National Bank in New York.[46] And when March 1 arrived, Chiang did not carry out his ultimatum of withdrawing all support. Instead, the Chungking government again provided the American Army with the necessary currency.

Moreover, there was a growing recognition on the American side that the huge Army expenditures were having a catastrophic effect on China's economy.[47] The Army refused to curtail its projects but at the same time it was now willing to approve a suggestion from H. H. Kung that $20 million in American currency be sent to China and that the Chinese government would sell it on the open market, thereby acquiring some part of the Chinese currency needed.[48]

On March 26 and again on March 28 Ambassador Gauss called for

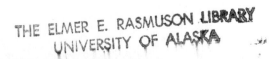

a new approach. He cited the fact that work on the airfields was going ahead. In return, the United States should not push for a final agreement. Gauss also advised against continued emphasis on a new exchange rate. It was, he said, of utmost importance to permit Chiang to save face. In turn, the United States, upon receiving Chinese currency, should deposit to China's account one dollar for each 100 to 200 *fapi* received. Adler, the Treasury's representative in Chungking, added the commonsense judgment it was "better to have bases and headaches after April 15 than headaches without bases."[49] This course found approval in Washington, and no pressure was exerted in the months ahead.

Finally, on May 19 the Chinese ambassador gave to Treasury Secretary Henry Morgenthau an *aide-memoire* which dropped the request for a loan, put forth proposals known to be acceptable to the United States, and suggested ways to get around the sticky exchange rate problem.[50] At the same time Kung's *memoire* made it clear that he expected assurance of postwar aid.

On June 8 Secretary Morgenthau wrote to President Roosevelt, "I should like to take this opportunity to congratulate you, as Commander-in-Chief of our Armed Forces, upon having faced and passed an important military crisis." The United States, he said, had its airfields in China and was now in a favorable position to bargain with the Generalissimo.[51]

Although this particular crisis seemed to be over, a final settlement of the immediate problem that led to the crisis was still months way. Relations with China entered upon a new stage in June 1944 when Roosevelt sent Vice President Henry Wallace to China to study the problems that were a cause of great concern. These included the question of relations between Chiang and Stilwell, the question of the Communists, and the absence of broadly based popular support for the Chungking government.

The regime had fallen victim to battle fatigue. The Nationalist Government could not fulfill the role assigned to it by the war. The Chinese economy lacked integration and therefore could not be mobilized to fight effectively against a highly efficient enemy. The war placed burdens on that economy which caused it to resort to inflation. Nor did the Kuomintang succeed in building an effective fighting force. The government of China recruited an army of three million men and failed to train them, equip them, or feed them. Both the poverty of China and the limits of Chiang's political control contributed to the weakness of the army. Chiang Kai-shek was not in a position to command his generals but only to bargain with them.

The crisis centered on economic questions and made clear for all to see the inefficiency of the economy. The government presided over but did not control the highly localized productive system. The war greatly increased the costs of government at the same time that the government suffered a loss of all customs revenue. The control of the seacoast ports by the enemy also cut off the goods China so badly needed. The end result was the printing of currency without reserves and an extreme shortage of goods, a combination that generated spiraling prices. The expenditures of the American Army added to the inflation. Inflation, in turn, worked a severe hardship on classes dependent on a fixed income and slowed down manufacturing. In this economic environment desperate people resorted to corruption, and the morale of the populace was eroded.

One measure of China's desperation was its inability to provide the paper necessary for the great volume of new currency. This had to be printed in the United States and flown in over the Hump. When the Chengtu airfields were under construction in the winter and spring of 1944, approximately 210 plane loads of the necessary paper money were flown in.

Finally, after the construction of the Chengtu airfields was completed, only twenty missions were flown from them. Nine of these were against Japan, and studies after the war showed they did almost no damage.

Notes to Chapter IV

1. Minutes of the Combined Chiefs of Staff, January 18, 1943, National Archives. Hereafter cited as C.C.S.

2. Ibid.

3. Roosevelt to Marshall, March 8, 1943, Franklin D. Roosevelt Memorial Library, Secret Map Room, Hyde Park, N.Y., Box 165.

4. Remarks by T. V. Soong on May 16, 1943, at the Third Washington Conference, *Foreign Relations of the United States The Conferences at Washington and Quebec 1943*, pp. 87-91, 138-39.

5. Minutes of the Joint Chiefs of Staff, November 22, 1943, National Archives. Hereafter cited as J.C.S.

6. Meeting of the Pacific War Council, May 20, 1943, *Foreign Relations of the United States The Conferences at Washington and Quebec 1942*, pp. 138-41.

7. J.C.S., November 22, 1943.

8. J.C.S., November 25, 1943.

9. Ibid.

10. Minutes of Meeting of Combined Chiefs of Staff, November 24, 1943, *Foreign Relations of the United States The Conferences at Cairo and Teheran*, p. 338.

11. Roosevelt to Chiang, Roosevelt Library, Secret Map Room, Roosevelt Memorial Library, Hyde Park, N.Y.

12. J.C.S., November 25, 1943.

13. *Foreign Relations of the United States The Conferences at Cairo and Teheran 1943* (Washington: Government Printing Office, 1961), p. 567.

14. Ibid., 674-78, 725.

15. Ibid., 856.

16. The Ambassador in China to the Secretary of State, February 21, 1944, File 893.00/15287, National Archives.

17. White to Morgenthau, January 11, 1944, *Morgenthau Diary*, Franklin Roosevelt Memorial Library, Vol. 693.

18. Stockwell to Frank T. Cartwright, March 1, 1944, Archives of the Board of Missions of the United Methodist Church.

19. Arthur N. Young, *China and the Helping Hand* (Cambridge: Harvard University Press, 1963), p. 281.

20. Ibid., p. 282.

21. Conversation of Morgenthau, White, and Friedman, January 1, 1944, *Morgenthau Diary*, Vol. 689, Franklin Roosevelt Memorial Library.

22. Secretary of State to the Ambassador in China, January 5, 1944, *U.S. Foreign Relations China* 1944, pp. 827-29.

23. Ibid., p. 828.

24. Ambassador in China to the Secretary of State, January 16, 1944, *U.S. Foreign Relations China* 1944, p. 835.

25. Young, op. cit., p. 302.

26. Ambassador in China to the Secretary of State, January 16, 1944, *U.S. Foreign Relations China* 1944, p. 838.

27. Ibid.

28. Ibid.

29. Ibid.

30. Ibid., p. 839.

31. Memorandum by the Director of the Office of Far Eastern Affairs, *U.S. Foreign Relations China 1944*, pp. 843-46.

32. Young, op. cit., p. 284.

33. Memorandum of Conversation, by Mr. Alger Hiss, January 19, 1944, *U.S. Foreign Relations China 1944*, p. 848.

34. Ibid., p. 849.

35. Conference in Secretary's Office, January 19, 1944, *Morgenthau Diary*, Vol. 695.

36. Ibid.

37. Memorandum of Conversation, by Alger Hiss, January 1944, *U.S. Foreign Relations China*, p. 849.

38. *Memorandum by the Chief of the Division of Financial and Monetary Affairs*, January 20, 1944, ibid., pp. 852-55.

39. Ibid., p. 854.

40. The Secretary of State to the Ambassador in China, January 20, 1944, ibid., p. 859.

41. The Ambassador in China to the Secretary of State, February 4, 1944, ibid., p. 869.

42. Ibid., February 12, 1944, pp. 871-72.

43. Ibid., February 24, 1944, p. 874.

44. Ibid., p. 875.

45. Memorandum of Conversation, Prepared in the Department of State, February 29, 1944, ibid., p. 876.

46.   Ibid., p. 889.

47.   The Acting Secretary of State to the Ambassador in China, March 3, 1944, ibid.

48.   Ibid.

49.   The Ambassador in China to the Secretary of State, March 26, 1944, ibid., 908 and March 28, 1944, ibid. (Adler to Secretary of Treasury), p. 909.

50.   The Chinese Embassy to the Treasury Department, ibid., pp. 921-22.

51.   The Secretary of the Treasury, June 8, 1944, ibid., 928.

General George C. Marshall   *(Courtesy of the U.S. Army)*

General Joseph Warren Stilwell   *(Courtesy of the U.S. Army)*

Major General Patrick J. Hurley
(Courtesy of the U.S. Army)

Ambassador Clarence E. Gauss
(Courtesy of the Department of State)

CHAPTER V

The Rise of the Chinese Communists

In the Winter of 1944 military considerations turned the attention of Americans to the Chinese Communists. Public impressions of the regime at Yenan, the Communist headquarters in the northwest province of Shensi, were vague at best. Twenty years earlier the Communists acquired a reputation for closing mission schools and colleges, villifying missionaries as the running dogs of imperialism, and kidnapping and on occasion murdering missionaries in areas they occupied. After 1938 the writings of Edgar Snow counterbalanced this one-sided view, but the public continued to consider the Chinese Communists as a dissident group of no great importance. The press gave only slight attention to their rapid growth during the early World War II years, in considerable part because the Central Government at Chungking did its best to hide internal divisions.

The absence of information was only one of several factors contributing to the distorted view. The most visible aspect of China in the 1930s was that of a defenseless and poor country struggling to hold back the Japanese invader. Internal problems attracted little attention at a time during which complicated political forces were at work. Few were aware of the continued struggle between the Kuomintang and regional warlords who resisted centralized control much like feudal barons of medieval Europe opposed the rise of the centralized monarchies. An equally small number had any knowledge of the tensions between classes or the distrust and dislike of the Westerners at whose hands the Chinese had so long suffered humiliation. Not having a grasp of these internal conditions, Americans could scarcely properly assess the strength of the Communists as they crusaded for a new social order and equality for China among nations.

Even the cosmopolitan *New York Times,* until well into 1944, treated Chungking as China and Yenan as a minor irritant among the many problems facing the Nationalists. In February 1943 Harold Callender, of the *New York Times,* reported that in the last two years there appeared to have been no recurrence of former hostilities between the Nationalists and Communists, that the large concentration of Nationalist troops in the Shensi region were there not to watch the Communists but to prevent a Japanese advance across the Yellow River, and that the Communists gained "their importance less from internal backing than from their link with Russia."[1] This report, while at odds with the facts, accorded with the Kuomintang's objective of minimizing the internal struggle so as to enhance its own prestige abroad. In reality, China was in the midst of a revolution and, in the eyes of the Nationalists, the Communists outranked even the Japanese as the enemy most to be feared. The Communists extended their control over a large part of North China at the very time that the American press ignored them.

China's Central Government could not long hide its difficulties from the outside world. One year after Callender's news story appeared, his colleague, Brooks Atkinson, *Times* correspondent in Chungking, provided one of the earlier glimpses into realities. Chungking's unrelenting censorship prevented the foreign correspondents in Chungking, increasingly restless and disillusioned, from telling the full story. Atkinson reported a press conference at which K. C. Wu, Vice Minister for Foreign Affairs, presided. Wu's effort to draw the curtain over the Communist issue led to what Atkinson described as "an engrossing and at times stormy discussion of the political topic that the Central Government reluctantly approaches." Wu denied that there was a blockade of the Communists. A Chinese colleague added that the conflict was nothing more than a family dispute "that can be amicably settled and does not need to be publicized." The foreign newsmen, insulted by this effort to mislead them, entered into a lively argument. At the close ten correspondents presented a letter addressed to the Generalissimo requesting permission to visit Yenan and other areas in Shensi in the immediate future.[2] The time had arrived when Nationalist censorship could no longer treat as a tea party what was becoming a full-scale revolution.

When the general American reading public began to have a fuller view of China's internal struggle, the exigencies of war distorted their picture. They had only slight interest in the Communist blueprint for a new society and the reasons for the Communist success. The concern of both diplomats and correspondents lay elsewhere. They were concerned about the ineffectiveness of the Nationalist armies against the Japanese and the fact that some 400,000 of the best troops were being used to block further Communist expansion at a time when American boys were fighting fiercely in the jungles of the south Pacific. They rejected the Nationalists' overwhelming concern with the rapid expansion of the Communists, and they denounced the leaders in Chungking for giving the highest priority to curbing the Communists. However legitimate this strategy was from the viewpoint of the Chinese Nationalists, to the American military it was nothing less than treachery on the part of an ally. Consequently, they directed their efforts toward having the Nationalists and the Communists unite against the foreign enemy. These efforts, in turn, led to the conclusion that it was the Nationalists rather than the Communists who were unwilling to subordinate domestic politics to the war against Japan.

In the summer of 1944 the adverse impact of K.M.T.-Communist rivalry on the war against Japan was the major American concern. This concern became ever more serious due to the successful Japanese military campaigns beginning in June and extending throughout the summer. The Japanese victories gave new impetus to other dissident political movements and to a general loss of public confidence in the Generalissimo's regime. It appeared that the government of China might collapse.

A new reason for American concern began to make itself felt during that same summer. Sino-Soviet relations had deteriorated sharply, and this raised the question as to whether the Soviets might not shift their support of the Kuomintang to the Communists.

The precise relations of the Russians and the Chinese Communists occasioned considerable speculation. The few scattered reports reaching Americans about Yenan told of one Russian doctor and numerous photographs of Lenin and Stalin, but there was no evidence of actual Soviet support. By the late summer of 1944, however, some Americans began to fear that if the Soviet Union entered the war against Japan and moved into Manchuria she would also assist the Communists in taking over control of both Manchuria and North China. In a report for the Secretary of State of a conversation with Chiang early in September, Gauss first raised this question. Chiang, wrote Gauss, did not appear to realize

> that if the Soviet Union should come to make war upon the Japanese and undertake hostilities in north China with the cooperation of the Chinese Communist forces and in Manchuria, defeat of the Japanese continental armies would probably leave the Communist forces and their regime in a strong political and military position in those areas, thus greatly extending their control and influence, and placing them in the category of a *de facto* regime for a very large section of this country having Soviet approval and probably Soviet support.[3]

Once this possibility entered into American thinking—and after January 1945 it came very much to the fore—then the question of the Chinese Communists was sharply distorted. The future success of the Chinese Communists appeared to depend on future Soviet moves rather than on their own strength. This was to mislead not only large segments of the American public but also some foreign service officers. Chinese Communist success was not dependent upon Soviet aid. As a non-Communist Chinese had stated as early as 1932, "The seed may have been Russian, but the present Communist crop has grown on rich Chinese soil."[4]

* * * *

The prevailing economic and political situation in China gave the Communists the opportunity to turn the war against Japan into a successful internal revolution. The tightly controlled party never lost sight of its ultimate goal—total revolution—and it shrewdly exploited the weaknesses of the Nationalist regime, seizing control of territory the Nationalists yielded to the Japanese, appealing to the aroused nationalistic feelings of peasants and students, and gaining the confidence of others by self-sacrifice and unprecedented moderation of its earlier extremism.

The party leadership was firmly committed to the tenets of Marxism-Leninism. The leaders never doubted that they were the true spokesmen for the proletariat and that the proletariat, in turn, was, by the dictates of the historical process, destined to usher in a new society. The party was, therefore, the voice of the inevitable. At the same time the party claimed that it was democratic because it alone spoke for the class destined to rule. Only the industrial proletariat had the experience providing the insights into the inner workings of modern technological society. It was the class that produced the wealth but which in the past had labored only to enrich others. Because the proletariat lived and worked at the heart of modern production it understood both the potential of the machine age and the needs of the people.

So said Marxist dogma. And the factory workers in China suffered grievances surpassing the most bitter experiences of the workers in Europe during the darkest days of the industrial revolution. But in China it was the peasants, simply because of numbers, who represented the greatest potential for revolution. Mao Tse-tung readily acknowledging this, built the party on the basis of the peasants although he continued to maintain that the Chinese Communist Party was the spokesman of the proletariat.

In the meantime, the leadership of the party came from various social classes. A study made in 1939 revealed that seventeen percent of the top seventy leaders were of proletarian origin, while seventy percent were "students from families of small farmers, professionals, merchants, and even aristocratic official families."[5] In this respect members of the very groups who were to be dislodged from control propelled the revolution, but their social origins mattered less than their conviction that the success of the revolution depended upon winning over the masses. The people were to rule, but the elite alone could be trusted to remain faithful to the true doctrine. Only the leaders possessed the infallible grasp of society's ultimate destiny. They could ill afford to permit the movement to be diverted from the goal by masses of people still subject to bourgeois attitudes and dreams of rising in the traditional social scale.

The party's firm faith in Lenin's theory of imperialism corresponded with the feelings of all Chinese humilitated by one hundred years' experience with foreign intruders. All imperialism was reduced to one source, the inevitability of capitalist societies seeking to rescue themselves from the inner contradictions of their economy by foreign investment. The intrusion of foreign capital led in turn to foreign control of transportation, of mining, and of banking, the heart of the subjugated country's economy. In 1936 American capital constituted only 8.6 percent of the total foreign investment in China, but the United States fell under the same censure as other nations.[6]

The Communists made the elimination of foreign economic control the rallying point for Chinese nationalism. This alone assured them of widespread support. By further setting themselves before the people as the only uncompromising foes of the Japanese, they could lay claim to being the most patriotic of all political contestants. They were no less confident that they were correct in their analysis of China's internal difficulties. Private ownership and control of capital had enabled a small group to reap the advantages of the labor of the country's millions of peasants. Peasants, burdened with heavy rents and usurious interest payments, found the explanation convincing. To this analysis of the evils of the present, the Communists added the promise of an egalitarian society where each would be rewarded according to his need. In short, as Benjamin Schwartz has put it, Marxism-Leninism, like divine revelation, provided the key to understanding the historical process, and the Communist Party was itself "the sole agent of historic redemption." Herein lay the dynamism of the Communists.

American correspondents and foreign service officers in China during the war years had no reason to take any interest in the Communist promises of relief from human bondage. They did take seriously the Communist claim to being the most aggressive opponents of Japanese aggression. Because the Communists appeared to be more effective than the Nationalists in fighting the common enemy of the United States and China, many diplomats and foreign correspondents developed some degree of admiration for them. General Joseph Stilwell, a reactionary in American domestic politics, was ready to join hands with the Chinese Communists because they gave promise of serving as an enterprising and determined ally against the Japanese.

Once the measuring rod became effective opposition to the dangerous enemy, the Communists had an advantage which gave promise of overcoming the long and deeply held American antipathy toward Communism. The inevitable hostility of the Communists to the United States as the chief capitalist power was lost to sight. Their determination to eliminate the foreigner's stake in China's economy disappeared from view. Their long-term plans for a socialist country came to appear remote. What mattered was successful prosecution of the war.

Ironically, at the same time this was taking place, some agencies of the American government became deeply apprehensive of Nationalist antagonism to the traditional foreign economic foothold. During the course of the war the Nationalists set their future course by establishing government monopolies. As the war progressed, they made further plans to exclude all foreign investments in banking and other key areas where foreign investment would lead to some degree of control of the Chinese economy. Washington watched these moves and protested with considerable vigor.[7] Nevertheless, military considerations overruled all others, and the Nationalists fell into disfavor, not because of their economic nationalism, but becasue they were laggards in the war against Japan.

The growth of the Communist movement after the outbreak of war with Japan attained proportions leading one observer on the scene to comment that it could not properly be described as expansion but only as an explosion. In 1937, at the time of the formation of the United Front, Communist troops numbered 40,000, which were confined to the remote part of northwest China.[8] Even in the early war years they made rapid progress in numbers and in area under their control. In late 1943 and the first six months of 1944 they increased so rapidly that they were almost as much the government of China as was Chungking. The Communists, equally dedicated to the defeat of the Japanese and to the creation of a new society, had turned the war into a locomotive of revolution.

Japan controlled the cities of occupied China but not the countryside. Japanese troops moved into the rural areas only on rare occasions to search out opposition and to assure the collection of the harvests. Japan needed to do no more than to deprive the Central Government of the economic resources of the occupied territory.

The peasants in these areas together with Chinese who had fled from the cities rather than serve the Japanese—their patriotism aroused by the harsh measures of the enemy—sought ways to continue resistance.[9]

The Communists had learned in the early days of the invasion of Manchuria that spontaneous resistance would emerge but it would be lacking in trained leadership and would need assistance. They moved into the void to fill both needs. As ardent opponents of the Japanese and because they were highly trained in underground activities, they were welcome. Before long they developed their own governing units, trained militia, indoctrinated large parts of the population, and recruited soldiers for their armies. They met little local opposition, for many of the better established families and former leaders had fled to other parts of the country. At the same time they were beyond the reach of the Nationalist forces. As Mao phrased it, the Communists went to the masses, learned from them, and then constructed a political and economic program that jibed with peasant feelings.

The Communists portrayed themselves as the true defenders of China and in their propaganda accused the Nationalists of betraying the country. Communists lacked the arms and equipment to take on the enemy in direct large-scale battle; therefore, Nationalist troops carried much more of the burden of fighting. But the records of the Japanese make it clear that they fought with great effectiveness, carrying on a nuisance guerrilla program and harassing enemy troops. They left no doubt in the mind of the local Chinese population of their military aggressiveness.

In the hands of the Communists, troops served as a major political instrument. Whereas the people had every reason to dread the presence of Nationalist troops, who made a practice of robbing them of their belongings, they found the Communist troops well-disciplined, friendly, and offering to assist them. Everywhere they showed a friendly attitude and approached the peasants as coworkers in a great cause. In March 1944 Everett Drumright of the American Embassy told of an interview with a Chinese Christian minister who lived near Yenan. The Chinese clergyman said some harsh things about the Communists but also testified that, in spite of other complaints, the people in the Communist-governed areas enthusiastically approved of the behavior of Communist soldiers and credited them with eradicating banditry.[10] A Roman Catholic missionary residing in a Communist area, although critical of the Communists, praised the behavior of the troops.[11] When American military observers surveyed conditions in Communist areas, they uniformly reported on the friendly relations between the armed forces and the people.

This was a new phenomenon in China, where troops traditionally harassed the people. The change came about because of the Communist indoctrination program. Every unit of the Communist armies, from the highest echelon to the lowest brigade, included well-trained political officers who prepared literature, taught classes, and directed political theatricals. Peasants for the first time learned to read, and the primers used in teaching them stressed the importance of hating the Japanese and of distrusting the Kuomintang. Peasants likewise learned that their highest duty was liberation of their countrymen. At higher levels there were "universities," where young people were taught correct political thinking. The Communists placed as great an emphasis on political education as they did on military training.

A Communist soldier was not only a military man but also an exemplar of the new society. The life style of the officers set the example. They received very little more pay than the privates, lived on the same diet, and shared the same modest quarters. In some respects the Communist military organization was less military than it was political. The subordination of the individual was no less real than in other armed forces, but it was subordination to a cause. All were instruments for the realization of something infinitely greater than the individual or even the sum total of individuals. Because officers exemplified this subordination and because the cause extended far beyond immediate military victory, the army was much more than a military arm of the society. In fact, no sharp line existed between the military and the political, between the soldier and the civilian. Every military officer and every soldier was as much a political instrument as he was a fighting man. This union of military and political ends transformed the army into the grand host of the immutable processes of history.

In the daily governance of the body politic the spirit was less Cromwellian. Leaders recognized that old values and traditional attitudes persist in spite of heavy indoctrination. The United Front of 1937 marked a change in this respect. It constituted less of a political accommodation with the Kuomintang than it did a strategy whereby class enemies were to be gradually weaned away from long-established values. People were to be permitted to pursue their old ways until such a time as they became barriers to the transition. The United Front suspended class warfare and put in its place the gradual building of a peasant political base adequate for the eventual launching of the new society.

Outside observers often looked upon the movement as an imposition of a foreign ideology. On the contrary, as Chalmers Johnson made clear in *Peasant Nationalism and Communist Power,* the revolution was a peasant awakening brought about by war with Japan. Communists enjoyed more striking successes in mobilizing peasants in the early 1930s than Johnson suggests, but it is nevertheless true that the war and a more moderate program speeded up the process. After the Japanese moved into China and sought to tie the peasant's productivity to Japan's needs and interfered with the peasant's security, peasant nationalism was aroused. Prior to this the peasants were largely outside the nationalistic movement which tended to be largely a movement of the educated and business classes. The Japanese invasion caused the peasants to look beyond their immediate locale. At the same time they began to organize local resistance movements only to find that they needed outside aid. The Communists, before moving in to offer aid, acquired complete information about local leadership and prejudices.

The aim was unity. If the enemy were to be weakened and finally defeated, it would be necessary to transform the community into a broadly based cohesive unit. Therefore, the Communists were prepared to recognize group interests, to make concessions to these interests, and to postpone basic and more radical reforms. To gain the confidence of merchants, craftsmen, and small landlords, their anxieties had to be relieved. Consequently, the Communists followed a course of moderation, reducing the heaviest burdens of rent and interest rates for the peasants and at the same time assuring the petty creditor class that they would receive payment. Only by this means could there be thoroughgoing social mobilization. Mao put it this way:

> Our old program of land confiscation—modified, inasmuch as the land-
> lord got a share—was not bad at the time. The basic demand of the
> masses was concentrated on their desire for land. Sun Yat-sen ad-
> vocated it. But it is not suitable for war time because the landlords wish
> to be anti-Japanese, but a policy of confiscation may drive them into
> the other camp. The peasants see the simple truth that rent reduction
> makes it possible for the landlords to remain and helps to isolate the
> Japanese. After a few experiences of land confiscation in some areas
> early in the war, the peasants saw that this policy ultimately harmed
> them. A policy of rent concessions by the landlord and guarantee of
> payment of rent by the tenant results in successful and genuine coop-
> eration. This policy is not merely opportunistic it is the only possible
> one.[12]

Communists prided themselves on being democratic. In practice, democracy meant subordination of individual interests to party goals and the bringing of the Chinese into participation in local govern-ment councils and wide range of organizations. There were elections of representatives to local governing councils. To promote the confi-dence of groups that might otherwise be hostile, it was provided that not more than one-third of a council should be Communist, another third was to be made up of representatives of other parties, and a final third from those who had no affiliation. In addition, there was widespread discussion of all questions. Representatives of the landed interests and of the merchants freely participated in the village gov-ernments in the border areas, but the alliance between the Commu-nist Party and the masses of peasants gave to the party the determin-ing voice.[13] Able and highly persuasive Communists readily turned the views expressed by illiterate peasants into support of their own measures. The broadly based participation did not prevent the only organized political party from dominating proceedings.

The Communists provided a series of organizations in which the people participated. These mass organizations aimed at embracing all and excluding no one. Through them social mobilization was made possible and a high degree of nationalist self-consciousness achieved. The organizations brought together peasants, workers, teachers, merchants, women, and young people. Among the more prominent were the Peasants' National Salvation Association.[14] The militia served much the same purpose. Membership was not limited to Communists. Michael Lindsay, who resided in Yenan for a period of years, cited figures released in 1942 claiming that there were over ten and a half million in the civil organizations and eight million in the military organizations.[15]

These activities did not add up to democracy as understood in the West. Behind the maze of organizations and the elections to local governing bodies was the Communist Party with an elitist group controlling basic policy. This in no way diminished the sense of belonging that flowed from the participation in elections and the highly organized activities. The elite ruled, but they did so with the approval of the masses who found in their program the nationalistic appeal of a new and strong China and great economic gains. The ideology served as the myth whereby all Chinese were to be reconciled for the first time to a new and greater society.

The dynamism of the movement and the conditions peculiar to the war resulted in what must constitute one of the most remarkable political transformations of modern times. By the close of 1939, according to the estimate of the Japanese army, the total number of individuals involved in the several types of military organizations was 800,000. A study by the Japanese Political Affairs Bureau placed the number connected with the Communist military in the occupied areas of North China at the close of 1939 at 120,000 regulars and 160,000 guerrillas. The same bureau at the end of September 1941 estimated that regulars and guerrillas in northern and central China was not less than 350,000.[16] This estimate did not include those active at the village level. Mao Tse-tung estimated the population under Communist rule in 1936 at 9 million. In April 1945 he placed the figure at 95,500,000.[17]

Other statistics confirm the rapid growth. Japanese authorities estimated the number of hsien in North China under the Communists in January 1938 to be 18 and in July 1941 at 355. Another 104 hsien were Communist controlled in central China by October 1941.[18] Estimates vary as to the size of Communist forces during the final year of the war. Boyd Compton placed the figure at 910,000, while Japanese believed it to be 1,028,293.[19] These figures roughly correspond to the estimates of several American military observers, but Military Intelligence in July 1945 concluded that 83,061,836 were under Communist rule and that the armed forces numbered 475,000.[20] The variance in the estimates indicates the difficulty of arriving at precise figures, but all support the conclusion that the Communists had remarkable success in mobilizing support.

Foreign observers generally gave credence to Communist claims to taking the offensive against the Japanese while at the same time having to defend themselves against repeated Nationalist attacks. This favorable picture of their roles was not beyond challenge. John Kullberg, in a military intelligence report issued in July 1945, gave the Communists credit for their great political success and treated all aspects of the Communist program with a high degree of objectivity. However, Kullberg disputed the Communist portrayal of themselves as the unrelenting foes of Japan who were always taking the offensive and he likewise challenged the Communist version whereby they were the innocent victims of Nationalist offensives and only fought the Kuomintang in self-defense.[21]

*   *   *   *

From Pearl Harbor to the summer of 1944 the United States followed a policy of taking no stand and giving no advice on the problem of disunity in China. By late winter of 1944 this policy was changed. The ineffectiveness of Chinese forces in fighting the Japanese provided the initial impetus. Anxiety over a possible civil war and long-range fear that such a conflict could entrap the United States in hostilities with the Soviet Union hastened reexamination of the established policy. By July the change was underway, and on the 24th of that month Joseph Grew, Director of the Office of Far Eastern Affairs, explained the change to Secretary of State Cordell Hull. "You will, of course," Grew wrote, "understand that we are not presuming to pass upon the merits of points of issue between the National Government and the so-called Chinese Communists." He stated, "This Government has no suggestions to offer with regard to the character of a settlement with the Communists." In conclusion, Grew expressed the hope "that the institution of President Chiang's democratic program might serve to unify support of the Government and revitalize war activity, and at the same time facilitate settlement of the special Communist problem."[22] Grew was doing no more than recognizing a change that was well underway.

The first step in the new direction had taken place in February when President Roosevelt sent a message to Chiang Kai-shek stating that it would be necessary to fight the Japanese in North China and Manchuria and that the United States had only the most meager information about conditions in those areas. Therefore, the message read, an Observers' Mission should "be immediately dispatched to North Shensi and Shansi provinces and such other parts of North China as may be necessary."[23] One month later the foreign correspondents in Chungking gained Chiang's reluctant consent to go to Yenan. In May, Lin Tsu-han, newly arrived Communist representative in the negotiations taking place in Chungking, notified Ambassador Gauss that American observers would be welcome in Yenan. In late June, at a conference with Henry Wallace, the Generalissimo gave way to American pressure and agreed to having American military observers visit Yenan subject to the stipulation that they should be accompanied by an official of the Chinese government.[24]

The sending of the mission to North China constituted a victory for the Communists. The recognition of their importance by the United States added to their status and likewise compromised the position of the central Government as the only recognized authority. Chiang yielded only under pressure and having done so sought to have the United States instruct its mission that it should insist that the Communists accept the direction of the Kuomintang.[25] Everyone from Secretary Hull to Ambassador Gauss looked upon Chiang's laying down this condition as a piece of arrogance unworthy of notice and as evidence of the Generalissimo's having learned little from either the eroding of his position at home or the weakening of his reputation in the United States.[26]

The instructions to David Barrett, in command of the Observer Group, were hastily drafted immediately preceding the departure of the first group and consisted of a long list of items. Included was the gathering of information on the "most effective means of assisting Communists to increase the value of their war effort."[27] Once in Yenan, Barrett was highly impressed with what he saw. "My strongest impression," he wrote "is that these people are interested mainly in two things, fighting the Japanese and gaining the support of the people." Barrett had come armed with doubts and had "long regarded with a jaundiced eye the reports of the many foreigners who have gone all out in the support of the Chinese Communists."[28] By August 27 Barrett wrote to Army Headquarters that he thought the question of whether or not to aid the Communists should be decided. He observed that the K.M.T. would always be opposed, but that in his view the time had come to experiment with furnishing "some fundamental equipment to see what would happen."[29]

Ambassador Gauss hung back. He warned Washington that any direct aid to the Communists would in all probability bring about the Kuomintang's downfall.[30] Nor was Gauss sanguine about bringing about a compromise between the Nationalists and the Communists. On the other hand, some military men entertained the hope that cooperation with the Communists on even a limited scale would force the Nationalists to seek a restoration of the United Front.

In sending the mission, the United States opened the door to a change in policy but it by no means committed itself to aiding the Communists. Only a minor step had been taken at a time of baffling indecision in the face of the possible demise of China's Central Government. The future would depend upon the ability of the tottering Nationalist regime to pull itself together. The United States, in rejecting the recent request for a loan and in overruling Chiang's opposition to the sending of the Observers' Mission, was clearly determined not to be used by the Nationalists merely for the purpose of perpetuating their own control when they had lost the confidence of their own people. The United States was mindful too of a long series of reports during the summer of 1944 of plans for the overthrow of the Chiang regime. One movement was led by Li Chi-shen in Southeast China. Li was in communication with other military commanders and likewise with leaders of the Communists and the Democratic League. Li was seeking American assistance.[31]

On July 22 the first group of American military observers left for Yenan. A second group left on August 5. The Americans received a flattering welcome. Mao greeted them at a reception, and this was followed by a dinner, a concert, and dancing. During the next few weeks top leaders of the party, including Chou En-lai and General Chu Teh made themselves freely available for discussions. Their openness, accessibility, self-confident demeanor, and frankness made a highly favorable impression. This first estimate was reinforced by the news correspondents, who had already been there for many weeks.

After six days John Service sent a report describing the behavior of people in Yenan. The highest leaders and people of the lowest rank, he observed, mingled freely. Relations between them were open, direct, and friendly. There were no beggars and no signs of desperate poverty. All were dressed more or less alike. Young people appeared to be busy and many of them spoke of eventually returning to their villages to carry on their work. "There is everywhere," Service wrote, "an emphasis on democracy and intimate relations with the common people." He noted further "There is a surprising political consciousness." He found that no matter who was questioned—barber or farmer or room attendant—he could give a good description of the Communist program. Service summed it up, "To the sceptical [sic], the general atmosphere in Yenan can be compared to that of a rather small sectarian college—or a religious summer conference." He wrote, "There is a bit of the smugness, self-righteousness, and conscious fellowship."[32]

Moralistic fervor, social equality, and enlistment of the masses in a cause was new to China. Service, like so many others who were accustomed to traditional Chinese ways, was impressed. Here was a China without brothels, without opium, without squeeze, and without beggars.

Service continued to send long reports giving his observations. He wrote about the practicality of the Communists and their lack of interest in pure theory. He told too of their systematic orderliness. He also noted that there was an effacement of individuality, uniformity of thought, and a lack of humor.[33]

Scores of others in the months and years ahead made the same observations. Service sought to go beyond the outward behavior of the Communists and to determine why they were pursuing a policy of moderation. He speculated that the Communists were led by their dialectic to believe that their society must pass through a series of stages of economic development. They must first move from the present primitive stage and then through the capitalistic stage before the dictatorship of the proletariat could be established. Another explanation might be that the Communists recognized that moderation was the most effective way to achieve power. If this were true, then they were likely to revert to their program of Communism.[34]

Having considered these two possibilities, Service leaned toward the first. The Communists expected to reach their goal only after passing through a series of stages of economic development. This, in turn, led him to conjecture that "the policies of the Chinese Communist Party will not run counter to the interests of the United States in China in the foreseeable future, and that the Party merits, so far as possible, a sympathetic and friendly attitude on our part."[35] He affirmed this view in the weeks ahead. He came to the conclusion that the Communists would cooperate with the United States if the United Staes cooperated with them. Service recommended that full consideration be given to whether or not the gains would justify "the overcoming—or disregarding—of [this] Kuomintang opposition." He concluded that large-scale military cooperation should be entered into.[36]

The long-term diagnosis of Service failed to answer the more immediate questions of concern to United States Army Headquarters in Chungking. Eventually the scene of battle would shift to North China and the coastal areas. It was of vital importance to have accurate answers as to the strength of Japanese forces, as to the strength of the Communists, and as to whether the Communists would cooperate with the Americans or align themselves with the Soviet Union. The Communists were not unprepared to answer questions along this line.

Their readiness to answer marks the high point in American-Chinese Communist relations for the next quarter of a century. They had good reason to be cooperative. If they could convey to the Americans how really strong they were, then the United States could be expected to reassess the situation and realign their policy to fit the facts of power. Moreover, the Americans might be induced to provide the desperately needed arms. They had still another reason for taking a cooperative stance. As they saw it, the Kuomintang would be strong enough to wage a civil war if the United States provided supplies only to the Central Government. They were wholly confident of winning the civil war if it came, but they preferred to avoid it. On the other hand, if the United States took action that forced the Kuomintang to consent to a coalition government, they were fully confident that they would soon control it.

Consequently, the Communists spared no effort in providing the Observer Group with information. The better the Americans grasped the facts of both their military and political success the more likely that the United States could be swayed. American military observers gained ready access to factual information and were soon able to report on the strength and location of Communist army units, the nature of guerrilla units, their effectiveness, and the prospects of the Communists having the support of the people in the areas where the fighting was likely to take place. The Communists claimed that 86,000,000 people were living in the areas under their control, that they had an army of 470,000 regular troops and a militia of 2,000,000. The militia had less training than regular troops, and they spent most of their time in production. At the base of the defense structure was the Self-Defense Corps. This included all able-bodied people, male and female. The members were not armed and had no military training but they were called upon to assist with the care of the wounded, to do sentry duty, to carry messages, and to collect intelligence. The reports from outlying areas prepared by American officers and soldiers confirmed these claims.[37]

John Service prepared the reports on the political situation. These told of the Communist strategy of moving in behind the Japanese lines, rendering assistance to groups of students and liberals who fled the cities in order to take up the cause against Japan, the winning of popular support by following a policy of moderation, the program to have soldiers aid the peasants and thereby win a good name, and the strenuous efforts to help the peasants understand the Communists plans for resisting the enemy.[38] Studies made since the war confirm these findings. Service placed major emphasis on how the Communists used the army for political purposes. He pointed out "that in the minds of the Communists leaders there is no definite distinction between military and non-military spheres." He observed, "To create the conditions which can win popular support and thus make possible their continued and successful operations the Communists have had to be a political army."[39] The political, economic, and military branches of government were so dependent upon each other that actually the same men carried out policies in all these areas.

The Communists, Service reported, held elections and one third of the posts were allotted to the Communists, one-third to the Kuomintang, and one-third to nonparty members. The Kuomintang did not participate, but former members of that party did run for office under the party name. The system of elections in no way weakened Communist Party control, for it was the only party with an active organization. The other candidates were not committed to any one party platform. Moreover, the political arm of the party, namely the army, was wholly in the hands of the Communists. Service concluded that the Communists were the chief initiators of the policies followed by the base governments.

Service viewed the system as democratic and noted that because the economic program led to the improvement of living conditions for the great majority, there was no significant or organized opposition.[40]

Reports from military observers in areas far removed from Yenan placed greater emphasis on the hatred for the Kuomintang, the determination of the Communists to expand south of the Yangtze River, and the nature of the party rhetoric. In outlying areas there was also greater emphasis on building the party on a peasant base and bolder pronouncements on the role of the party as the voice of the revolution. In many respects these reports provided a truer picture of the party dictatorship and the totalitarian nature of the regime.

On August 23 Mao, in a long interview with Service, pushed hard for an arrangement with the United States. He began by proposing that the United States use its influence to compel the Kuomintang to establish a provisional national congress which would replace the system of one-party rule. The congress would govern the country until a new regime was established. It was also to serve as a constitutional assembly. Mao also stressed the necessity of some form of cooperation between the United States and the Communists when the armed forces of the United States landed on the China coast.

The Kuomintang, warned Mao, would launch a civil war resulting in "long years of ruin and chaos for China." Only if the United States took action to discourage the Kuomintang could this tragedy be avoided.[41] Chiang must be forced to take a conciliatory course. His only interest was in perpetuation of his own control. The nationalist Government was under the domination of reactionary cliques only interested in preserving their own power.

Mao wanted to know what the future policy of the United States would be. Would the United States return to a policy of isolation and simply sit by while the Chinese tore themselves apart? Was the

United States concerned about the wholly undemocratic character of Chiang's regime? Was the United States prepared to use its influence to bring about the establishment of a government in China that was more broadly representative? Mao thought a new government might be composed of 50 percent of Kuomintang representatives and 50 percent of representatives from other parties. If the United States would try to bring this about, it could probably be achieved and then civil war would be avoided.

Mao then explained how the United States could achieve this objective. The United States should support all sides actively fighting Japan. Its course up to now, said Mao, had been to support only the Kuomintang. Service interjected a question that would in the next few years inhibit any change in American policy. How was the United States to withdraw recognition from the existing government when that government had taken no overt action to provide a basis for such a decision? Mao seized the occasion to charge that one-sided support to one party constituted interference in the internal affairs of China. The United States had followed this course even though the recognized government had used blackmail in its dealings with Washington. Service then raised the question as to how conservative American business interests who looked upon Communism as satanic were to be won over to working with a Communist regime. Mao retorted that American business interests had no reason to be afraid. The Communists followed a policy of moderation. They had lowered interest rates and rent but only within reason and, in turn, they had assured Chinese businessmen of receiving payment. After the war, he continued, China would need foreign capital for purposes of reconstruction and development, and China would have to import goods.[42]

At this stage Mao exuded cordiality. He had much to gain by winning American support. Apart from his desperate need for supplies, American cooperation would almost inevitably force the Kuomintang to agree to a new all-party government. He had good reason to believe that such a government would shortly be under the control of his own party. On the other hand, if the United States continued to supply the Kuomintang alone, civil war was inevitable and if the United States sided with the Kuomintang in that war, the war would be drawn out and highly destructive.

Events of the future were to confirm Mao's analysis. At the time Americans held conflicting views, and the outcome was by no means as clear as it appeared to Mao. Ambassador Gauss differed from Service, asserting the Communists sought control of all China. Their attitude of cooperation, said Gauss, was dictated by their seeking time to strengthen their position. Gauss warned that any support of the Communists was likely to bring about the collapse of the Kuomintang.[43] Yet, Americans desperately wished to avoid a civil war and recognized the danger that the United States would become involved. On this point there was agreement. How the war was to be avoided constituted the second question. To this there was no generally agreed-upon answer.

John Service believed that the American aim could best be achieved by further cooperation with the Communists. His reasons were these: the weakness of the Kuomintang and its unwillingness to suffer further attrition of its forces at the hands of the Japanese; Communist belief that the more aggressive they were in fighting the Japanese, the greater the public support would accrue to them; continued support of the Kuomintang alone would encourage the Kuomintang to launch a civil war; support of both would compel the Kuomintang to reform; and finally, aid to the Communists would "almost certainly make it impossible for the Kuomintang to start a civil war." To these considerations Service added that the strength of the Communists assured a maximum return on any aid given to them.[44]

Service had found himself at the center of a discussion of an issue with consequences almost beyond the range of the imagination. He was not at the center of decision making. He could only hope that the clarity of his reports and the realities they portrayed would alert his readers to the gravity of the situation.

During the same days Service met with Mao in Yenan, Roosevelt followed through on his efforts to have General Joseph Stilwell placed in command of all forces in China. In a plea for prompt action the President, on August 21, spoke of the gravity of the military situation. In an indirect reference to the Communists, Roosevelt took the position that as to the question of which forces should be under Stilwell's command, all forces "who will kill Japanese" should be employed "when the enemy is pressing us toward possible disaster. . . ."[45]

Ten days later the Generalissimo called in Ambassador Gauss and took sharp issue with the President's proposal.[46] The day was rapidly approaching when the two leaders would have to come to terms on whether the war against Japan or China's civil strife had the higher priority.

Chiang's position in China was already in serious danger. The weaknesses of the Central Government led to a serious movement to displace him. On August 10 Stilwell cabled Washington reporting the threat of an explosion. The plot aimed at placing Marshal Li Chi Shen in power, former Chairman of the Kweilin Office of the Central Military Affairs Commission, a man regarded by Stilwell as unsuitable. He preferred Pai Chung hsi, a man of character, ability, and common sense.[47] Roosevelt was fully informed of this development at the time he sought to have Chiang agree to working with the Communists.

Chiang had failed to grasp the fact that Roosevelt was now in a position to be independent. During the first years of the war this had not been true, and the Chinese Nationalists had exploited the situation to their advantage. Now the United States had other avenues for attacking Japan, and its armed forces were already well on the way to the final target. Nor did Chiang recognize that he was rapidly losing his second asset in dealing with the United States. American officials' goodwill toward Chiang and his government was rapidly giving way to distrust as the public became aware of the question of the exchange rate, of the corruption in China, and of the failure of the Chinese to fight aggressively.

*   *   *   *

The decline of the Kuomintang was paralled by the growing strength of the Communists. This fact was generally recognized by Americans in China regardless of their political bias. In later years the reports of John Service were to be seized upon by those seeking to explain the final victory of the Communists as a product of conspiracy. Not only was the Communist triumph not dependent upon what the United States did or failed to do but it seems most unlikely that the reports of Service had any great influence on decision making in the higher echelons. In this connection it should be noted that the Army intelligence report of July 1945 had a much wider circulation. The report differed in part from the reports of Service but it also emphasized the strength of the Communists. That report presented the following conclusion:

> Practically all impartial observers emphasize that the Chinese Communists comprise the most efficient, politically well-organized, disciplined, and constructive group in China today. This opinion is well supported by facts. It is largely because of their political and military skill, superior organization, and progressive attitude, which has won for them popular support no other party or group in China can equal, that they have been expanding their influence throughout the past seven years. This expansion has now reached the point where many of the best informed observers believe that no anti-Communist group in China can longer hope to eliminate them. Some of the keenest observers go so far as to predict the ultimate ascendancy of the Chinese Communists in China 'if the present reactionary groups in Chungking are allowed to continue in power.'[48]

The Army G-2 report of July 1945 did not spare the Generalissimo's regime. "We are facing a situation, it must be candidly admitted, where we are backing a government in China which, though it may be militarily stronger than any other independent Chinese regime, has lost much of its popular following," the report stated. To this it added the judgment that the regime was a "widely hated 'political machine.' "[49] The report pointed to the strong non-Communist opposition to the Central Government and held that the Communists at many points followed and acted upon the principles of Sun Yat-sen while the Kuomintang opposed any party or group which sought to put those principles into practise.[50]

At two points of major importance the intelligence report differed in tone and emphasis from the reports of other observers. It contended that the Communist program of moderation was wholly consistent with the party's firm adherence to Marxism-Leninism. This view was based on careful analysis of what Mao Tse-tung had stated in his book *New Democracy* in 1941.[51] No American foreign service officer had ever described the Communists as merely agrarian reformers, but some had speculated that the policy of moderation might become permanent. The Army intelligence report argued that the proponents of this view were doomed to disillusionment; the Communists, it maintained, were genuine Communists.

Secondly, the report argued that there was a strong affiliation between the Soviet Union and the Chinese Communists. In a carefully documented section it was shown that the Communist leaders had, beginning with the Nazi-Soviet Pact of 1939, endorsed every major move of the Soviet Union.[52]

The differences between the conclusions and speculations in the G-2 report and the reports of some other observers were overshadowed by what all agreed upon, namely the strength of the Communists and the almost complete lack of public support for the Nationalists.

NOTES TO CHAPTER V

1.   *New York Times*, February 18, 1943.

2.   Ibid., February 17, 1944.

3.   Gauss to the Secretary of State, September 4, 1944, *Foreign Relations of the United States China 1944*, pp. 544-45.

4.   Frank Rawlinson to A.L. Warnshuis, November 28, 1932, Enclosure: "The Chinese Soviet Republic," Missionary Research Library, Union Theological Seminary.

5.   Chalmers Johnson, *Peasant Nationalism and Communist Power, The Emergence of Revolutionary China* (Stanford University Press, 1962).

6.   Chi-ming Hou, *Foreign Investment and Economic Development in China* (Cambridge: Harvard University Press, 1965), p. 17.

7.   Memorandum for the President, August 15, 1944, prepared in the Far Eastern Division and signed by John Carter Vincent, Department of State Archives, File 893.00/8-15-44.

8.   Johnson, op. cit., p. 73. The author gives consideration to several different estimates of the number of Communist troops and acknowledges that the number may have been greater.

9.   Ibid., see Chapter II "The Japanese Role in Peasant Mobilization."

10.   Everett Drumright to the Secretary of State, March 16, 1944, Department of State Archives, File 893.00/7-22-44.

11.   Edward E. Rice to Secretary of State, July 22, 1944, Department of State Archives, File 893.00/7-22-44.

12.   Quoted in *The Chinese Communist Movement*, Military Intelligence Report, July, 1945, Volume I, p. 28. Military Records Branch, National Archives.

13.   Ibid., p. 70.

14.   Johnson, op. cit., p. 77.

15.   Ibid., p. 76.

16.   Ibid., Notes, p. 192.

17.   Ibid., p. 193.

18.   Ibid., p. 213.

19.   The intelligence report reads:

       There can be no doubt that in many cases Kuomintang troops have attacked the Communists, forcing them to make counterattacks in self-defense. In granting this it would seem, however, that simple logic would prove conclusively that the Communists have been the chief attackers against the Kuomintang forces throughout the past eight years. From its tiny original base in North Shensi the Eighth Route Army has spread out into vast areas of the coastal provinces of North China within and beyond the Great Wall, and the new Fourth Army has spread its influence over great areas of central China. . . . p. 101.

20. The Chinese Communist Movement, Vol. I, Military Records Branch, National Archives, p. 283.

21. Ibid., p. 101.

22. Memorandum Prepared in the Department of State for the Secretary of State, *Foreign Relations of the United States China 1944*, pp. 484–85.

23. Roosevelt to Stilwell and Chiang, February 9, 1944, Franklin D. Roosevelt Memorial Libarary, Secret Maps Room, Box 16.

24. *Memorandum of Conversation, by the Second Secretary of Embassy in China*, June 23, 1944. *Foreign Relations of the United States China: 1944*, pp. 460-64.

25. Memorandum by Gauss, August 31, 1944, *Foreign Relations of the United States: China 1944*, p. 546.

26. Hull to Gauss, September 9, 1944, ibid., pp. 567-69.

27. David D. Barrett, *Dixie Mission: The United States Army Observer Group in Yenan, 1944* (Berkeley, California: Center for Chinese Studies, 1970), p. 28. Also Gauss to Secretary of State, August 25, 1944, *Foreign Relations of the United States: China 1944*, pp. 515-16.

28. David D. Barrett to the Commanding General Forward Echelon, August 14, 1944, File on Dixie Mission, Modern Military Records Branch, National Archives.

29. Ibid., August 27, 1944.

30. Gauss to the Secretary of State, September 8, 1944. *Foreign Relations of the United States: China 1944*, pp. 559-62.

31. The movement in the southern provinces at first appeared to be aimed at forcing Chiang to remove reactionary leaders rather than at the overthrow of Chiang. However, after July 14 the reports indicated that Chiang was to be overthrown. A report from Kunming stated that The Federation of Democratic Parties was now taking the position "that the Generalissimo is solely responsible for China's critical situation; that there is no hope of saving the situation through his regime; that he and his regime are doomed and must be opposed." *Memorandum by the Director of Far Eastern Affairs*, July 31, 1944. The Consul at Kunming, Philip Sprouse, wrote lengthy reports which were summarized and forwarded to Wash-

ington. After one month in Kunming, Sprouse wrote that his most striking impression of the political situation was "the bitter criticism of Chiang by all liberal elements including Kuomintang members." Gauss to the Secretary of State, July 31, 1944.

32. Gauss to the Secretary of State, August 26, 1944, Enclosure: *Report by the Second Secretary of Embassy in China*, July 28, 1944. *Foreign Relations of the United States: China 1944*, pp. 517-20.

33. *Report by the Second Secretary of Embassy in China*, September 4, 1944, *Foreign Relations of the United States: China 1944*, pp. 551-56.

34. Ibid., August 3, 1944, pp. 562-67.

35. Ibid.

36. Gauss to the Secretary of State, September 28, 1944. *Foreign Relations of the United States: China 1944*, pp. 599-602.

37. George Atcheson to Secretary of State, November 24, 1944, Enclosure: "Medical Organization and Equipment of the Chinese Forces Behind the Japanese Blockade Line," by M.S. Casberg, Major, U.S.M.C., October, 1944, O.S.S. Reports, National Archives, File 106022.

38. John Service to Commanding General, "The Development of Communist Political Control in the Guerrilla Bases," September 10, 1944, Hurley Papers.

39. John Service to Commanding General, "Summary of the Situation in North China," August 15, 1944, Hurley Papers.

40. In September, 1944 Gauss forwarded a summary of an article written by C. Y. Hsu who had recently been in Yenan. Hsu presented a careful analysis based on his study of Communist resolutions, writings of Mao, and his own observations. Hsu concluded, "The Chinese Communists claim that they adopt the principle of democratic centralization in organization but factually there is more centralization of power in the party than in democracy." C.E. Gauss to Secretary of State, September 15, 1944. Enclosure: Central China News Agency Release. Department of State Archives, File 106021.

41. In the interview with Service, Mao spoke as follows:

We Communists know civil war from bitter experience. We know that it will mean long years of ruin and chaos for China. China's unity, her stabilizing influence in the Far East, and her economic development will be delayed. Not only the Chinese but also all nations having interest in the Far East will be affected. *China will become a major international problem.* This vitally concerns the United States. One thing certain is that we Communists dread civil war. We abhor it. We will not start it. We will do our best to avoid it—even though we know that as things now are (provided the K.M.T. does not receive foreign help) we would eventually win. . . .

Service to Commanding General, "Interview with Mao Tse-tung," August 27, 1944, Hurley Papers.

42. Ibid.

43. Gauss to Secretary of State, September 8, 1944, *Foreign Relations of the United States: China 1944*, pp. 559-61.

44. Ibid., August 29, 1944, Hurley Papers.

45. Roosevelt to Chiang Kai-shek, August 21, 1944. Map Room, Franklin Roosevelt Memorial Library, Box 20.

46. Gauss to Secretary of State.

47. Harry Hopkins to the President forwarding message from Stilwell, August 10, 1944, Franklin D. Roosevelt Memorial Library, Map Room, Box 19.

48. *The Chinese Communist Movement*, Volume I, p. 3.

49. Ibid., p. 238.

50. Ibid., p. 78.

51. Ibid., pp. 6-8.

52. Ibid., pp. 183-94.

CHAPTER VI

The Crisis Mounts
"Vinegar" Joe Stilwell and Patrick Hurley

Total confusion faced the United States and China in the summer of 1944. Mao Tse-tung might well have found more than ample illustrations for one of his favorite topics of discourse, the problem of contradictions within society. On the one hand was General Stilwell, a loyal devotee of China who deeply respected the Chinese but who as a tenacious infantryman, was determined to abide by his early conclusion, "My safest course is straight down the road."[1] There was the contradiction of Chiang himself, distrustful of foreigners and yet ready to use them to support his regime. There was also the ironic paradox of Stilwell who came to China determined to fight Japan and the Generalissimo who was equally determined to limit the fighting.

Above all, there was the American government caught in the contradiction of having determined not to pass judgment on the internal strife in China when at the same time many of its leaders took sides by describing the leaders of the Central Government in perjorative terms. At the peak of this schismatic situation the same government named Patrick Hurley as its chief emissary, a man who after two months denounced the leaders of the Central Government as pro-Fascist and accused them of favoring a dictatorship and who at the same time described the Communists "as the only real democrats in China" and the party that cooperated in the American effort to restore a united front.[2]

The confusion arose out of the staggering problems rather than the network of individual inconsistencies. Individual preferences came into conflict with national and political interests. Men found themselves despising the present and timid about the future. Wide gulfs emerged between well established national aims and the means by which they were to be achieved. For the United States the only test of measures, except when the first priority given to the defeat of Hitler was challenged, was whether a measure seemed likely to contribute to the defeat of Japan. This simplified American decision making but it led straight to difficulties with China.

The Central Government in China faced a more complex task than simply defeating the Japanese. The defeat of Japan was a matter of lesser concern to the Chinese leadership, who felt confident that the United States would take care of that problem. The government in Chungking, in mapping strategy in its struggle against Japan, was forced to give consideration to what effect each move would have on its own relations with the semiautonomous Chinese warlords. These regional military leaders would resist assignments that would weaken their forces and thereby make them vulnerable to control by Chiang's government. In addition, the Chungking government faced the Communists, who had rolled over ever greater stretches of territory and had established their own local governments. To complicate matters still further the Kuomintang was sharply divided within itself. The most powerful elements sought only to preserve their own interests, had but little sympathy with Chiang's determination to build a united China, and viewed the Japanese invaders, like previous conquerors, as inevitably being swallowed up in the sea of Chinese superiority and greatness of numbers. To preside over this delicate balance of forces and make headway toward unity required a ruthless approach, and meant that those who had no power would be sacrificed when necessary and that little or no attention would be paid to the grave economic and social burdens of the masses.

The presence of the United States made the political problems infinitely greater. Thousands of American soldiers complaining of corruption, of the inefficiencies, and of the methods of the police state threatened the regime. The sudden influx of thousands of army officers serving as military advisers, but to a considerable extent exercising command functions in Chinese divisions, ran counter to the widespread distrust of the foreigner. The American military's determination to have the Chinese fight the Japanese and the failure to recognize that China was scarcely capable of fighting a highly efficient modern nation created endless tensions. These conditions were to overwhelm individual Americans responsible for working with China, and they were to lead to problems of foreign policy that did not lend themselves to solution. Quite appropriately Secretary Morgenthau once commented to General Somervell, during the loan discussions in March 1944, "Well, it's practically the same as invading a country."[3]

The political reactionaries and military leaders most powerful in the Chinese government were guided by attitudes, interests, and outdated conceptions of government. Allied with that group was the Soong family, modern and western in outlook, highly capable, confident that it should hold the reins of power, and subject repeatedly to charges that it used both its power and its financial know-how to enrich itself. The family was sharply divided so that T. V. Soong fought major battles with his two sisters, Madame Chiang, the Generalissimo's wife, and Madame Kung, who fought continuously to protect her husband, H. H. Kung, the Minister of Finance. Madame Kung was prepared to use any means to prevent her brother, T. V. Soong, from achieving a dominant position. If T. V. should gain ascendancy he would oust H. H. Kung from his post. (A third sister had been married to Sun Yat-sen.) This political alignment meant that the United States government had to deal with powerful figures whose social and political views were almost diametrically opposed to its own. It was likewise a political alignment that in the absence of popular support China sought to strengthen its position by making extreme and endless demands of its ally, the United States.

In November 1942 a prominent American who had served in China in the diplomatic corps and who had years of experience in China, Ernest B. Price, warned Lauchlin Currie, Roosevelt's administrative assistant, of the situation the United States confronted. Price advised him that the United States must take the Chinese "in as full partners in this war" but it must also be aware of the difficulties inherent in such cooperation. He spoke of corruption and perfidy. "We cannot deal with even the best of them on any other basis," he wrote, "than the most cold-blooded and cool-headed realism; on the basis of a matter-of-fact realization of what is our *mutual* best interest."[4] Price's view, as a matter of fact, already held sway in the Roosevelt administration, although the President warned against taking a superior attitude and urged that Chiang be treated with respect.

By the summer of 1944 the ties of alliance, subjected to tortuous strains, seemed about to fall apart. Observers, such as foreign correspondents and visiting members of Congress, could view the situation with philosophical tranquility or could indulge in harsh moralistic judgments; however, those bearing the burdens of direct responsibility could only hope that the decisions they must make would carry them through the present crisis. And the present crisis was manifold: Japanese armies were pushing through Hunan, capturing the important city of Changsha, taking over the air bases from which Chennault's 14th Air Force operated; Chiang was in deep trouble and faced a movement to overthrow him; the best Chinese divisions were engaged in blockading the Communists and not in fighting the Japanese; the Burma campaign had narrowly escaped disaster when Chiang interfered with Stilwell's command and refused to send his Yunnan troops to hold off the Japanese; inflation was reaching new peaks; peasants in Honan, bitter over the treatment they had received at the hands of the army during the 1943 famine, turned on the Chinese troops and disarmed 50,000 of them. And Chiang's biggest asset, the goodwill of the American public, was rapidly eroding under an avalanche of reports of corruption, callousness, ineptitude, and the failure of China to carry its weight in the war.

The time had come to pay more attention to China. In June 1944 Roosevelt, hoping to appease the Chinese with a show of concern and also to gain time, sent Vice President Henry Wallace to China. The mission fulfilled its limited aims, but Wallace's report simply corroborated what was already well known.

On July 4 the Joint Chiefs of Staff sent a memorandum to the President that rang with alarm. The memorandum stated that the situation in China was deteriorating at rapid rate. "If the Japanese continue their advance to the west," the Joint Chiefs warned, "Chennault's 14th Air Force will be rendered ineffective, our very long-range bomber airfields in the Chengtu area will be lost and the collapse of China must inevitably result." They recommended that drastic measures be taken immediately "in an effort to prevent disaster to the U.S. effort in that region." The message cited the impotence of the Chinese forces, pointed to the lack of leadership, bitterly criticized Chiang's insistence on giving the highest priority to building up Chennault's air force and for pursuing the practice of giving equipment and supplies to the ground forces only incidentally. The Japanese were free to move into any area they wished to occupy. This situation could be remedied only when every resource, "including the divisions at present confronting the Communists," was devoted to the war against the Japanese. "The time has come, in our opinion," said the Joint Chiefs, "when all the military power and resources remaining in China must be entrusted to one individual capable of directing that effort in a fruitful way against the Japanese." The only man qualified to fill this position, according to the Chiefs of Staff, was General Stilwell.[5]

The President responded with vigor and was shortly prepared to move along three fronts: the imposition of firm American leadership over the Chinese military, including the Communists, the promotion of a unified effort of all Chinese military forces against Japan, and the keeping of China in the war. On July 6 President Roosevelt made the first bold move; he urged the Generalissimo to recall Stilwell from Burma and place him in command of all military forces in China with full authority to distribute lend-lease materials.[6]

*   *   *   *

The unification of all the armed forces under Stilwell brought to the fore once again this controversial figure. The President was fully aware of the long feud that had existed between Chiang and "Vinegar" Joe. Lauchlin Currie, Special Assistant to the President, who served as Liaison with China, after a trip to Chungking in August 1942 began his report by observing that Sino-American relations were steadily deteriorating. American officials in China were losing patience with the Chinese, and the Chinese were disillusioned because the Americans were not able to turn the tide of the war at once.

Currie stated that Ambassador Gauss was unpopular with all Chinese officials and "his contacts with them are of the most perfunctory sort."

The most serious difficulty, according to Currie, was the unhappy relationship between Chiang and Stilwell. Chiang insisted that Stilwell was only an adviser, while Stilwell insisted on the authority to command. The difference, Currie thought, might have been bridged, but Stilwell "has no respect or esteem for the Generalissimo and believes that his conceptions, strategy and tactics are ghastly. . . ." Worse still, the American general made no effort to conceal his feelings. Currie recommended his recall.[7] When questioned about Currie's charge, Stilwell said Currie had distorted the situation. Currie, said Stilwell, was wrong. His personal relations with Chiang were friendly and, moreover, he, Stilwell, was far from indifferent about training thirty divisions.[8]

A part of the difficulty lay in Stilwell's insistence that he would not become involved in Chinese domestic politics. The corollary to that was that decisions must be made on military grounds without regard to political considerations. Chiang could not follow such a rule for his very survival was dependent upon retaining the support of the generals and political cliques. Vinegar Joe's other major fault was his determination to fight the Japanese. Finding his plans and operations ensnarled in the complex machinery of political bargaining, he gave way to frustration and to blunt language. On March 15, 1943, he wrote to his good friend and loyal supporter, General Marshall, complaining of delay, interference, and deliberate thwarting of his work. And the corruption angered him. In Yunnan, where Stilwell was busy training Chinese troops, there was opposition; and Stilwell attributed this to fear that the American presence would interfere with the smuggling racket.[9] He had high praise for the Chinese soldier and respect for many officers but he was contemptuous of the military leadership. "It is the gang of Army 'leaders,' " he wrote, "that is the cause of all our grief."[10]

However, the conflict between Stilwell and Chiang did not arise wholly out of differences on questions of strategy. Vinegar Joe antagonized a great many of his own American generals. Among these was General Boatner, who was equally critical of Chiang and the Kuomintang regime and who likewise sided with Stilwell on questions of strategy. Boatner, years later, told of how abusive and unreasonable Stilwell could be, wrote bitterly of his love of publicity, and his posing as the tough private who despised rank; he also criticized him for being unwilling to acknowledge his mistakes.[11]

Stilwell made no allowance for the problems faced by the Chiang regime and took such a strong negative view that he irritated his superiors in Washington. After being in China for six months he thought the United States was being played "for a sucker" and took the position that "we should stop fooling and get out of here entirely, or we should lay down certain conditions which they must meet." This irascibility caused Secretary of War Henry Stimson to write in the margin of Stilwell's report: "This is what we are really up against, in view of the impossibility of replacing Stillwell [sic]."[13]

The distinguished, able, and cautious General William Slim presented the most balanced picture of the controversial general. This British officer participated in the retreat of the armies in Burma in 1942 along with Stilwell, worked with him in the campaigns on the Indian-Burma border in 1943, and served as Stilwell's commanding general in the campaign to recapture North Burma in 1944. Slim liked Stilwell, but found him a stubborn man who would hold tenaciously to his own view at staff conferences. He noted, too, that Stilwell loved publicity. He found him abusive on occasion.[13] At the same time he praised Vinegar Joe for his ability as a tactician and admired him for his imagination and drive. Concerning Stilwell's role in preparing for the later campaigns in Burma, Slim wrote: "Stilwell was magnificent. He forced Chiang Kai-shek to provide the men; he persuaded India to accept a large Chinese force, and the British to pay for it, accommodate, feed, and clothe it."[14]

In the spring of 1943 Roosevelt, disturbed by reports that Stilwell was depriving Chennault of supplies, wrote to George Marshall stating that this was wholly the wrong approach.[15] Marshall, ever loyal to Stilwell, replied in a two-page letter defending him. He acknowledged that Stilwell had undoubtedly been overly blunt in speaking to the Generalissimo and he assured the President that action was being taken to give Chennault his supplies, but the brunt of his statement was a defense of Stilwell's strategy. Defense of the air bases depended upon proper training and equipment of Chinese army units. The Japanese would attack the air bases as soon as they were seriously hurt by air attacks. No significant air effort could be carried out from China until a land route through Burma could be opened. The Chinese forces now being trained, said Marshall, would play an extremely important part in that operation.[16]

The reply to the President went to the heart of both the question of strategy and the long controversy over Stilwell. Chennault had convinced both the President and the Generalissimo that air power could hold back the Japanese forces in China and that eventually the 14th Air Force, from bases in China, could destroy Japan and force her to surrender. Both leaders found it convenient to accept this theory, the President because he was under attack in Congress by the Republicans, who were charging him with neglecting China. In agreeing with Chennault and the Generalissimo and in giving highest priority to supplies flown in over the Hump to Chennault's Air Force, the President warded off his domestic opposition. The Generalissimo likewise found it infinitely easier politically to emphasize the development of the 14th Air Force than to reorganize China's ground forces. However, in 1944 a large-scale Japanese offensive against the unprepared and weak Chinese armies demonstrated the validity of Marshall's and Stilwell's views.

Marshall's defense of Stilwell followed a deliberate effort by Chennault's staff officer, the well-known newspaperman, Joe Alsop, to have him removed. In a twenty-page letter, dated March 1, Alsop argued that Stilwell was starving the 14th Air Force and he stressed the harmful results of Stilwell's approach. The general, wrote Alsop, insisted on control down to the lowest level. Because of Stilwell's affection for the Chinese, this was tolerable, but it had the effect of inculcating in the hundreds of American officers serving as advisers a readiness to take command. These advisers, unlike Stilwell, distrusted the Chinese, had no hesitancy in taking sides on internal issues, and became enmeshed in Chinese politics.[17]

The following December Alsop wrote again to Harry Hopkins charging that Stilwell was responsible for the unfortunate attitude his ground officers took toward the Chinese. The vast majority of them, according to Alsop, "regard the Chinese as so many thieves, traitors, incompetents and savages."[18] He wrote, "I cannot ever hope to describe to you the atmosphere and as they make no secret of their opinions in public or private, and as at least 60 percent of what they

say is immediately carried back to the Chinese leaders by the innumerable agents of the Chinese secret service, the political results are
already serious." He also denounced Stilwell for supporting the proposed campaign against Burma. Alsop thought it would be so lengthy
an operation that it could not be completed before the summer of
1945.[19] Within another six months Alsop managed to gain access to
Henry Wallace and to convince him that Stilwell should be recalled.

Two months before Alsop's second letter Stilwell was in serious
difficulty. In the summer of 1943 T. V. Soong had concluded that
Stilwell must be recalled. He opened his campaign in Washington,
where he had strong allies, among them Harry Hopkins. He appealed
to Roosevelt, who sent him to Marshall. Rebuffed by Marshall, he
went to Chungking and presented his plan to the Generalissimo.[20]
A friendly observer stated that Soong saw in Stilwell a major barrier
to good relations between the two countries and knowing that China's only hope lay in future American support wished to remove the
man who was so blunt about China's shortcomings.[21] The Generalissimo, offended by Stilwell's constant reminders of the deficiencies of
the Chinese governing group and more recently upset by Stilwell's
proposal for a joint operation with the Communists in the northwest,
agreed to ask for his recall.

At this point Soong's plan became known to Madame Chiang and
her sister, Mrs. H. H. Kung, wife of the Minister of Finance and Vice
President of the Executive Yuan. Kung, according to his critics, had
no understanding of government finance and he was unscrupulous
in building his own fortune. Mrs. Kung, by reputation powerful and
the friend of reactionaries, was determined to undermine the position of T. V. Soong. Cyril Rogers, of the Bank of England, after a
conference with Kung, said no one could take his views on financial
matters seriously.[22] In Chungking his chief reputation was for corruption. His speculation and investment in American shipments of
gold were well known in Washington. Madame Kung and Madame
Chiang, seeing their own futures threatened by Soong's moves, ral-
lied to Stilwell. So did Lord Mountbatten, newly appointed Supreme
Allied Commander of the Southeast Asia Command.

General Somervell arrived in Chungking in October in time to be
present at the session where Mountbatten and Madame Chiang defended Stilwell. The meeting, Somervell recorded, became "all love

and kisses" and then to his amazement Chennault, Stilwell, and Madame Chiang became involved in a heated controversy over a whorehouse.[23] The establishment had come to the attention of Stilwell as a center of smuggling. Chennault acknowledged to Stilwell that he had known about it. On further investigation, Stilwell concluded that Chennault had close connections with it.

This temporary diversion of the discussion had no lasting importance, but the controversy generated by T. V. Soong's effort had far reaching results. Soong was not only wholly eliminated from the government, but his life was in serious danger. His removal, according to one thoughtful American observer in Chungking, had a disastrous effect on the government, leaving the reactionary elements in control. This estimate must be balanced against the fact that T. V. Soong was far from liberal in his political views even though he had an understanding of both modern finance and international affairs.

Shortly after this crisis, relations between the Gimo and Vinegar Joe improved. Both were ardent advocates of the proposed Burma campaign, However, after the Cairo Conference in November, Stilwell was deeply troubled by his role and questioned his own usefulness. He recognized that his post as chief of staff to Chiang "was simply a paper one, without staff, directive, or duties."[24] He had been largely ignored. Therefore, he took off for Burma in January and threw all his great energies into the newly launched campaign to take control over northern Burma. With the strong support of Mountbatten and excellent cooperation from General William Slim, the Britisher, he was able to carry out a most difficult campaign but not without further difficulties with Chiang. The Generalissimo was most reluctant to send his Yunnan troops into Burma even when they were desperately needed. Stilwell appealed to General Marshall and warned that it would take pressure from the President to change the situation. By this time Roosevelt was no longer partisan to Chennault nor was he prepared to readily accede to the Generalissimo. The President sent a cable stating that it was inconceivable that the American trained and equipped Yunnan forces were unable to advance. If these were not used in the common cause, said the President, it meant that "our most strenuous and extensive efforts to fly in equipment and to furnish instructional personnel have not been justified." This implied threat to cut off lend-lease brought action.[25]

The campaign in upper Burma moved ahead. The American-trained Chinese troops distinguished themselves. Stilwell went to the front and, as General William Slim said, gingered up the Chinese wherever they stalled and did so with great success.[16] In a message to Marshall, Vinegar Joe proudly reported that now that they had learned that they could defeat the Japanese the Chinese really had their tails up.[27]

The Burma campaign brought both praise and criticism for the hard-fighting Stilwell. Some Americans questioned his strategy, but it was the British who took sharp issue with him. General Slim questioned the value of the drive north and also held that it should have started far to the south so that all Burma could have been cleared of the enemy. Slim acknowledged that he saw it from the British viewpoint, namely that the reconquest of Burma was an end in itself. The Americans looked upon the reconquest of northern Burma as a means of opening up the supply route to China. However, this was not the only difference. Slim believed that the American island-hopping campaign in the Pacific was moving at a pace that meant the enemy would be reached from that direction long before effective assaults could be launched from China.[28] This view was also held by some Americans.

Stilwell's target was Myitkyina far to the north. The campaign around that point stalled for months. General Boatner laid the blame on Stilwell, charging him with greatly underestimating the strength of the Japanese in the area. Vinegar Joe was not ready to acknowledge this and he placed the blame on his subordinates. Commenting on Stilwell's frustration in the face of delay, General Slim wrote that Stilwell was caustic, accused his American commanders of not fighting and of filing false reports, criticized the Chindits and held that they were not obeying his orders, and he demanded of the various units the impossible.[29] These setbacks were temporary. Myitkyina fell on August 3. Toward the close of the campaign, Major General Thomas T. Handy wrote to Marshall describing the operation as a masterpiece. "Beset by a terrific struggle with the jungle, the monsoons, the Japanese, logistics, to say nothing of mite typhus complications," observed Handy, "he has staged a campaign that history will call brilliant."[30]

The final stages of the hard fighting in Burma took place as the

Japanese armies in China were capturing Changsha and taking airfield after airfield. Chennault called for more supplies, and Stilwell grudgingly gave him what he asked for but with the conviction that air power could not redress the balance of Japan's great superiority in ground troops. On May 24 Stilwell again asked for Marshall's advice. Central China was on the verge of collapse. It was perhaps too late to bring about the military changes demanded by the situation. Stilwell pointed out that he had been sent to China with instructions to promote a program for strengthening the Chinese ground forces so that they could protect airfields to be used in the bombing of Japan and so that the Chinese armies would be able to defeat the Japanese armies on the mainland of Asia. Was this still the strategy? If so, it necessitated complete reorganization of the Chinese forces, an end to the present danger that the Nationalists and the Communists were about to engage in civil war, and the establishment of new leadership.[31]

Stilwell was now in a highly favorable position. The President was ready to support him. Not only had his strategy been proven right by the disaster facing China but by his success in Burma.

*   *   *   *

This was the background of the Stilwell issue when Roosevelt, on July 9, 1944, urged Chiang to place Stilwell in command of all Chinese forces, including the Communists. By this time Vinegar Joe was ready to work out an arrangement whereby the Communists would receive limited amounts of supplies to aid them in carrying out guerrilla attacks against the Japanese in North China. Stilwell was likewise prepared to carry out a complete reorganization of the Chinese armed forces. The incompetents in the higher echelons would be rooted out; and every effort would be made to reduce the number of troops so that they could be fed, trained, and equipped. All these moves had tremendous political implications, and Stilwell's record made it clear that political considerations would not stand in his way.

Chiang could not lightly reject Roosevelt's proposal. In July 1944 his regime was on the edge of collapse, his armies in retreat, the public disillusioned, and moves were underway to replace him. His own future depended upon continued support from the United States. Chiang continued to profess respect for Roosevelt and confidence in the President's goodwill, but now he faced a request that threatened his regime. Faced with this dilemma, he sought time and a way around the American demand. On July 13 he cabled Roosevelt asking that he send a personal emissary with full authority to speak for him. The Gimo was obviously seeking to have a man appointed with whom he could work and to have that man outrank Stilwell.

Admiral Leahy promptly wrote in his diary that it was difficult to find "a candidate who is qualified for this proposed appointment."[32] General Marshall was deeply concerned over the probable naming of a man who would outrank Stilwell and possibly weaken his position. On August 3, while Roosevelt was making a trip to Hawaii, Marshall cabled Stilwell stating that he thought it probable that the President would agree to Chiang's request for a special emissary. He explained:

> In order to precipitate a decision and also lay the ground for a workable arrangement for you, the thought has occurred to us here that in view of the President's past use of General Hurley in the Middle East, and of Hurley's admiration for you and his previous contact with you and the Generalissimo in China, we might propose to the President that he designate General Hurley as his personal representative without defining his authority and with the understanding here to Hurley that his job was to facilitate your relations with the Generalissimo.[33]

Marshall added that Hurley was efficient and suave and "could pour more oil on the troubled waters out there. . . ." Stilwell in return cabled: "I would welcome the help of your candidate. It takes oil as well as vinegar to make good French dressing."[34]

Shortly thereafter Roosevelt appointed Hurley. The President's directive informed him that his principal mission was "to promote efficient and harmonious relations between the Generalissimo and General Stilwell, to facilitate General Stilwell's exercise of command over Chinese armies placed under his direction."[35] In veiw of later developments, this instruction is worthy of emphasis. The aim of the United States was a unified command of all Chinese armies under Stilwell. In this way the Nationalists and the Communists were to be brought together for effective action against the Japanese and, during the future course of military developments, the two parties were to achieve a political settlement. Military unification and then political unification were to be achieved in that order.

On August 21 Roosevelt urged Chiang to hasten the appointment of Stilwell. The gravity of the military situation, said the President, demanded action. As to the question of which forces should be under his command, Roosevelt thought this should only be limited by their availability to fight the Japanese. When "the enemy is pressing us toward disaster," he argued, "it appears unsound to refuse the aid of anyone who will kill Japanese."[36]

On the last day of August the Generalissimo summoned Ambassador Gauss. For an hour and a half he explained why he was troubled by the American proposal to send supplies to the Communists. The Communists, encouraged by the possibility of receiving American supplies were, said Chiang, becoming more arrogant and difficult and they now refused to negotiate with the government. He contended, that the Communists did not need American prompting to fight the Japanese. They would be repudiated at once by the Chinese people if they failed to oppose Japan.

Ambassador Gauss rejected Chiang's view that the recent negotiations with the Communists had broken down because of proposals made by the United States. They had, as a matter of fact, come to a standstill many times in the past. Then Gauss explained the exact position of the United States. His government was not interested in the Communist cause; "however, we are interested in seeking a prompt solution of a Chinese internal problem which finds the armed forces of China facing one another instead of facing and making war upon Japan," and, Gauss added, "in the present critical period of the war this is of outstanding importance."[37]

Gauss gave a full report of this interview to Secretary of State Cordell Hull, who discussed it with the President. Roosevelt and Hull were particularly pleased that Gauss had proposed to the Generalissimo that a solution to the internal problem "might be found in some measure which would bring competent representatives of other groups or parties to participation in the government, . . ." Hull encouraged Gauss to pursue this proposal. He was to inform Chiang

that the President and I feel that your suggestion is practical and timely and deserving of careful consideration; that we are concerned, not only regarding non-settlement with the Chinese communists, but also with regard to reports of discontent and dissidence in other parts of the country among non-communist Chinese, . . .

Gauss was further instructed to inform Stilwell, Hurley, and Nelson "of the matter and, if you consider that a useful purpose would be served, you are authorized to invite one or more of them to accompany you to call on Chiang."[38]

General Patrick Hurley had served as Secretary of War under Hoover and had then served as legal counsel to the Sinclair Oil Company in its negotiations with Mexico over the question of compensation for its oil properties. Hurley succeeded in bringing about a settlement satisfactory to the company and thereby added one million dollars to his personal fortune. His experience gave him full confidence in his ability to negotiate. During the early years of the war he carried out a number of missions for Roosevelt in the Middle East. He was not a military man; his rank had been bestowed upon him to strengthen his bargaining position at the time he went to the Middle East. He approached the problem of bringing unity out of discord in China as dependent upon securing the assurance of the Soviets that they would not support the Chinese Communists and would instead act in a manner that would cause the Chinese Communists to be more amenable to reason. In turn, the United States would use its influence to promote the view in Chungking that it need not fear the Soviet Union and that the Soviet Union was not engaged in promoting an internal revolution in China. He entered upon his task after a briefing in the department of State as yet unaware of the complex currents stirring in the Chinese caldron and with no proper appreciation of the fact that he was about to deal with extremely able negotiators and with even less appreciation of the infinite distrust that stood in the way of genuine cooperation between the two Chinese parties.

In his discussions with the President, Hurley had gained his approval of a visit to Moscow prior to going to Peking for the purpose of learning the Soviet View on the internal dissension in China and of winning Soviet support for the American effort. The only hope, as Hurley saw it, lay in the Soviet Union restraining the Chinese Communists at the same time that the United States dampened the inclination of the Kuomintang to solve the Communist problem by military means. In Moscow, Stalin and Molotov assured Hurley that they approved of his mission, told him that the Chinese Communists were not really Communists, and stated that the Soviets were prepared to work with the Kuomintang.[39]

Hurley arrived in Chungking in early September and became involved at once in negotiations with Chiang in regard to the President's proposal to appoint Stilwell commander of the Chinese theater with the authority to do what was necessary to bring about effective prosecution of the war. On September 10 Chiang presented an *aide memoir* in which he stated that he could not appoint Stilwell because he lacked confidence in his military ability.[40] Stilwell, he complained, had insisted on the second Burma campaign in spite of the fact that the British had refused to provide an amphibious force. This had weakened the position of the ground forces in China itself and facilitated the current Japanese capture of Chinese airfields.

The discussions about Stilwell continued. Hurley remained hopeful that the appointment could be made once a clear understanding had been reached about the limits of Stilwell's authority. Then, on September 19, came a radio message from the President to the Generalissimo.[41] Hurley and Stilwell saw it briefly before Stilwell handed it to Chiang, who was in conference with several of his top leaders and with Hurley. The message, phrased in tones of a reprimand, cited past failures to move ahead, called for prompt decision, and urged that Stilwell be appointed with unrestricted powers. Stilwell noted in his diary, "the harpoon hit him right in the solar plexus, but, although he turned green, he never batted an eye."[42]

The Generalissimo was both stunned and angry. For some days he entertained the notion that Stilwell had drafted the note and sent it to the President for signature and transmittal.[43] Hurley and Stilwell, while aware of Chiang's anger, went ahead drafting proposals outlining the limits of Stilwell's authority and some of his plans for the future. Stilwell, believing that control of lend-lease was standing in the way of his appointment, included a proviso whereby Chiang was to be in full control of lend-lease. He likewise stated that Chiang was probably worried about proposed cooperation with the Communists. If so, Stilwell was willing to postpone cooperation with them. These last days of anticipation of a new era came to an abrupt end on September 24 when the Generalissimo told Hurley that he could not appoint Stilwell.[44] Chiang then sent a message to Roosevelt that was even less diplomatic than the one he had received. Roosevelt delayed making a decision as to his next move. On October 4 the Joint Chiefs again urged the President to push the appointment of Stilwell.[45]

On October 11 Hurley sent a message advising the recall of Stilwell. He stated that he had found that "the two men are fundamentally incompatible and they are mutually suspicious of each other." Hurley thought Chiang receptive "to logical persuasion and leadership." However, Chiang reacted violently, wrote Hurley, when he believed he was being confronted with a squeeze play or ultimatum. Stilwell had made the mistake of seeking to coerce. Not to accept Chiang's recommendation, wrote Hurley, could only mean American withdrawal from China.[46] Roosevelt reluctantly accepted Hurley's advice but he notified the Generalissimo in frank language of his disappointment. The reply, drafted in the War Department, bluntly challenged the Generalissimo. It was modified at the White House but still strong.[47]

Chiang had offered to appoint some other American to the overall command position he denied Stilwell. Roosevelt, undoubtedly influenced by the hostility generated in the War Department by the rejection of Stilwell, stated that given the deplorable condition of the military siutation in China he thought it would be quite improper to ask any American to accept responsibility for reorganizing China's defenses.[48] This accorded with the views of Stimson and Marshall. The Secretary of War had said that the Generalissimo's refusal to appoint Stilwell amounted to a catastrophe.[49] After Stilwell's recall Lieutenant General Albert C. Wedemeyer was appointed to his post as Commanding General, China Theater.

In effect, Roosevelt's refusal to appoint some other American canceled the first part of the instructions to Hurley, who then proceeded to seek political unification. This was an even more prodigious task and constituted a free-wheeling interpretation of his instructions. Hurley's action gave some reason to critics to charge that he rewrote his own instructions. The charge is not without justification, but the fact remains that President Roosevelt never questioned Hurley's action.

The Stilwell episode gave rise to considerable criticism in the United States. Those who were critical saw a surrender to Chiang as a compromise with democratic principles. Critics of Chiang came to see in it a victory for Chiang that greatly increased the chances of civil war. Having won this round, the Generalissimo would not compromise with the Communists, and the result would be fratricidal strife. Admiral Leahy, on the other hand, noted that Stilwell had failed completely to adjust himself to the authority of Chiang as Generalissimo and President of China.

General Slim thought the only thing that was surprising was that the breach had not come sooner.[50] Stilwell's contempt for Chiang, whom he called "The Peanut," was no secret. Stilwell had expressed his harsh judgment in public, and it was obviously known to the Generalissimo. Yet, Stilwell was surprised and deeply hurt. He poured out his feelings to Marshall in a series of cables and protested vigorously that acceptance of Chiang's decision meant that he had no intention of cooperating in the war effort. The objections to his personality, said Stilwell, did not constitute the real reason why the Gimo had refused to appoint him. The real reason was that Chiang did not wish to employ his forces against the Japanese.[51] In a cable to Marshall on September 26 he had charged bitterly that Chiang had no intentions "of making further efforts to prosecute the war." The aggrieved general stated, "Anyone who crowds him toward such action will be blocked or eliminated." Nor did Chiang, according to Stilwell, have any intention of "instituting any real democratic reforms or of forming a united front with the Communists." Stilwell continued, "He himself [Chiang] is the main obstacle to the unification of China and her co-operation in a real effort against Japan."[52]

An extremely able general and a devoted friend of China had given Chiang adequate grounds for refusing to appoint him. But the harsh judgments voiced by Stilwell were not unwarranted. If Vinegar Joe had failed to work a change in the situation in Chungking, it was no less true that the oil administered by Stilwell's successors served only to perpetuate the fiction that the Chiang regime could unify China and restore life to a moribund government.

In the meantime, Hurley was urging Chiang to take steps that would strengthen his government by bringing in men of a more liberal persuasion. Some shifts took place. H. H. Kung was removed as Minister of Finance and General Ho Ying-shin was removed as head of the military forces. Hurley acknowledged that these represented only a slight shift in direction but he did his best to convince others that Chiang had turned a significant corner and was sincerely interested in ending the long years of one-party control.

On October 19 Hurley reported to the President in the most sanguine of spirits. With the approval of the Generalissimo and upon the invitation of Mao Tse-tung, he had carried on conversations with representatives of both parties. He had found the Generalissimo conciliatory toward the Communists, a change Hurley attributed to his having convinced Chiang that the Soviet Union desired good relations with the Chungking government. "Russia's attitude," Hurley told the President, "is the chief factor that makes possible a settlement between Chiang Kai-shek and the Communist leaders."[53] His optimism may have been more official than real, for he wrote to his secretary in Washington, "I have ridden many an outlaw broncho in my day but I am riding a dragon now and believe me he is giving me some ride."[54]

On November 7 Hurley flew to Yenan, where he greeted his hosts with the Comanche war cry and according to stories circulated later, addressed the leader of the Communist party as "Mr. Moo." His hosts were quite willing to permit him his eccentricities and greeted him graciously. During the next two days, with Hurley participating, the Communist leaders hammered out a five-point proposal for a settlement. At the close of one session he confided to an American naval officer who was present that he would have no more difficulty in dealing with the Chinese than he had experienced with the Mexicans and he knew how to handle them. Hurley left Yenan with the Communist leaders fully expecting that he would support the agreement.

Colonel David Barrett, who was present at the conferences between Mao and Hurley, has told the story of what took place. Hurley delivered a proposal from the Nationalists that included five points. These called for: a unified effort against Japan, the Communist forces to carry out the orders of the Nationalist government, both parties to adhere to the principles of Sun Yat-sen, one government and one army, and legalization of the Communist Party.[55] Mao at once assailed this program and questioned Hurley as to whether the Generalissimo had agreed to it. At a second session the same day Mao launched into a denunciation of Chiang, charging that it was the Kuomintang that had blocked the way to multi-party rule and insisting that there must be a complete reorganization of the government.[56] Hurley wisely chose to avoid a direct confrontation and shifted the discussion to the question of what the Communists saw as an acceptable arrangement. Mao asked for time to consider this, and the next session did not take place until the afternoon of the following day. What the Communist proposal included is not recorded, but Hurley asked for time to study the terms, suggested that they impressed him as entirely fair, and told Mao that he thought they should "go farther." David Barrett's understanding of this gesture from Hurley was that he thought that they could rightfully ask for more favorable terms.[57]

According to Barrett's later and fuller account, Hurley took the proposed draft and worked it over and then presented it to the Communists the following afternoon. Included in the revised draft were the individual freedoms guaranteed in the American Bill of Rights. The Communists were delighted with the revised version. Whereupon Hurley suggested that the draft should be signed by Mao and by himself.[58] Thereupon the proposal, with its two signatories, became the proposal of Hurley as well as of Mao and committed Hurley to its support. He had shown himself as eager to win the goodwill of Mao and Chou as he had in so readily agreeing to Chiang's demand that Stilwell be repudiated. In both cases he apparently did not grasp that his innocence of the sound and fury of Chinese politics was being turned to the advantage of parties engaged in a ruthless internal struggle.

The Communists' five points set forth in polite rhetoric pious statements as to future cooperation. The real meat in the dish coming from Yenan lay in points two and four. Point two provided for the establishment of a coalition government which was to initiate "A new democratic policy providing for reform in military, political, economic and cultural affairs. . . ." All anti-Japanese armies were too be under a Military Council consisting of representatives from the armies. Point four referred again to this Military Council's authority and closed with the bland but explosive statement, "The supplies acquired from foreign powers will be equally distributed."[59]

The willingness of the Communists to take the road of coalition was a measure of their confidence. If their revolution could be accomplished without long and difficult fratricidal strife, so much the better. They had good reason to believe that in a coalition government and with their own party made legal and free to carry out its organizational program throughout the provinces, they would emerge in control. Moreover, it would be a great gain if their army, dependent upon the limited weapons and munitions they could manufacture and take over from retreating Kuomintang forces and the Japanese, were able to draw upon American supplies. In addition, Mao and Chou were clearly mindful that adoption of their program, with the United States as its underwriter, would have the effect of neutralizing the United States in any future civil war and thereby remove the danger, which they feared, of American support of the Kuomintang after the war.[60]

On his return to Chungking, Hurley spent the weekend with Chiang at his mountain retreat. He wrote to Roosevelt, "I know that it will be apparent to you that nearly all of the basic principles recited in the proposed agreement are ours." He also stated that there would have to be reform within the government before the Communists would reach an agreement. Chiang showed him a proposal he would offer to the Communists. "I have had to advise him," said Hurley, "that his basis would not, in my opinion, be acceptable to the Communists at least not until his own government had been reformed and reorganized."[61]

Chiang asserted that Hurley had been misled by the Communists and that their proposal was unacceptable. On November 21 the Nationalists offered their own three-point program. It, too, included euphemistic declarations about opposing Japan and support of democratic freedoms after the war, but the commitments the Nationalists were prepared to make would have the effect of excluding the Communists from having an effective voice in the government. After incorporation into the National Army the Communist forces were to receive equal treatment in respect to pay, allowances, munitions, and other supplies but before this could take place the Communists must "give over control of all their troops to the National Government, through the National Military Council." This Council was to include one high-ranking Communist officer appointed by the Nationalist government.[62]

On the day that the Nationalists presented their offer, Hurley notified Roosevelt, "Find situation more complicated than anticipated."[63] The next several weeks provided him with further instruction in the complexities.

The Communists reacted with vigor to the Nationalists' offer. It was, Mao and Chou told Barrett in Yenan, further evidence of the unwillingness of the Kuomintang to abandon one-party rule. The repetition of the demand presented so many times in the past that the Communist Army must be absorbed under the Nationalists was offensive and showed that the Nationalists had not changed. The Communists had always made this conditional on changes in the makeup of the government so that the government would be something else than their dedicated enemy. They pointed out that the National Military Council had not met in a long time, that it possessed no authority, and that it was meaningless to offer a place on it to the Communists. The fact that Hurley had defended this part of the Nationalist proposal angered them. Barrett recorded that they stated, "We beg to differ with General Hurley, and we assure him we know whereof we speak when we say a Communist on the National Military Council would know no more about its workings than an outsider and would have no more voice in its councils."

Mao and Chou believed that Hurley had betrayed them. At Yenan, Hurley had not only thought their proposal was fair but he had suggested much of it. Then, when the Generalissimo had rejected the terms, Hurley asked the Communists to accept the counterproposals. Their faith in the emissary had been destroyed. Barrett wrote, "Chairman Mao's attitude throughout the interview was recalcitrant in the extreme." Barrett recorded: "He was not discourteous to me, but several times he flew into a violent rage. He kept shouting, over and over again, 'We will not yield any further,' 'that turtle's egg, Chiang,' 'If Chiang were here I would curse him to his face.' " Finally, in his report, Barrett wrote ruefully, "I left the interview feeling that I had talked in vain to two clever, ruthless, and determined leaders who felt absolutely sure of the strength of their position."[64]

Ironically, Hurley privately continued to hold to the views he had expressed at Yenan although he had permitted Chiang to place him in the position of supporting the Generalissimo's proposal. In a message to Roosevelt on December 14 Hurley accurately stated the Communist position that their rights could only be protected "if they are accepted on a basis of equality and a genuine coalition government formed. . . ." Then Hurley went on to state he had told Chiang "that he and his government have failed to take advantage of the opportunities offered by the Communist party for a settlement."[65]

This was only a few weeks after he had sent a message to Morgenthau stating that the leaders of the Central Government were pro-Fascist in their views and that they favored a dictatorship, while the Communists were the only real democrats in China.[66]

There is no record as to how Roosevelt assessed the internal political struggle in China. However, it is clear that he was disillusioned with the Central Government. The hard-pressed President certainly had no wish to be swept into that fast-moving maelstrom, but he could not close his eyes to its impact on the Pacific war. He persisted in putting pressure on Chiang to lend his hand to finding a working arrangement so that his own troops and the North China forces could expedite "the objective of throwing the Japanese out of China."[67]

On December 16 Chou En-lai, who had retained his customary composure during the interview with Barrett, addressed a politely phrased letter to Hurley.[68] Chou was unyielding in his criticism of Chiang but he refrained from criticizing the American participants. On December 28 Chou sent Hurley four additional proposals calling for the release of all political prisoners, the withdrawal of the Kuomintang troops from the border region and the cessation of attacks on Communist forces elsewhere, the abolition of all curbs on the people's freedom, and the closing down of secret police activity.[69] Chiang immediately protested that the Communists upped the price when agreement was in sight.

The Communists continued to show an interest in cooperating with the United States, but Mao and Chou also stated flatly that "we cannot be expected to pay the price which the Generalissimo demands for his permission for us to receive this help." They added:

> If on his record, the United States wishes to continue to prop up the rotten shell that is Chiang Kai-shek, that is her privilege. We believe, however, that in spite of all the United States can do, Chiang is doomed to failure. . . . We are not like Chiang Kai-shek. No nation needs to prop us up. We can stand erect and walk on our own feet like free men.[70]

While the negotiations were far from over, the United States had unwittingly become involved in a larger project than it intended. The Roosevelt administration sought only some temporary working arrangement that would facilitate the carrying on of the war against

Japan. The negotiations had promptly moved from this modest objective to the grander aim of a coalition government in China. The first and more modest aim was a legitimate interest on the part of a wartime ally; the second, in spite of efforts to avoid it, dragged the United States into involvement in working out the nature of China's future government and social and economic system.

Late in the fall of 1944 the War Department, the Office of Strategic Services, and General Wedemeyer, Stilwell's successor, almost succeeded in putting the mission back on the track of limited goals. The OSS had long viewed working with the Communists as useful to the gathering of intelligence and to the prosecution of the war by means of increased guerrilla activity against the Japanese. The plan agreed upon called for a limited number of Americans to work with the Communists behind the Japanese lines in destroying installations, outposts, and transportation lines. The United States was to provide limited amounts of material. General McClure, who had come from Washington as Wedemeyer's chief of staff, was in charge of making the plans. These were discussed with Hurley who gave his approval.

The Communists welcomed the plan with enthusiasm, but Chiang insisted that implementation would be subject to approval by the National Government.[71] This was made clear to the Communists.[72] Tai-li, chief of China's secret espionage service and his close friend, Admiral Miles of the United States Navy, who had bitterly opposed all OSS activity in China, immediately launched a campaign in opposition, focusing their efforts on Chiang and Hurley. They won over Hurley, who then killed the plan, charging that members of the American military were working with the Communists behind his back.[73] They had, said Hurley, entered into negotiations with the Communists which undermined his efforts to build a coalition.

NOTES TO CHAPTER VI

1.   Anonymous report on Stilwell's views, Stilwell File No. 2—Yoke Force, Hurley Papers, Box 86, University of Oklahoma.

2.   General Hurley's message to Secretary Morgenthau, November 15, 1944, *Morgenthau Diary*, Vol, 801, Roosevelt Memorial Library.

3.   *Morgenthau Diary*, Vol. 689.

4.   Ernest Price to Lauchlin Currie, November 3, 1942, Private Secretary's File, Box 91, Roosevelt Papers, Roosevelt Memorial Library.

5.   Record Group 165, Records of the War Department General and Special Staffs: OPD 384 T5 (Case 47).

6.   Roosevelt to Chiang, July 6, 1944, Copy in the Hurley Papers, Box 88.

7.   Report of Lauchlin Currie, August 24, 1942, Contemporary Military Records, National Archives.

8.   Stilwell to Marshall, October 18, 1942, OPD Executive 10, Item 22, Military Records, National Archives.

9.   Stilwell to Marshall, March 15, 1943, Map Room, Box 165, Roosevelt Memorial Library.

10. Ibid.

11. After the publication of Barbara Tuchman's biography of Stilwell, General Boatner prepared a lengthy essay on Stilwell charging that the author had ignored the criticisms he had made of Stilwell in a series of interviews while she was preparing the book. General Boatner forwarded a copy to the Asian Studies Center at Harvard. In his paper, Boatner argues persuasively that Stilwell put on acts for the press, abused his subordinates when things went wrong even though the mishaps were a product of his own errors, that he neglected his staff work, and that he made serious mistakes in judgment. These observations were confirmed by others.

12. Memorandum for Mr. Currie from General Stilwell, August 1, 1942. War Department 711134, National Archives.

13. Field Marshall Viscount Slim, *Defeat into Victory* (New York: David McKay Company, 1961), p. 36.

14. Ibid., p. 118.

15. Roosevelt to Marshall, March 8, 1943, Map Room, Box 165, Roosevelt Memorial Library.

16. Marshall to the President, March 16, 1943, Division of Military Records, National Archives.

17. Joseph Alsop to Harry Hopkins, March 1, 1943, Hopkins Papers, Box 138, Roosevelt Memorial Library.

18. Ibid., December 22, 1943.

19. Ibid.

20. Barbara W. Tuchman, *Stilwell and the American Experience in China, 1911–45* (New York: The Macmillan Company, 1971), pp. 390–91.

21. Top Secret Memorandum, "The Politico-Military Situation in China," October 26, 1944. Hurley Papers. This document, author unknown, presents a highly knowledgeable account of developments in Chungking. The facts presented are verifiable but, of course, it is impossible to ascertain the motives of T.V. Soong. The author, friendly to Soong, views Soong as seeking to improve Sino-American relations by removing Stilwell. Barbara Tuchman takes a less charitable view (p. 390). In all probability Soong identified an improvement of relations as dependent upon increasing his own influence in Chungking. To get rid of Stilwell was to make himself the chief liaison between the two governments.

22. Tuchman, op. cit., p. 321.

23. Lt. General Brehon Somervell to Marshall, October 24, 1943, Map Room, Box 165, Roosevelt Memorial Library.

24. Charles F. Romanus and Riley Sunderland, *China-Burma-India Theater: Stilwell's Command Problems, United States Army in World War II* (Office of the Chief of Military History, Department of the Army, Washington, D.C., 1956), p. 78.

25. Roosevelt to Chiang, April 3, 1944, Map Room, Box 16, Roosevelt Memorial Library.

26. Slim, op. cit., p. 219.

27. Marshall to the President, January 29, 1944, OPD 381 CTO, Military Records, National Archives.

28. Slim, op. cit., p. 215.

29. Ibid., p. 242.

30. Romanus and Sunderland, op. cit., pp. 368–69.

31. Ibid., pp. 362–63.

32. Entry to July 13, 1944, Leahy Papers, Library of Congress.

33. Marshall to Stilwell, August 3, 1944, OPD, Executive 10, Item 59, Military Records, National Archives.

34. Stilwell to Marshall, August 5, 1944, OPD, Executive 10, Item 59, Military Records, National Archives.

35. Roosevelt to Hurley, [no date] OPD, Executive 10, Item 59, Military Records, National Archives.

36. Roosevelt to Chiang, August 21, 1944, Map Room, Box 20, Roosevelt Memorial Library.

37. Gauss to Hull, August 31, 1944, *United States Relations with China with Special Reference to the Period 1944–1949* (Washington: Department of State, 1949), pp. 561–63.

38. Hull to Gauss, September 9, 1944, ibid., pp. 563–64.

39. Hurley to Roosevelt, October 19, 1944, Hurley Papers, Box 88.

40. *Aide Memoire* from the Generalissimo to Hurley, September 10, 1944, Hurley Papers, Box 88.

41. Romanus and Sunderland, op. cit., pp. 444–46.

42. Ibid., 5.

43. Ibid., p. 447.

44. Ibid., p. 450.

45. Leahy Memorandum for the President, October 4, 1944, Contemporary Military Records, National Archives.

46. Hurley to the President, October 13, 1944, Hurley Papers.

47. Proposed Message from the President to the Generalissimo, Contemporary Military Records, National Archives; Romanus and Sunderland, op. cit., p. 459.

48. Marshall to Stilwell, October 5, 1944, OPD, Executive Documents, Military Records, National Archives.

49. Marshall to Leahy, October 4, 1944, OPD, Executive Documents, Military Records, National Archives.

50. Slim, op. cit. p. 318.

51. Stilwell to Marshall, October 10, 1944, OPD, Executive 10, Item 60, Military Records, National Archives.

52. Stilwell to Marshall, September 26, 1944, OPD, Executive 10, Item 60, Military Records, National Archives.

53. Ibid., October 19, 1944, Hurley Papers, Box 88.

54. Hurley to Mrs. Carter, October 12, 1944, Hurley Papers.

55. David D. Barrett, *Dixie Mission:* The United States Army Observer Group in Yenan, 1944 (Berkeley, California: Center for Chinese Studies, 1970), pp. 58–59.

56. Ibid., pp. 59–60.

57. Ibid., p. 62

58. Ibid., p. 64.

59. Hurley to the President, November 16, 1944, Hurley Papers.

60. Ibid.

61. Ibid., November 17, 1944.

62.   Ibid.

63.   Ibid., November 21, 1944.

64.   Barrett to Wedemeyer, December 10, 1944, Hurley Papers.

65.   Hurley to Roosevelt, December 14, 1944, Map Room, Roosevelt Memorial Library.

66.   Hurley to Morgenthau, November 15, 1944, *Morgenthau Diary,* Vol. 801.

67.   Roosevelt to Hurley, November 17, 1944, Map Room, Box 11, Roosevelt Memorial Library.

68.   Chou En-lai to Hurley, December 16, 1944, Hurley Papers.

69.   Ibid., December 28, 1944, Hurley Papers.

70.   Barrett to Wedemeyer, December 10, 1944, Copy in Hurley Papers.

71.   Hurley to the President, January 14, 1945 and Hurley to the Secretary of State, January 31, 1945, Hurley Papers.

72.   Wedemeyer to Marshall, January 19, 1945, Copy in Hurley Papers.

73.   R. Harris Smith, OSS *The Secret History of America's First Central Intelligence Agency* (Berkeley: University of California Press, 1972), pp. 273–74.

CHAPTER VII

"This Seemingly Innocent Proposal"

John Davies

Some form of coalition of the political groups would have relieved the United States of the pressing problem of disunity in China and it would probably have avoided the future distressing divisions in American domestic politics. Hopes of achieving unity kept the proposal alive in spite of deep skepticism on the part of many, including Ambassador Gauss. Whatever the slim prospects of success, Patrick Hurley, quite unintentionally, not only killed those prospects but he also followed a course that reduced the United States to a faithful suitor of an aging and calculating lady without friends.

During his first few months in China, Hurley showed no hostility to Communist leaders in Yenan but he became increasingly distrustful of them. The change in his attitude may have been due to the influence upon him of the Nationalist leaders in Chungking or the toughness shown by Mao and Chao in the discussions in December. The President's emissary, named Ambassador to China after Gauss' resignation in November 1944, vetoed his own program of reform in China by taking the position that because the Chiang regime was the duly recognized government it was neither to be threatened with moves endangering its retention of power nor faced with a possible withdrawal of American support. In addition, Hurley repeatedly took the regime's point of view on disagreements between the K.M.T. and the Communists, thereby further assuring Chiang of continued support. Bolstered in this fashion against mounting hostility within China, the reactionaries dominating the Central Executive Committee of the Kuomintang simply held on to the reigns of power and saw no need of reforming. Hurley's course served as a tranquilizer at a time when most observers believed that only major surgery could restore the health of the government.

Assured of the United States continuing support, the Kuomintang, dominated by the C-C and Whampoa military cliques firmly opposed all compromise. Chiang did not refuse to negotiate but he adhered to conditions which he knew were unacceptable to the Communists. Prior to any reform of the government the Communists were to submit their army to the control of the Nationalist Government. As to government reforms, for the time being these were to be limited to a few appointments, little more than gestures. There was to be no sharing of power with either the Communists or genuinely democratic dissident groups. Hurley raised no objections. He expressed sympathy with the Nationalist position that political reorganization must be delayed and that no move should be made until the Communists surrendered control of their army. Chiang's offers were nothing more than tokens, and Hurley supported these. He repeatedly affirmed that this stance was in accord with his instructions.

Hurley's instructions were in large part oral. Both at the time he left for China in August 1944 and again during his visit in Washington in February 1945 he discussed his mission with Roosevelt. He interpreted his instructions to mean that he seek to establish cooperation between the contending parties in China and seek to strengthen the Chinese government and keep China in the war. Historians have not disputed this part of Hurley's interpretation. What seems more questionable was Hurley's viewing his instructions as affording ground for almost wholly taking the side of Chiang. The instructions did not warrant this course.

Given the nature of Chinese society, the loss of public confidence in the Central Government, and the amazing success of the Communists in building a broad political base, Hurley's basic assumptions added up to serious miscalculations. Worse still, his partisan role in the superficially neutral effort to bring about unification helped lead his country down the tortuous path that led to twenty-five years of support of a regime long after it had lost all credibility in its own territory.

This original blunder in Sino-American wartime relations occurred in spite of the fact that scores of Americans in official positions perceived at an early date that Hurley was following a dangerous course. Upon his arrival in Chungking Hurley learned that Ambassador Gauss did not believe it possible to achieve even the more limited aim of military cooperation between the two Chinese camps and that the Ambassador thought a collapse of the Kuomintang regime was most probable, a probability Gauss viewed as offering the possibility of a new and effective government.[1]

When Hurley found that many foreign service officers differed with his own prognosis, he quickly concluded that they were wrong. Hurley did not close his eyes to the weaknesses of the Chiang regime but, unlike the foreign service officers, he believed that the existing government would remedy its weaknesses and that it was the only government strong enough to unify China. The foreign service officers differed with Hurley on two basic issues: they were convinced that the Chiang regime would only institute reforms if the United States applied great pressure and that the weaknesses of the government were so basic and far reaching that short of a fundamental reordering of the political structure it was destined to collapse. As the emissary of the President and reporting directly to Roosevelt, Hurley considered himself to be independent of the State Department. Had this not been true he would have been compelled to observe the department's instructions or face removal. As it turned out, he largely ignored the department and was still permitted to continue. This unhappy circumstance became readily apparent during the early months of 1945.

Those in disagreement with Hurley, men such as John Davies, differed with him on two major points.[2] First, Davies and others placed a lower estimate on the ability of the Kuomintang to restore public confidence in its administration and they likewise believed that the Communists had achieved sufficient strength so that short of a major transformation of the central government in a direction which would give them an effective voice they could well afford to refuse to compromise. Second, the Communists would turn to the

Soviet Union for assistance if this was the only recourse left to them. Therefore, the proper course for the United States was to exert great pressure on the Kuomintang and to work in a limited degree with the Communists in order to make this pressure effective. Short of bringing about a basic reordering of the Central Government there could be no compromise, and the result would be civil war. Civil war posed two dangers. The strife might end in a divided China, and this would be an invitation to outside powers to interfere. Civil war might also result in an alignment of the Soviet Union and the United States on opposite sides and their involvement in a new world catastrophe.

The contestants held to their positions with the greatest tenacity. In this struggle of opposing views the question was never whether or not the Chinese Communists were genuine Communists, but rather which strategy for achieving unification promised success. Hurley believed in negotiating with the Communists but he also believed that any indication to them that the United States might cooperate with them short of approval by the Nationalists would cause them to turn a cold shoulder on the negotiations. Consequently, he saw those who would cooperate with the Communists as enemies of the negotiations.[3] His distrust and hatred of them mounted until he could not bring himself to accept the fact that they were equally devoted to the interests of the United States.

Those who differed with Hurley were not prepared to circumvent the Nationalist Government, as he asserted, but they believed that only rigorous pressure from the United States could bring about reform. Subordination of American interests to the wishes of Chiang Kai-shek would reduce the United States to a hostage of the Central Government and leave that government free to pursue a course that could only lead to civil war.

Personalities sharpened the fray. Hurley was not a good listener and he failed to perceive that as head of the Embassy it was his responsibility to promote good working relations among its members. Largely ignored by their chief and offended by his highhanded treatment of them, their personal grievances served as a leaven that enlarged the differences on strategy that separated them from him. Hurley's pride, his eccentric ways, and his unwillingness to draw upon their much greater experience in China undermined their confidence in him.

China, in spite of American wishes to the contrary, moved toward fratricidal war and, as she did, it was necessary to take the realities into account. In December General McClure and a group of officers at Army Headquarters in Chungking drafted a plan for the use of Communist troops in a huge guerrilla operation against the Japanese. Twenty-five thousand American paratroopers were to participate, and the United States was to furnish supplies. All troops were to be under the command of Americans. The targets were Japanese lines of communications, outposts, railroad bridges, culverts, and railway equipment.[4] Hurley insisted that these plans must be subject to the approval of the Generalissimo. Later Hurley asserted that he implacably opposed the whole operation.[5] After gaining only very tentative approval from the Minister of War, General McClure gave his consent to discussion of the plan with the Communists. The Army wished to get to them before the O.S.S. intruded. It was made clear to the Communists that the plan must first be approved by the United State government.[6] When Hurley learned of this, he attributed the recent Communist offensive to their hopes of American aid and also charged that it explained the recent Communist intransigence in the negotiations.[7] Both parties had been consistently intransigent, and negotiations had broken down many times before. Hurley's charge originated in his hostility to his subordinates. At any rate, the Generalissimo vetoed the operation. Hurley's opposition did not prevent the Joint Chiefs from issuing its order in late January giving General Wedemeyer freedom to cooperate with any Chinese faction that might be present in an area where landings took place.[8]

Other puzzling and stubborn questions haunted the policy makers by January 1945. Hurley had worked indefatigably and sincerely to bring about a compromise but in the process he had come to recognize that a genuine coalition meant the end of the Kuomintang. Chiang and T.V. Soong believed that this was true and they adamantly opposed even use of the term "coalition."[9] In a cable to Stettinius on December 24, 1944, Hurley betrayed his misgivings explaining why coalition was unacceptable to the Nationalists. He was sufficiently troubled so that he outlined alternatives to a political coalition and he, in fact, returned to the earlier idea of a single military command. The best alternative, said Hurley, might be "an American military command of all Chinese forces." He reported that it was understood that both Chiang and the Communists would agree to this. Such a command, added Hurley, would make it possible to provide limited supplies of ammunition and demolition material to the Communists, and they would use it effectively.[10] But he promptly backed away from this approach. Instead he stressed that his instructions directed him to prevent the collapse of the National Government. Seeking some firm footing from which to negotiate, he turned his instruction to keeping China in the war into a dictum to preserving the Chiang regime. This interpretation rested on the fact the government in Chungking was the recognized government and the United States must deal with it in good faith. This left Hurley in the position of assuring Chiang that the United States would continue to support him against the domestic enemies as well as against Japan. Therefore, Chiang need not compromise with the Communists nor need he in any way weaken one party control.

Hurley's shift coincided with a growing conviction among others that Chiang would not compromise and that at the same time he could not unify the country by either political or military means. John Davies, in a memorandum in January, described the hope that Chiang could unify China as a fiction. The Communists, said Davies, could do so. Therefore, as he saw it, the United States had missed the boat, and only the Soviet Union could be happy.[11] John Carter Vincent, Chief of the Division of Chinese Affairs, also expressed doubt that unification would take place under Chiang but he had not lost complete faith in the Nationalists. Vincent held that "with regard to the short-term objective, Chiang appears to be the only leader who now offers hope for unification." Having so stated, Vincent went on to say, "With regard to our long-term objective, it is our purpose to maintain a degree of flexibility which would permit cooperation with any leadership in China that would offer the greatest likelihood of fostering a united, democratic, and friendly China."[12]

"Flexibility" came to be the leading guideline in the Department of State. If Chiang did not survive, as many believed most likely, it naturally followed that there must be a willingness to change course in the event his fall took place. Not all believed that the fall of Chiang would be immediately followed by a Communist takeover, for there were several movements afoot by combinations of warlords and leaders of minor parties to stage a coup.

Military considerations also dictated flexibility. The plans of the Joint Chiefs of Staff after October 1944 no longer hinged on large-scale operations by the Chinese armies or heavy bombardment of Japan from airfields in China, but they did include a landing in the vicinity of Ningpo south of Shanghai.[13] Intelligence reports indicated that in this area the American troops were likely to encounter Chinese who were independent of Chungking.

What should be done? In mid-January the Division of Chinese Affairs in the Department of State, in a memo for the Joint Chiefs, warned that the Central Government would probably fall if the Japanese tried and succeeded in capturing Chungking and Kunming. If the Japanese tried and failed, then the standing of the Nationalists would be strengthened. If the Japanese did not attack "the situation would probably continue much as it is with a gradual deterioration of conditions and of the Central Government's position." To these observations the memo added that the Division of Chinese Affairs held no hope that there would be a coalition of the Kuomintang and the Communists. Finally, the Joint Chiefs were advised that it would be undesirable and a breach of faith to supply arms to any dissident group as long as the United States continued to recognize the Central Government as the legally constituted government of China. However, in the event of American landings in areas where Central authority was not existent, then extension of aid on an ad hoc basis for the purpose of meeting exigencies would be desirable.[14] It was on the basis of this recommendation that on January 29 the Joint Chiefs issued an order incorporating this recommendation.[15] Flexibility was on the way to becoming policy, but it was not the policy of Hurley.

February saw a continuation of the attitude of caution. Although desirable, unification of China appeared to be more and more unlikely. The Chinese Communists were now rapidly expanding into areas south of the Yangtze and along the coast. On February 7 Raymond P. Ludden cabled the Assistant Chief of Staff of Military Intelligence giving the findings of the Military Observer Group. He stressed the determination of the Communists to expand as the forces of the Central Government withdrew in the face of the Japanese advance. "The further one proceeds east in Communist controlled areas of North China," Ludden stated, "the more outspoken and bitter become the criticism of the Kuomintang Government."[16]

Within a month John Service reported that the Communist Fourth Army was rapidly expanding into Anhwei, Kiangsu, and Chekiang, the provinces west, south, and north of Shanghai.[17]

At the close of February both the Nationalists and the Communists gave strong signs of moving toward a clash. As the Communists drove hard to control more territory, the Nationalists made less effort to conceal their unwillingness to compromise. In a meeting before the State Council one representative asked Chiang a question about unification and did so in a manner that indicated he favored it. The Generalissimo "became enraged and delivered a stinging reprimand." He also seized the occasion to criticize Sun Fo. Chiang, it was reported, was red with anger "and his voice and his hands shook."[18] On March 1 before the preparatory commission for the inauguration of constitutional government, Chiang, in a speech devoted in large part to denouncing the Communists, announced that the National Assembly would meet on November 12.[19] This body, elected nine years earlier and before the Communists had made their strong gains in popular support, would clearly seek to perpetuate one party rule. The Communists labeled Chiang's announcement as a declaration of war.

Neither side was ready to compromise, although as one observer noted both parties usually clothed their public statement in conciliatory language. If Chiang was intransigent, so were the Yenan leaders. On April 1 John Service met with Mao, Chou, and Chu Teh. Mao, in good spirits, said that the failure to achieve unity was misunderstood abroad. The failure was not due to the mere bickering of two political parties. The issues were "basic and vital." He outlined the principles for which the Communists had been fighting throughout the war: union on the basis of resistance to Japan, the granting of democratic rights, and the full mobilization of the people. They continued to defend boldly these principles as they had before there were Soviet and American victories. "Our objectives," said Mao, "are unchanged but our voice gets louder as the situation in China becomes more desperate and more urgent and as more and more people see that we are right." Mao had not used the words "basic and vital" lightly.[20]

On February 27 the American Joint War Plans Committee made a significant recommendation. The committee favored continued efforts at unification but called for steps to be taken "to coordinate guerrilla activities by the Chinese Communists with the operations of China Theater Forces and U.S. forces in the Pacific." Then the committee stated:

> Continued support of the National Government to the exclusion of the Communists may lead us into conflict with Russia after the present war. There is little doubt that a very close tie exists between the Chinese Communists and Russia, although proof of this is not at hand.[21]

The committee's expectation of civil war in China and its assumption that a close relation existed between the Chinese Communists and the Soviets did not in itself answer the question of what policy the United States should pursue. Several options remained open. One of these was to try to lure the Communists away from their ideological brothers in the Soviet Union. Not to do so would be to make them wholly dependent on the Soviet Union. The United States might also choose to give the Nationalists support or withdraw and accept whatever might be the outcome of a civil war.

Postwar considerations began to move to the forefront as wartime strategy for defeating Japan receded. The committee's conclusions agreed with those of John Davies, but he was more deeply conscious of the domestic political implications than was the committee. Consequently, he sadly observed that the American public still adhered to the fiction of Chiang unifying China and providing a stabilizing force. Davies was well informed as to separatist schemes of various Chinese leaders, knowing how the forces of Yu Han-mou, Chang Fa-kuei, and Tsai Feng-kai in the southeast had deliberately avoided engaging the Japanese in their recent drive because they wished to keep their forces intact so as to be able to set up a new regime.[22] He was equally aware of the vitality of the Communists. He not only entertained few fictions regarding China but he was no less realistic concerning the possibility of contradictory pressures in the United States bringing about delay. He feared unsatisfactory compromises contrived to meet the pressures of American domestic politics. In a memo of January 4 Davies wrote, "It is further evident that the necessary sensitivity in a democratic system of the administration to public opinion makes it unlikely that American policy can be anything other than a vacillating compromise between realism and wishful thinking."[23]

Davies himself did not engage in wishful thinking. The War Plans Committee believed that there was a close tie up between the Soviet Union and the Chinese Communists.[24] Patrick Hurley was one of the few who believed the contrary. A number of developments fostered the assumption that the Soviets would gain a dominant position. The mounting criticism of the Soviet Press against the Kuomintang during the winter and spring of 1945 led many to believe that a shift in Soviet policy was about to take place. The hard bargaining of Stalin at Yalta and the behavior of the Soviets in the countries occupied by the Soviet armies supported the same estimate.[25] Davies, cynical about the Soviet Union, believed that the Soviets would pursue a highly imperialistic policy in Asia. His report seemed to imply that Marxism-Leninism created ties that reduced national and cultural identity to a nullity.

These estimates of the relationship between the Soviet Union and the Chinese Communists sadly underestimated the strength of Chinese nationalism now dressed in Communist clothing. Friendship between Yenan and Moscow on ideological grounds, however real, eventually failed to override either Chinese or Soviet national interests. The scant testimony existing on wartime relations between the two suggests that the relationship was far from close. The Soviets were popular in Yenan, but there was no evidence of close cooperation.

On March 1 John Service met with several of the leaders in Yenan on a series of occasions and sought out their views on future relations with the Soviet Union. The Communists' spokesmen took for granted that Russia would enter the war and based this conclusion on the self-evident fact that Soviet national interests in Asia dictated Soviet participation. The Communists did not believe that the Soviet Union would seek to control Manchuria but they did think she would want a friendly government and easy access to trade. They also told Service that they did not expect aid from the Soviets, but Service reported that they clearly expected that Soviet forces would cooperate with them in Manchuria. Mao, in tones of philosophical tranquility, explained the danger of accepting foreign aid. Aid from abroad, he thought, would encourage the Chinese to depend on foreign assistance and promote a state of mind characterized by a feeling of dependence and inferiority. The present war, said Mao, was a war of national liberation, one in which they gained faith in themselves and in which hardships were turned into assets.[26]

The inner drive of the revolution in China sufficed to propel it; it was not dependent upon support from outside. Neither the Soviet Union nor the United States were to influence China's course significantly, but neither was fully prepared to accept this. The corollary to this was that both feared that the other would act in such a way in relation to the civil war looming ahead that they would clash. Both were Pacific powers. Both sought stability in the area. Both faced the question of who would fill the vacuum that would result once Japan had been crushed. This concentration on the changing configuration of world power caused them to see the China question from the outside rather than from the inside.

During the anxious winter and spring of 1945 Hurley labored in the oppressive dampness and chilling cold of Chungking to find a basis for unification. He met with Chou En-lai and then with the Nationalist leaders, T.V. Soong, Acting President of the Executive Yuan and Minister of Foreign Affairs, Wang Shih-chieh, Minister of Information, and General Chang Chih-chung, of the National Military Council. The sessions, while not finally productive, provided temporary rays of hope. Soong sought to bring about the only kind of unification tolerable from the Nationalists' point of view, Communist representation in a few positions, but with control residing with the Kuomintang. To surmount the Communist objection to unification of the armies under the Central Government, Chiang proposed to appoint an American officer to command the Communist army.[27] Chou En-lai contended that the time had come to return the government to the people and that the necessary first step was the formation of a coalition government.[28] Soong argued that to establish a wholly new government in wartime would throw China into chaos.[29] There were moments of optimism. On February 3 Wang presented a draft which led Chou to say that for the first time he felt that they were reaching a basis on which they could all cooperate. The draft called for convening representatives of the several parties to study the ways for ending the period of one-party tutelage and of establishing constitutional government. The committee was to draw up a common political program, provide for unification of the armed forces, and determine the form in which members of other parties than the Kuomintang would take part in the National Government. Only if the committee reached unanimous agreement was the proposal to be submitted to the National Government for approval and execution.

The hopes died quickly. Chiang and his party promptly laid down two conditions, first that the Communists must turn over control of their army prior to any steps being taken and, secondly, that there would be no changes in the one-party government at the present time. When, some eleven days later, Chiang announced that the National Assembly would meet in November he thereby informed the Communists that he wholly rejected the major points of the conditions they deemed essential.

Hurley recorded no feeling of impatience with Chiang as he turned his back at this moment on the seemingly greatest hope for the negotiations. He retained the position he had stated one month earlier when he had met with a committee of the Kuomintang and found them committed to one-party rule. At that time he had noted, "I, of course, had deep sympathy with him [Chiang] because I well understand that the National Government must be maintained."

From the beginning differences between Hurley and his staff and between Hurley and the Department of State were attributed by the Ambassador to intrigue. Shortly after Hurley returned to the United States in February 1945, the Embassy in Chungking proceeded to give its views of the situation. George Atcheson, Jr., Chargé, sent a lengthy memorandum embodying these views. He stressed Chiang's increasing intransigence, his appointment of extreme conservatives in recent weeks, and the conclusion by the Communists that "we are definitely committed to the support of Chiang alone, and that we will not force Chiang's hand in order to be able to aid or cooperate with them." Atcheson recommended that the situation be put before the President and that he inform the Generalissimo "in definite terms that military necessity requires that we supply and cooperate with the Communists and other suitable groups who can assist, . . ."[30] The cable asked that this matter be discussed with Hurley and Wedemeyer while they were in Washington. Hurley saw this as a stab in the back.

However, Atcheson's cable received careful attention in Washington. Acting Secretary of State Joseph Grew sent it to President Roosevelt with a memo explaining the dangers in recent developments in China.[31] When Hurley attacked Atcheson's views in an interview in the Office of Far Eastern Affairs, Joseph Ballantine, Deputy Director of the Office of Far Eastern Affairs, took exception and in a telephone conversation with Hurley the following day said he did not see "how Atcheson's recommendations, if adopted, involved recognition of the Communists as armed belligerents or were inconsistent with our recognition of the National Government as the government of China." Ballantine sought to persuade Hurley that Atcheson "had done his duty in giving his estimate of the most recent developments and of the thought of the Embassy in that connection."[32] In the course of the exchange Hurley's position became clearer than ever. Asked what he thought of Chiang's March 1 speech, Hurley replied that "he had understood Chiang Kai-shek perfectly and that he thought it very natural that Chiang Kai-shek should take a stronger line as his position became more solid." Unfortunately, there is no record of President Roosevelt's response to Hurley's opinions.

By April the cleavage between Hurley and the Department of State had widened. Laurence E. Salisbury had recently written two articles for the *Far Eastern Survey,* journal of the American Council of the Institute of Pacific Relations, charging that all-out support of Chiang had played into Chiang's hands and was getting in the way of unification. He attributed this mistake in strategy to Hurley. Grew asked Edwin F. Stanton, Deputy Director of the Office of Far Eastern Affairs, to give him his opinion of Salisbury's argument.[33] Stanton agreed with Salisbury. On April 28 Stanton sent Grew a memorandum in which he was highly critical of Hurley. He charged that Hurley was intransigent and inflexible, that he had given Chiang blank check support, and that he was extremely suspicious of and disliked foreign service officers.[34] On April 23 Grew had already cabled Hurley "it is most important that we maintain complete flexibility repeat flexibility with regard to achieving them [long-term objectives] and that we must make it entirely clear to the Generalissimo and his Government that our support of them is not of the 'blank check' variety."[35] Two weeks later, on May 7, Grew cautioned Hurley again. While the United States continued to support the National Government, Grew advised that "in pursuance of the long-term objective and against the possible disintegration of the existing government, we aim to maintain a degree of flexibility to permit cooperation with any other leadership which may give greater promise of achieving unity and contributing to peace and security in east Asia." The United States, said Grew, was not prepared to commit itself to future military support "until we are convinced that the government is making progress toward achieving unity and solid popular support."[36]

These warnings only suggested to Hurley that some disloyal elements were at work in the State Department. His attitude toward his superiors in the Department had their origin in part in the fact that Roosevelt had appointed him as his special emissary and that he was independent of that branch of the government. He received further advice on May 28 from the State-War-Navy Coordinating Committee, the highest level group short of the President. The three cabinet members composing this committee began by reaffirming that the long-range goal was a China serving as a stabilizing factor in the Far East "with a government representative of the wishes of the people." The instructions went on to say that "should the authority of the existing government disintegrate, we would reexamine our position in the light of the manifested wishes of the Chinese people and regard sympathetically any broadly representative government or movement which gave promise of achieving unity and of contributing to peace and security in eastern Asia."[37]

Hurley's estimate of Chiang's strength differed from that of the great majority of observers. Others stressed the increasing strength of the Communists, who were now on the verge of controlling a very large part of the area behind the Japanese lines from the Yangtze through North China. Unfortunately, Hurley did not indicate why he believed that the Nationalists had strengthened their position, but it is probable that he was influenced by the cutbacks in the size of the army, by the efforts to strengthen the morale in the armed forces, and by a limited effort to reform the administration. What American policy should be obviously depended upon estimates of the staying power of the Kuomintang and the difference between Hurley and others on this score explains at least in part their clash on policy questions. This clash eventually reached far beyond Hurley and those immediately involved and finally served to divide the American public.

Hurley did honestly inform his superiors in Washington of the stalemate he confronted. In a cable to the Secretary of State giving his observations of the Kuomintang Party Congress, held early in June, Hurley reported that while there was considerable outspoken criticism, it was also true that the reactionary C-C Clique had gained in strength by about ten percent of the CEC and CSC and indirectly have a majority in both committees.[38] In forwarding a six-page memorandum from Everett Drumright, Hurley stated that great obstacles lay ahead, but that the situation was definitely improved. However, Drumright's report provided no basis for even restrained optimism.[39] The old stumbling blocks to successful negotiation remained, namely Nationalist insistence that the Communist Army be incorporated into the Nationalist Army prior to political reform and equal Communist determination that political reform must precede the unification of the armies. Drumright found relations between the Nationalists and the Communists steadily deteriorating and he cited steps taken by the Communists for the express purpose of countering the Nationalists' refusal to reform the government so as to give the Communists a meaningful voice. These steps included a speeded-up program of territorial expansion, the making of plans for setting up a separate state, and stronger criticism of the Kuomintang.

Late in June, Hurley had a three-hour conference with General Wang Ja-fei, the then ranking member of the Communists in Chungking. Wang readily acknowledged that the ultimate aim of his party was the establishment of a Communist society. He was equally frank in stating that the Communists sought reform on the basis of the original four points agreed upon at the time of Hurley's first visit to Yenan. Hurley, in turn, when asked by Wang to urge Chiang to accept these, said he would not do so, and he gave as his reason that once these had been accepted, the Communists would be free to dominate and they would not find it necessary to enter into any agreements with the Nationalists. Action on the four points, said Hurley, should come after and not before an agreement with the armed Communist Party.[40]

The negotiations had long since reached the stage of being no more than a tedious repetition of points. The two sides were worlds apart in their political and social philosophies. Neither accepted the possibility of some arrangement for sharing power as a desirable end.

Both believed in one-party rule although quite willing to claim that each alone stood for a multi-party system. And these basic political convictions had been strengthened by almost twenty years of warfare. Now the Communists saw victory within their grasp and the Kuomintang, aware that it had lost the battle at the political level, could only desperately fend off their rivals and place their faith in another military suppression campaign.

"The seemingly innocent proposal" was not withdrawn. The futile gesturing in Chungking continued. However, the energy of the American leadership was directed to other ways of achieving a strong and friendly China capable of serving as a stabilizing force. Success now seemed to depend upon developing satisfactory relations between Soviet Russia and Nationalist China. China's fortunes had so long been determined by foreign powers that no one appeared to have contemplated the possibility that it would determine its own destiny.

Of the many American participants in Chungking and Washington few exhibited optimism, whether they agreed or disagreed with the American Ambassador in Chungking. Hurley was almost alone in believing that his mission was successful. At a luncheon with the United Press Bureau Chief in Chungking in April, upon his return from Moscow, Hurley suggested to his guest, "Wouldn't it be a great thing for me to get the Nobel Prize for settling the Civil War."[41]

In the course of the seven months preceding the termination of the war the most perceptive overall analysis of the dilemma confronting the United States was that provided by John Davies. In a lengthy dispatch from Moscow on April 15 he refrained from recommending a future course. Given the situation as he saw it, there was, indeed, no course to recommend. On the question of establishing a coalition, Davies concluded that Chiang, given his earlier experience with the Communists and recognizing the weaknesses of his regime, knew that in a coalition he would lose. The Communists, on the other hand, saw in a coalition a cheap way to achieve victory. No coalition was to be achieved. Secondly, it was possible that, with far-reaching, all-out foreign support, the Kuomintang might achieve victory in a civil war. However, the Kuomintang must first bring about reforms to marshal popular support. Choice of this course, support of the Kuomintang, likewise assumed that the American public would willingly sustain an extremely costly and long drawn out effort. Thirdly, the Communists might or might not cooperate with the United States. Davies had serious doubts that they would, but their disillusionment with the Soviet Union because of the scabby treatment they had received at the hands of the Kremlin made this a possibility. Yet, some factions among the Communists would be unalterably opposed. Finally, there was the probability of the Soviet Union entering the war and invading Manchuria to strike at the Japanese. If the United States set out to win the cooperation of the Communists, she would face the necessity of "competing with Russian drawing-power rather than seeking to block it off." Davies asked "Even if the Yenan regime is willing to cooperate with us . . . and we undertake with maximum possible effect a campaign to capture politically the Chinese Communists, what would happen should the Red Army move into North China?" Wherever the Russian army had gone in Europe, political domination had followed. Moreover, he observed, "it should not be surprising if those Chinese sympathetic to the United States were liquidated and American aid and cooperation effectively obstructed or eliminated."[42]

Hurley's formula had been rejected by the Department of State in a large part during the winter and spring of 1945. Yet there was no change, for neither Roosevelt during his last months nor Truman chose to terminate Hurley's appointment nor to demand a change in the course he was following. The records available do not indicate why this was so. Hurley's continuance stands as one of those unfortunate incidents when for inexplicable reasons the hard decision of changing the course failed to be taken.

NOTES TO CHAPTER VII

1. Memorandum of Conversation at Ambassador Hurley's house, June 15, 1945, Hurley Papers.

2. Memorandum by John Davies, [no date] Second Secretary of Embassy, *Foreign Relations of the United States 1945*, Vol. VII, *The Far East China*, pp. 155–57; Memorandum by Davies, April 15, 1945, ibid., pp. 334–38;Memorandum by Davies, July 10, 1945, ibid., pp. 928–32; Memorandum by Raymond Ludden and John Service, February 14, 1945, *U.S.F.R. 1945*, pp. 216–18; Atcheson to the Secretary of State, February 28, 1945, *U.S.F.R. 1945*, pp. 242–46.

3. At a meeting of Hurley with five of his subordinates on June 15, 1945, these men made clear their position about providing reports on the situation as they saw it. Hurley, in an emotional state, did what he had done before and was to do again, namely cite them as enemies seeking to undermine his policy. Memorandum of Conversation at Ambassador Hurley's house, June 15, 1945, Hurley Papers.

4. Memorandum of Colonel B. F. Taylor, Army Headquarters in Chungking, Hurley Papers, File 308, Document 105.

5. Hurley to the Secretary of State, January 31, 1945, Hurley Papers, File 308, Document 107.

6. Memorandum of Colonel B. F. Taylor, Hurley Papers, File 308, Document 105.

7. Hurley to Roosevelt, January 14, 1945, Hurley Papers, Box 98, File 1.

8. This order is referred to by Hurley in a draft of a letter to the President. The draft is undated. Hurley wrote that Wedemeyer had received two memoranda which he regarded as directives authorizing him "to start arming the Communists now." These memoranda were two of the enclosures transmitted with an instruction dated February 8. Hurley Papers, Box 92-F1.

9. Hurley's telegram of December 24 was summarized by Secretary of State Stettinius and forwarded to the President. Stettinius to Roosevelt, January 4, 1945, *U.S.F.R. 1945*, p. 154.

10. Hurley to the Secretary of State, December 24, 1944, *U.S.F.R. 1944*, p. 745 and Hurley to Roosevelt, January 14, 1945, Hurley Papers.

11. Memorandum by John Davies, [no date], *U.S.F.R. 1945*, pp. 155–57.

12. Memorandum of Vincent to the Acting Secretary of State Joseph Grew, January 29, 1945, *U.S.F.R. 1945*, pp. 37–39

13.   Minutes of Joint Chiefs of Staff, Report of Joint Staff Planners, February 27, 1945, National Archives.

14.   Memorandum Prepared in the Division of Chinese Affairs for the Joint Chiefs of Staff, [undated but about January 12], U.S.F.R. 1945, pp. 169–72.

15.   Minutes of Joint Chiefs of Staff, Report of Joint War Plans Committee, February 27, 1945, National Archives.

16.   Ludden, Second Secretary of Embassy, to Assistant Chief of Staff, G-2, February 7, 1945, Hurley Papers.

17.   Service report "The Present Communists Attitude Toward the Central Government," March 11, 1945, 893.00/3-2145, Department of State, National Archives.

18.   Atcheson to Secretary of State, February 26, 1945, U.S.F.R. 1945, p. 240.

19.   Ibid., March 2, 1945, U.S.F.R. 1945, pp. 254–58.

20.   Memorandum of Conversation of John Service with Mao Tse-tung, Chou En-lai, and Chu Teh, April 1, 1945, U.S.F.R. 1945, pp. 311–17.

21.   "Report of Joint War Plans Committee," February 27, 1945, Minutes of the Joint Chiefs of Staff, National Archives.

22.   Memorandum by Davies for Vincent, January 5, 1945, U.S.F.R. 1945, pp. 159–62.

23.   Memorandum by Davies for Vincent, [no date but apparently written early in January], U.S.F.R. 1945, pp. 155–57.

24.   Report of Joint War Plans Committee, February 27, 1945, Minutes of the Joint Chiefs of Staff.

25.   Several reports in the winter and spring of 1945 speculated on the ties between the Chinese Communists and the Soviet Union and the probable course the Soviets would follow in Asia. Among these are Memorandum by the Chief of the Division of Eastern European Affairs, May 10, 1945, U.S.F.R. 1945, pp. 863–65 and Proposed Memorandum by the Acting Secretary of State to President Roosevelt, March 27, 1945, U.S.F.R. 1945, pp. 305–306. The developments in eastern Europe after the Yalta Conference aroused such deep concern that on May 12 the Acting Secretary of State asked both Secretary of the Navy James Forrestal and Secretary of War Henry Stimson if the Yalta decision in regard to the Far East should be reconsidered. Acting Secretary of State Grew to the Secretary of Navy, May 12, 1945, U.S.F.R. 1945, pp. 869–70.

26.   Report by Service, March 14, 1945, U.S.F.R. 1945, pp. 279–83; Report by Service, March 23, 1945, U.S.F.R. 1945, pp. 301–304; Memorandum of Conversation, by Service, April 1, 1945, U.S.F.R. 1945, pp. 311–17.

27.   A seven-page statement of the offer presented by the Nationalists

was given to Hurley by T.V. Soong on February 16, 1945. Hurley Papers, Box 98-F2.

28. Copy of Chou En-lai's statement rejecting the offer which was first presented by Wang Shih-chieh. Hurley Papers, Box 98-F2.

29. Hurley to the Secretary of State, February 18, 1945, *U.S.F.R. 1945*, pp. 223–30.

30. Atcheson to the Secretary of State, February 28, 1945, *U.S.F.R. 1945*, pp. 242–46.

31. Grew to Roosevelt, March 2, 1945, *U.S.F.R. 1945*, March 2, 1945.

32. Memorandum by the Director of the Office of Far Eastern Affairs, March 6, 1945, *U.S.F.R. 1945*, pp. 260–62.

33. Stanton to Grew, April 25, 1945. Department of State, National Archives, 711.93/4-2745.

34. Memorandum by Stanton, April 28, 1945, *U.S.F.R. 1945*, pp. 348–50.

35. Grew to Hurley, May 7, 1945, Department of State, National Archives, 711.93/5-745. In this cable Grew cites his message of April 23.

36. Ibid.

37. Memorandum Concerning United States Post-War Military Policies with Respect to China, original State Department paper dated April 3, 1945; dispatch by State-War-Navy Coordinating Committee on May 28, *U.S.F.R. 1945*, pp. 74–79.

38. Hurley to the Secretary of State, June 16, 1945, *U.S.F.R. 1945*, pp. 413–14.

39. Hurley to the Secretary of State, June 23, 1945, Department of State, National Archives, 893.00/6-2345.

40. Hurley to the Secretary of State, June 30, 1945, Department of State, National Archives, 893.00/6-3045.

41. Alvin Ravenholt, in an interview in November 1944.

42. Memorandum by the Second Secretary of Embassy in the Soviet Union (Davies), April 15, 1945, *U.S.F.R. 1945*, pp. 334–38.

CHAPTER VIII

Frustrations on the Eve of Victory

The spring of 1945 witnessed the defeat of Germany and left the powerful Allies free to concentrate all of their forces in the war against Japan. Cautious estimates of military strategists placed the surrender of the Japanese more than a year away and plans were laid for an invasion of the enemy's home islands. The future success of the atomic bomb was as yet unknown and the losses of the Japanese merchant marine, crippling in their effect on Japan's war effort, were underestimated. Consequently major attention was focused on the military battles that lay ahead.

However, American statesmen were now compelled to give thought to pressing questions. China's desperate economic straits led to another bitter series of negotiations. At the same time relations with the Soviet Union entered upon a period of mutual distrust. Russian moves in eastern Europe led to American charges that they were not abiding by the agreements negotiated at Yalta. The Russians, in turn, were made distrustful by the abrupt end of lend-lease and the American power play whereby pro-Nazi Argentina gained admission to the United Nations. During that same spring representatives of the United States, fearful of new Chinese moves to limit foreign enterprise in China, sought assurance that the regulations being discussed would not prevent American business from playing an active role.

As early as January the Chinese placed pressure on the United States to renew large-scale gold shipments. These shipments were to be deducted from China's account, namely the remaining balance of the $500 million dollar loan extended to it early in 1942. The Chinese, in support of these requests, maintained that only by selling gold in China could they absorb some of the excess currency and avoid galloping inflation. Adler, Treasury representative in Chungking, recommended against granting the request. He based his recommendation on two grounds: that it was a mistake for China to dissipate her foreign exchange in this fashion since she would desperately need it for postwar reconstruction and that the sale of gold was not effective in countering inflation.[1] Ambassador Hurley, although opposed to cutting off present gold shipments, and Secretary of the Treasury Morgenthau agreed with Adler's recommendations.

China's argument that she needed the gold to counter a sharp rise of inflation did not impress Morgenthau or top officials in the State Department.[2] They, too, demonstrated deep concern over the rapid rise of prices in China and fully appreciated the danger of a complete collapse and consequent fall of the Central Government, but they were convinced that only a broad program could prevent the collapse and that the sale of gold was only a palliative.

The rapid decline in value of Chinese currency heralded an extreme inflation. At a meeting of representatives of the many American agencies in Chungking on February 20 Adler stated that preliminary reports indicated that prices in that city had risen 50 percent since January 1 and they had risen 100 percent in Kunming.[3] This rapid inflation continued throughout the spring months. At another meeting of the same representatives in the chancery in Chungking on June 12, C. F. Remer of the Division of Financial and Monetary Affairs of the State Department, observed that during the first four months of 1945 prices rose at the rate of 20 percent a month, a more rapid increase than for any four-month period since 1937. Remer noted that the cost of living rose 100 percent and the cost of food by 125 percent.[4]

The causes of the mounting inflation were related to the surge in the war effort. The Nationalist Government was seeking to remedy the deplorable conditions prevailing in the army in 1944 and therefore sharply increased both pay and food allowances of men in the armed services. At the same time a new Chinese Service of Supply purchased greatly increased amounts of supplies and equipment so as to assure the army's readiness for the campaigns planned against the Japanese forces along China's coast. This took place concurrently with the surge of activity by the China War Production Board that had been established in November 1944. The Board, aiming at putting new life into the badly sagging war industries was reported to have extended loans of CN $2.5 billion in March and CN $4.5 billion in May. In addition, the American armed forces spent some CN $55 billion during the first four months of the year.[5] To meet these increased expenditures the Central Government printed more currency.

American opposition to the shipment of more gold gained ground. On March 11 Adler reported that the government was selling gold at the rate of 350,000 ounces per month but even so this covered only 25 percent of the monthly deficit. The government, he observed, was selling gold "at an absurdly uneconomic price."[6] There was also a conviction among Americans that the sale of gold had led to speculation and that stories of how few had profited enormously was undermining confidence in the government.[7] These stories broke into the headlines on May 19, and the Control Yuan called for severe punishment of the manager of the Central Bank and several high officials in the Ministry of Finance.[8]

Throughout March and April leading American officials urged upon China a very broad-range anti-inflation program. Adler, after working in close collaboration with General Almstead and Calvin N. Jayner of the Foreign Economic Administration, drafted a long memorandum dated March 19. This warned that galloping inflation was now at hand, barter transactions were beginning to take the place of the usual transactions in currency, and that by the end of the year monthly government expenditures would exceed revenue by CN $50 billion. "There is no simple panacea which will bring the inflation to a halt," said the memorandum, and "the pouring out of gold unaccompanied by any other measures would be merely throwing 'chicken feed into the maw of the dragon' of inflation." The measures recommended were far-ranging, including the abolition of price control to encourage production, the prompt release of supplies stored by the government, stern measures against private hoarding, and the import of much-needed goods, particularly cotton textiles and trucks. The sale of gold should be at a higher price. The memorandum also called for reform of the government administration. "An excellent start has already been made in this direction, which should be continued by the abolition and fusion of redundant government agencies and further reduction in the number of government employees," the memorandum advised.[9] Contrary to an earlier recommendation by Leon Henderson, Adler and his colleagues recommended deferment of a currency stabilization fund. These recommendations became the basis for the negotiations later conducted in Washington by Morgenthau and T.V. Soong.

Sometime in late April T.V Soong, now Minister of Foreign Affairs, went to Washington to present China's case. He called for the shipments of $200 million in gold, 4,000 trucks, and 176,000,000 yards of cotton textiles. Soong, far from timid in declaring what China needed, also presented the demands in terms of the United States agreeing or facing a catastrophic collapse of China.[10] He received a sympathetic hearing regarding trucks and textiles, and the Foreign Economic Administration made every effort to meet his demands.[11] Cotton textiles were not available in sufficient quantity, and an effort was made to secure the balance from Brazil and Mexico.

The question of gold shipments was another matter. Representatives of both the Treasury and State Departments opposed the granting of Soong's request because they were convinced gold sales were no solution and because they distrusted how the gold would be used. In a memo for Soong, dated May 8, Morgenthau strongly opposed gold sales and recommended that instead China's balance of the 1942 loan be used to establish a Currency Stabilization Fund.[12] In a memo the following day, Soong pushed aside the stabilization fund proposal and then hit the Secretary of the Treasury with the unpleasant fact that Roosevelt had promised to make available to China $200 million in gold out of the $500 million loan and that this promise had been confirmed by no one less than Morgenthau himself in a letter dated July 27, 1943.[13] Having nailed the Secretary of the Treasury to the wall on the gold issue, Soong unabashedly picked up Morgenthau's proposal for a stabilization fund, observed that of course it would take more than $500 million and that he was ready to enter into negotiations.[14] Morgenthau, had been outmaneuvered. Hurley, in Chungking, who had been insisting that any concession on gold shipments should be made only after China had been committed to reforms, was appalled.[15] Not until he learned that Morgenthau had forgotten his letter of July 1943 and that this letter deprived him of bargaining power could Hurley grasp the nature of what had taken place. In the meantime, the first gold shipments backed up by the 1942 loan arrived in China.

In July the American representatives in Chungking were cha-grined by another move by China's Talleyrand. On June 26 the Central Government suspended gold sales. In addition, on July 30 the Supreme National Defense Council, upon recommendation by Soong, placed a 40 percent tax on all unmet gold commitments.[16] These actions stood in sharp contradiction to Soong's assertions in Washington less than two months earlier that unless China could continue gold sales it faced immediate collapse.

Soong had managed to get what he wanted largely under the false pretense that the gold was to be used to combat inflation. His maneu-ver further undermined the confidence of American leaders. Mor-genthau and his advisers had long been distrustful of both Soong and his brother-in-law H.H. Kung. By August, Hurley had developed an equal distrust of Soong. He acknowledged that upon his arrival in China he had turned to Soong because Soong understood the Ameri-can situation and was useful in helping him understand the General-issimo. However, Hurley now concluded that Soong was prepared to take advantage of rivalries and conflicts within the American govern-ment and he reported that Soong openly boasted that he could get what he wanted by threatening to get it from other countries if the United States refused. "In other words," Hurley wrote, "every favor that Dr. Soong requests is accompanied by a threat of damage to the United States unless his request is immediately fulfilled."[17]

*   *   *   *

By the spring of 1945 there was added reason to give attention to the probable future role of the Soviet Union. The American military had long viewed Soviet entry into the war against Japan as desirable. At the end of the long route of island-hopping campaigns across the Pacific, the American military expected to confront the inner circles of Japan's defense including yet powerful Japanese armies both on the home islands and in North China and Manchuria. Soviet assistance would hasten final victory and save countless American lives. At Teheran Stalin agreed to enter the Far Eastern war after the defeat of Germany. In anticipation of this, Roosevelt had already sounded out Chiang Kai-shek at Cairo as to what compensations the Soviets would demand and what concessions would be reasonable.

At Yalta, in February 1945, the Americans, British, and Russians reached agreements, subject to China's eventual approval, whereby the Soviet Union would gain a leasehold of Port Arthur, Dairen would be a free port but the preeminent interests of the Soviet Union would be recognized, and the Chinese Eastern and South Manchurian Railways would be controlled by a board to be made up of representatives of both the Soviet Union and China. The Yalta agreement committed both the United States and Great Britain to support the Soviets when they entered into negotiations with China.[18] Realistic considerations dictated these decisions. The American participants had good reason to believe that China would pay a higher price if left to face the Russians alone.[19] There were also those who, like Stimson, stressed that Russia was in a military position to seize what they had been conceded at Yalta and that the Soviets were not likely to be influenced by political inducements proferred by the United States.[20] An even more important consideration, perhaps even the controlling one, was the desirability of improving relations between Chungking and Moscow so that the Soviets would continue to cooperate with the Nationalist Government rather than support the Communists and that the U.S.S.R. would use its influence to persuade the Chinese Communists to accept reasonable Kuomintang proposals.[21]

After Yalta the deterioration of Soviet-American relations aroused greater concern as to what course the Soviets would pursue in Asia. Secretary of the Navy Forrestal, in a meeting of the State-War-Navy Committee on May 1, asked: "How far did we wish to go in destroying Japan? Is Japan to be readmitted to family of nations after her demilitarization? What is our policy on Russian influence in the Far East? Do we desire a counterweight to that influence? And should it be China or should it be Japan?"[22]

On May 12 the Acting Secretary of State, Joseph Grew, asked James Forrestal and Henry Stimson a series of questions concerning future policy regarding the provisions of the Yalta agreement relating to the Far East. The memorandum asked:

1. Is the entry of the Soviet Union into the Pacific war at the earliest possible moment of such vital interest to the United States as to preclude any attempt by the United States Government to obtain Soviet agreement to certain desirable political objectives in the Far East prior to such entry?

2. Should the Yalta decision in regard to Soviet political desires in the Far East be reconsidered or carried into effect in whole or in part?

3. Should a Soviet demand, if made, for participation in the military occupation of the Japanese home islands be granted or would such occupation adversely affect our long-term policy for the future treatment of Japan?[23]

Grew added that the State Department considered it desirable to have the Soviet Union assist in the unification of China under the National Government.

This memorandum led to an exchange of views that threw much light on the attitudes and opinions of American leadership. Secretary of War Stimson responded that the Yalta agreements only made concessions that were "within the military power of Russia to obtain regardless of U.S. military action short of war." He expressed little faith in an effort to have the Soviets reconsider the agreements reached at Yalta.[24] Secretary of the Navy Forrestal simply endorsed the views of Stimson.[25]

Grew followed this with a lengthy statement of the State Department's position with regard to the attitude to be taken. The document emphasized the importance of unification of China and stated that this required that the Kuomintang surrender its exclusive control over the government, give legal recognition to the Communists and other parties, and cooperate with all other parties "to create a representative, strong and stable government." Secondly, the State Department called for military unification under a war council representing all parties and the placing of all armed forces "under the operational command of an American commander assisted by a staff composed of Chinese, Soviet and British officers." Thirdly, the State Department looked to the Soviet Union to use its influence to bring about the cooperation of the Chinese Communists.[26]

Forrestal and the Assistant Secretary of War John J. McCloy pulled back. They were unprepared to commit the armed services to a program with such far-reaching implications. The Army statement did not, however, reject the proposal of unification of the Chinese military forces. The questions raised concerned Chinese willingness to accept the proposals and the workability of a combined staff. The Army favored continued efforts at political unification and military unification under an American commander with liasion teams of the Russians and the British.[27]

Fear of discord, nourished by the disagreements at the San Francisco Conference, caused Averill Harriman, Ambassador to the Soviet Union, and Charles Bohlen, Soviet specialist, to urge Truman that he ask Harry Hopkins to go to Moscow to talk with Stalin and Molotov. Hopkins, accompanied by Harriman and Bohlen, left for Moscow on May 23.[28] The meetings were frank but not uncongenial, and Hopkins returned reassured. Stalin was particularly encouraging regarding the Far East. He "would do everything he could to promote unification of China under the leadership of Chiang Kai-shek." No Communist leader, said Stalin, was strong enough to unify China. The Soviet Union would respect Chinese sovereignty in Manchuria and when Soviet troops entered that area he would welcome representatives of Chungking.[29]

By June the time had arrived to inform the Chinese of the bargain that had been struck at Yalta. Soong, who had been attending the San Francisco Conference, flew to Washington and on June 9 met with President Truman, Admiral Leahy, and Joseph Grew.[30] The President informed him of the agreements. Some days later, on June 14, Soong met with the President, Grew, and Bohlen and he was told of the assurances Stalin had given to Hopkins. Soong found most disturbing the provision calling for a lease of Port Arthur but he was also unhappy about the promise that the Soviet Union should have a preeminent interest in Dairen and the provisions concerning the Manchurian railways.[31]

Chiang was informed of the agreements on June 15. Apparently they came as no surprise, for Roosevelt had long before intimated what the Soviet Union would demand. Chiang did not protest but he immediately sought American and British participation in the prospective treaty negotiations with the Russians.[32] Truman promptly responded that this would conflict with the agreements signed at Yalta.[33] In brief, China was left to her own resources in the coming negotiations.

Soong, now confronting difficult negotiations in Moscow, hoped to stay in Washington until the return of Hopkins, with whom he had long been friendly, but the latter preferred to avoid seeing him. Consequently, Soong returned to Chungking at once and then went to Moscow. The negotiations revealed that Stalin's interpretations of the Yalta agreements did not square with those presented to Soong in Washington. Soong so informed Harriman, who was in daily communications with him.[34] President Truman and the new Secretary of State James Byrnes were so disturbed that they instructed Harriman to notify Soong that they expected to be consulted "before any agreement is concluded between the Soviet and Chinese Governments based on the Yalta Agreement."[35]

The divergencies in interpretation centered on the question of control of Dairen and the railways. The Soviet Union insisted on joint ownership of the railways by a Sino-Soviet Company, a majority of one of the board of directors and a Russian director.[36] The Russians likewise demanded that Dairen, along with Port Arthur, should be included in a military zone and that the city should be subject to Soviet control.[37] Soong contended for joint control of the railways and the stationing of Chinese troops in Manchuria to protect them. He also sought to have Dairen placed under Chinese control but with guaranteed access to ships of all nations. The Chinese yielded on the question of independence for Outer Mongolia in the hope of mitigating the settlement in Manchuria, but Stalin held firm. On July 12 Soong returned to Chungking, and the Soviet leaders departed for the Potsdam Conference. Soong could only take consolation in the fact that Stalin had agreed not to help the Communists.[38]

The Soviet posture brought different reactions from Americans. Secretary of War Stimson recognized the legitimate interests of the Soviet Union in the area and thought the concessions that had been made were reasonable. On July 16, he wrote:

> We can afford to permit Russia to have access to ports in Manchuria, and I interpret the Yalta Agreements as giving her full commercial access to Dairen, with the necessary facilities. Likewise, I understand the late President Roosevelt's willingness to permit the Russians to have what in effect is the lease of a naval base at Port Arthur.

But Stimson was adamant in maintaining that the United States should not agree to further concessions which would lead to closing the door in Manchuria to American trade.[39] Joseph Grew was ambivalent. On the one hand, he did not regret the concessions made at Yalta. These were the price China had to expect to pay for assistance in defeating the Japanese and for a Soviet commitment not to assist the Chinese Communists. But Grew also saw in the Soviet demands a return of the worst kind of imperialism and he wished to use American influence to modify the demands.[40] Averill Harriman, Stimson reported, "was much worked up over his fears of the Russian plans. . . ."[41] The most extreme alarm and the deepest distrust was exhibited by John Davies who had been transferred to Moscow. In a lengthy memorandum on July 10 Davies outlined what he believed to be the minimum objectives of the Soviet Union: domination or the voluntary allegiance of North China, Sinkiang, Inner Mongolia, Manchuria, Korea, southern Sakhalin, and the Kurile Islands and an opportunity to exploit politically the postwar situation in Japan. Davies also outlined the several possible strategies the Soviets would employ and one of these would be to use the Chinese Communists, who would have no other choice than to comply. He concluded with the observation that the Soviets would "be careful in performing its political surgery in Asia to cause during the next two or three years as little shock and pain as possible to the United States." He expected that the Soviet "anaesthetization" would be effective "in pretty much direct proportion to the degree of ignorance in which the American people are kept with regard to the issues involved."[42]

At the Potsdam Conference in July Averill Harriman initiated moves to have the Soviet Union modify the demands it made of Soong. He insisted that the United States must support China by confronting Stalin with the limitations of the Yalta concessions as understood at the time they were entered into. The United States, according to Harriman, had only agreed to a lease of Port Arthur, to making Dairen an international port open to the ships of all nations, and to granting the Soviets assurance of use of the Manchurian railways and a voice in their administration.[43] Harriman's views undoubtedly represented the understanding of other Americans who had been at Yalta, but the wording of those agreements left room for differences in interpretation. These differences were discussed only briefly at Potsdam, but on his return to Moscow Harriman took up China's cause.

On August 8 Harriman and George Kennan met with Stalin and Molotov. Stalin readily agreed to respect the Open Door policy but he insisted that the Yalta agreement assured the Soviet Union of a "preeminent" position in Dairen, and this meant a preferential position in the administration of the city. He and Molotov argued that it was necessary to place the city within the military zone of Port Arthur to assure the city's security. Harriman contended that the term "preeminent" meant no more than that the Soviet Union would be preeminent in trade.[44] The following day Stalin retreated to the position whereby the Soviet Union would exercise military authority in Dairen only in time of war and he also accepted the American contention that the government of the city should be in Chinese hands. However, the Chief of the port was to be a Soviet. Concerning the railways in Manchuria, Stalin likewise compromised and now proposed a board of directors with equal membership but with a Soviet manager.[45] On August 13 Stalin and Soong reached agreement. Harriman cabled Truman:

> Soong is quite encouraged today because he feels that he has succeeded in obtaining Stalin's agreement to basic principles that he was fighting for. He is also encouraged to feel that since Stalin has fought so hard over each point he intends to live up to the understandings reached. He is very grateful for our support and is convinced that unless we had taken an active part in the negotiations he would have had to concede to all Stalin's demands.[46]

Deep distrust and sharp irritation marked the exchanges in Moscow between Stalin and Harriman. The Americans believed that the Soviets were pushing the Yalta agreements considerably beyond their original meaning and that their unstated aim was domination of Manchuria. Stalin believed that the Americans were listening only to the Chinese and that the Chinese appeared to regard the Soviets as fools. The central point at issue was the term "preeminent." Stalin argued that this meant final control and cited how that term as used elsewhere in the Yalta agreements clearly meant a dominant position in administration. Harriman contended that the discussions at Yalta and the views expressed by Roosevelt on Dairen showed that the

President had intended no more than to acknowledge that free access to the railways and Dairen would result in the Soviet Union having most of the trade. At one point Stalin warned Soong that he had better come to an agreement quickly or "the Communists will get into Manchuria." In Washington Secretary of State Byrnes noted:

> We feel that the only compensatory advantage which the Chinese Government is being given in return for the concessions which it is asked to make is an unequivocal commitment on the part of the Soviet Government to withhold support from dissident elements within China.[47]

The day before the signing of the treaty Japan surrendered, but the American goal of a strong and friendly China capable of stabilizing relations in East Asia appeared as remote as ever. The strong China emerging behind the scenes was only vaguely visible. The recognized government in Chungking, regardless of varying estimates of its future, was at the moment impotent to restore its rule over occupied China and to a large extent had lost the confidence of its own people. Whatever prospects that government had for the long-term future, it was then so weak that even its immediate survival depended upon American assistance and upon restraint by the Soviet Union in the face of the vacuum left by Japan's downfall.

The part played by the United States in modifying Soviet demands made no significant difference. In a note of September 4 Harriman observed that Russia would not find it difficult, even after the withdrawal of Russian forces from Manchuria, "to remain master of the situation in all essential respects." The treaty did not so specify "but it was tacitly understood by both parties to the negotiations that Chinese officials in Manchuria would have to be, in the main, ones amenable to Russian influence." Harriman thought it likely that the Chinese Communists would enter Manchuria and that, amenable to direction from the Communist Party in Russia, would serve Russia's interests. He added that the treaty legitimized Soviet action and at the same time undermined any possible crusade by the United States and the Chinese Nationalists against Yenan. Harriman's assessment of the situation took into consideration the power of the Soviet Union and the fact that it would be willing to pay a considerable price for the protection of what the Soviets judged to be vital national interests in a country with whom it shared a five thousand mile border.

*   *   *   *

The beacons heralding victory only served to shed light on the vast disarray and reveal that, if war had avoided the worst evils, victory did not assure attainment of the oft-proclaimed goal of a strong and friendly China serving as a stabilizing force in the Far East. Repeatedly, Americans had observed during the winter and spring of 1945 that it appeared that the United States had fought with the aim of preventing Japanese domination only to find the place of the Japanese was about to be taken over by the Soviet Union. Constant tension and deep misunderstanding during the war had likewise created a wider gulf between the United States and China than had existed at any time since the Chinese Nationalist upheaval of the 1920s.

Since January 1945, as the allies became convinced that victory was near, interest in the postwar period increased. Two topics, closely related, gained close attention: proposed Chinese regulations of foreign economic enterprise within its borders and the draft of a new commercial treaty presented to China on April 2. The position of the United States rested on the Joint Declaration by Roosevelt and Churchill of August 4, 1941, calling for freedom to trade and economic collaboration. In the context of the Atlantic Charter and the restrictions on international trade by cartels that had characterized the 1930s, this declaration appeared to connote the opposite of economic imperialism. The war years and the increasingly conservative tone of the Roosevelt administration gradually shifted the emphasis. In September 1944 the President, in a letter to the Secretary of State, linked the Sherman and Clayton antitrust acts to the liberal principles of international trade and stated that the trade agreement program had "as its objective the elimination of barriers to the free flow of trade in international commerce."[48] In another letter to Leo Crowley, Administrator of the Foreign Economic Administration, the President wrote:

International trade on as full and free a basis as possible is necessary not only as a sound economic foundation for the future peace, but it is also necessary in order that we may have fuller production and employment at home. Private industry and private trade can, I am sure, produce a high level of international trade, and the Government should assist to the extent necessary to achieve this objective by returning international commerce to private lanes as rapidly as possible.[49]

This objective of freer international trade occupied a prominent place in the draft of the proposed commercial treaty. There was now considerable concern about future trade with China and investments in privately owned business in that country. The apprehension grew out of manifestations of an economic nationalism in China that favored strict regulations of foreign enterprise and a widespread conviction in the Kuomintang that China must industrialize quickly and could only do so if the government established government corporations to promote and operate monopolies in the fields of transportation, finance, mining, oil production, and some fields of manufacturing. These basic areas of the economy were to have a high priority in an extensive system of economic planning. The private sectors of the economy were to be subordinated to overall controls so that their activities did not come into conflict with the major goal of rapid industrialization of those areas of major importance in bringing about an improved standard of living. These aims enjoyed the advantage of being in accord with Sun Yat-sen's three principles.

During the visit of H. H. Kung in the summer of 1944 the Department of State encouraged interested business groups to make known their views, and a joint memorandum prepared by the National Foreign Trade Council and the China-American Council of Commerce and Industry was presented to him.[50] In November 1944 the Department sent Judge Milton J. Helmick to China to study the effects of Chinese laws, regulations, and courts on American companies. The memorandum presented to Kung stressed the advantages of private enterprise, set forth the view that China had more to gain by drawing upon private sources of American capital in promoting economic development, urged that American banks be given freedom to operate and that laws and rules concerning foreign trade be clarified and changed to facilitate the activity of foreign firms. By February, Helmick had completed his investigation and had drafted a list of suggestions.[51] This was presented to the Generalissimo in February.

The question of formulating a new set of Chinese regulations shortly became a matter of some urgency because foreign firms were required to register by June 30. The Chinese government announced that foreign firms should register and agree to comply with existing regulations, and these presented difficulties. While these American business representatives were led to believe that the new regulations being drafted would reflect Helmick's suggestions, it also became clear that the Chinese government was determined to control foreign firms. The State Department did not, at this stage, go beyond exerting its influence in favor of "simple and reasonable" regulations. A considerable part of the difficulty lay in the lack of clarity of existing regulations leaving foreign firms uncertain as to what was demanded of them. A second difficulty lay in the requirement of existing regulations that a company pay a fee based upon the amount of capital allotted to its branch or branches in China and, in lieu of this, pay a fee based upon half the total capital of the company. Because American firms would be subject to the latter, many of them protested that they would have to discontinue.[52] The State Department supported the complaints about the registration fee, and in June the Chinese government announced that collection of the fee had been postponed until the following December. The Legislative Yuan made only slow progress in drafting the new regulations during the summer of 1945. Chinese officials invited representatives of the United States to make their views known. American objections and suggestions were devoted almost exclusively to clarification of language in the provisions rather than to the substantive aspects of the regulations. On September 29 the Legislative Yuan completed its third reading of the bill. However, it was not promulgated into law. In November the Supreme National Defense Council reviewed it.

The new law, while not objectionable to the Embassy in Chungking left major questions unanswered. The right of a foreign firm to do business in China did not rest on compliance with the regulations and requirements enacted but on gaining the approval of the Ministry of Economic Affairs.[53] This feature was clearly recognized as leaving the door open for the Chinese government to control industry. No protest was launched against this feature of the new law, but by December the Secretary of State informed the Embassy that American businessmen were disturbed by some aspects of the new rulings and instructed the Chargé to lay the matter before Chiang Kai-shek.

The draft of the proposed commercial treaty had been presented to China on April 2, 1945. In May, discussions began in Washington between members of the Department of State and a representative of the Chinese Embassy. These discussions came to a close on July 9; they had been no more than an exchange of views for purposes of clarification. It was understood that the actual negotiations were to take place in Chungking. In the course of these discussions the Chinese representative had stressed the importance of mutuality. The history of China's foreign relations, marked by unequal treatment, made this absolutely necessary if the Chinese government were to approve the treaty. The Chinese representative had likewise emphasized that the provisions of the treaty must in no way limit China's freedom to formulate her own economic program.

At the time of the Japanese surrender the nature of economic relations between the United States and China remained undetermined, but the American business community, supported by the government, had demonstrated an avid interest. The anticipation of a lively trade and an opportunity to invest in China's postwar reconstruction gave momentum to efforts to secure from China assurances of a government policy and of regulations attractive to American merchants and capitalists. China, desperately in need of loans from the American government, was, nevertheless, equally determined to be in full control of her economic life and to be free to develop economic policies that accorded with her needs.

The economic realities in China scarcely justified American business dreams. This fact gained but little acknowledgment in the agencies in Washington. China needed goods, needed to rebuild, and needed capital, but the Chinese knew their requirements better than the foreigner and they placed primary emphasis on reordering economic life so that national interests received highest priority. In Washington this aspect of the question entered into the discussions of the Interdepartmental Committee on Economic Policy toward China. Edwin A. Locke, Jr., a man with broad business experience and a prominent member of the Roosevelt administration during the war, who served as Executive Assistant to Donald Nelson when he headed an economic mission to China, took the long view. In a letter to the committee on March 17, 1945, Locke pointed to the interests of the United States in a strong and economically healthy China. Such a China, he stated, would "be a large, permanent, growing and much needed market for United States goods—including capital goods, productive capacity of which has been especially expanded in this country during the war." But Locke also called attention to the undeveloped nature of China's economy, her scanty and primitive transportation, and her industrially untrained people. "Consequently," he observed, "the completed process of industrialization is bound to be a long one." He warned, "We cannot expect to pour a flood of industrial goods into China in the hope of transforming her in a few years into an industrial giant." Capital investment and capital goods would be needed and American businessmen would participate only if assured of a fair return and security. "Yet," Locke advised, "foreign investments must be consistent with the overall needs of Chinese development, and must avoid infringement of China's national integrity."[54]

NOTES TO CHAPTER VIII

1. Hurley to the Secretary of State, January 17, 1945, *U.S.F.R. 1945*, pp. 1056–57. The message, sent under Hurley's name, was from Adler, who summarized both his own and Hurley's views.

2. Memorandum by the Secretary of the Treasury to the Chinese Minister of Foreign Affairs, May 8, 1945, *U.S.F.R. 1945*, pp. 1081–83.

3. Memorandum by the Second Secretary of Embassy (Boehringer) of discussion at meeting of representatives of U.S. agencies on February 20, 1945. *U.S.F.R. 1945*, pp. 1060–62.

4. Hurley to the Secretary of State, July 9, 1945, *U.S.F.R. 1945*, pp. 1110–13.

5. Ibid., p. 1111.

6. Atcheson to the Secretary of State, forwarding report by Adler, March 11, 1945, *U.S.F.R. 1945*, pp. 1063–64.

7. In a memorandum to Soong, dated May 8, Secretary of the Treasury Morgenthau advised that China should investigate and cancel sales to speculators and illicit purchasers and noted that the impression in the United States was the sale of U.S. dollar certificates and bonds and the sale of gold "have gone into relatively few hands with resultant large individual profits . . ." Morgenthau to Soong, May 9, 1945. *U.S.F.R. 1945*, pp. 1082–83.

8. Hurley to the Secretary of State, May 27, 1945, *U.S.F.R. 1945*, p. 1097.

9. Chargé in China (Briggs) to the Secretary of State, April 12, 1945, Enclosure, Memorandum by Adler "A Program for Retarding the Inflation in China." *U.S.F.R. 1945*, pp. 1067–72.

10. Soong to Morgenthau, May 9, 1945, *U.S.F.R. 1945*, pp. 1083–85.

11. Memorandum by the Administrator of the Foreign Economic Administration, May 3, 1945, *U.S.F.R. 1945*, pp. 1079–80.

12. Morgenthau to Soong, May 8, 1945, *U.S.F.R. 1945*, pp. 1081–83.

13. Soong to Morgenthau, May 9, 1945, *U.S.F.R. 1945*, pp. 1083–84.

14. Ibid., May 9, 1945, *U.S.F.R. 1945*, pp. 1086–87.

15. Navy Department to the Department of State, June 6, 1945, Enclosure, Hurley to Morgenthau, *U.S.F.R. 1945*, pp. 1100–02.

16. Hurley to the Secretary of State, August 7, 1945, *U.S.F.R. 1945*, pp. 1117–18.

17.   Hurley to the Secretary of State, August 18, 1945, *U.S.F.R. 1945*, pp. 1125–28.

18.   Robert E. Sherwood, *Roosevelt and Hopkins An Intimate History* (New York: Harper & Brothers, 1948), p. 867.

19.   Joseph Grew outlined at length his views concerning the Yalta agreements as they related to Asia in a memorandum dated July 13, 1945. Grew regretted the provisions relating to railroads and Dairen, "which, if carried out in full, would represent a reversion to a situation which was one of the most pernicious foci of imperialism . . ." But Grew also noted: "At the same time the fact cannot be lost sight of that the National Government of China stands to gain much by Russian participation in the war against Japan and by Russian agreement not to support the Chinese Communists." Grew to the Secretary of State, July 13, 1945. *Foreign Relations of the United States Diplomatic Papers The Conference of Berlin 1945*, (Washington: Government Printing Office, 1960), Vol. I, pp. 870–71.

20.   Stimson to the Acting Secretary of State, May 21, 1945, *U.S.F.R. 1945*, pp. 876–78.

21.   Assistant Secretary of War (McCloy) to Acting Secretary of State, May 27, 1945, *U.S.F.R. 1945*, Enclosure 2, pp. 886–87.

22.   *The Forrestal Diaries*, ed. Walter Millis (New York: The Viking Press, 1951), p. 52.

23.   Grew to Forrestal, May 12, 1945, *U.S.F.R. 1945*, pp. 869–70.

24.   Stimson to Grew, May 21, 1945, *U.S.F.R. 1945*, pp. 876–78.

25.   Forrestal to Grew, May 21, 1945. *U.S.F.R. 1945*, p. 878.

26.   Grew to Forrestal, May 21, 1945. *U.S.F.R. 1945*, pp. 878–83.

27.   Assistant Secretary of War John H. McCloy to the Acting Secretary of State, May 27, 1945. *U.S.F.R. 1945*, pp. 884–87.

28.   The document prepared by the Department of State was given to Bohlen for use in the meetings in Moscow but the negative responses of the Army and Navy caused Grew to cable Harriman instructing him not to discuss the proposal. Consequently, the discussion with Stalin was limited to a very general exchange of views.

29.   Memorandum of Conversation at Meeting in Kremlin, May 28, 1945, attended by Hopkins, Harriman, Bohlen, Stalin, Molotov, and Pavlow. *U.S.F.R. 1945*, pp. 887–90.

30.   Memorandum of Conversation, by the Acting Secretary of State, June 9, 1945. *U.S.F.R. 1945*, p. 896.

31.   Ibid., June 14, 1945, *U.S.F.R. 1945*, pp. 901–903.

32.   Hurley to the Secretary of State, June 14, 1945. *U.S.F.R. 1945*, pp. 903–904.

33. Acting Secretary of State to Hurley, June 18, 1945. *U.S.F.R. 1945*, p. 907.

34. Harriman to President Truman, July 3, 1945. *U.S.F.R. 1945*, pp. 912–14.

35. Byrnes to Harriman, July 6, 1945, pp. 916–17.

36. Memorandum by Charles Bohlen of Meeting of Truman and Stalin at Babelsberg, March 28, 1945, *U.S.F.R. The Conference of Berlin*, Vol. II, Appendix D, p. 1586. Hereafter this volume is cited as *U.S.F.R. Berlin*.

37. The Special Assistant to the Assistant Secretary of State (Dooman) and the Chief of the Division of Chinese Affairs (Vincent) to the Assistant Secretary of State, July 19, 1945, Subattachment 2. *U.S.F.R. Berlin*, p. 1232.

38. Memorandum by the Ambassador in the Soviet Union (Harriman) July 18, 1945, *U.S.F.R. 1945*, p. 944.

39. Stimson to Truman, July 16, 1945. *U.S.F.R. 1945*, p. 943.

40. Grew to Secretary of State, July 13, 1945. *U.S.F.R. Berlin*, Vol. I, pp. 870–71.

41. Footnote cites entries in Stimson's diary. *U.S.F.R. Berlin*, Vol. II, p. 1224.

42. Memorandum by John Davies, July 10, 1945. *U.S.F.R. 1945*, pp. 928–32.

43. Dooman and Vincent to the Assistant Secretary of State, Attachment 2, memorandum by Harriman, July 18, 1945. *U.S.F.R. Berlin*, Vol. II, pp. 1237–41.

44. Memorandum of Conversation, by the Minister Counselor in the Soviet Union (Kennan), August 8, 1945. *U.S.F.R.1945*, pp. 960–65.

45. Harriman to Truman, August 11, 1945. *U.S.F.R. 1945*, pp. 967–69.

46. Ibid., August 14, 1945. *U.S.F.R. 1945*, pp. 970–73.

47. Byrnes to Harriman, August 11, 1945. *U.S.F.R. 1945*, pp. 969–70.

48. Secretary of State to the Ambassador in China, February 16, 1945, Enclosure 2, Memorandum to the Embassy at Chungking for Use in Negotiating Treaty of Friendship, Commerce and Navigation. *U.S.F.R. 1945*, p. 1300.

49. Ibid., p. 1301.

50. The Secretary of State to Hurley, January 23, 1945. *U.S.F.R. 1945*, pp. 1206–1207.

51. Hurley to the Secretary of State, February 15, 1945. *U.S.F.R. 1945*, pp. 1209–11.

52.   Memorandum by Joseph Keating of the Division of Commercial Policy, June 11, 1945. *U.S.F.R. 1945*, p. 1218.

53.   Chargé in China (Robertson) to the Secretary of State, October 17, 1945. *U.S.F.R. 1945*, pp. 1243–46.

54.   Locke to John E. Orchard, March 17, 1945. Hurley Papers, Box 91 F-4.

CHAPTER IX

Peace and War

The political and social revolution released by eight long years of war continued to roll like the great swells that follow a storm at sea. Which group of political leaders was best prepared to make it serve their ends was already an established fact. The Communists, by the close of the war, had established a political base with amazing success.

The most conservative elements at the moment continued to control the Kuomintang, although liberal groups were within the party. Most of them had as their first aim preventing the foreigner from ever again gaining a stranglehold. These same liberal and leftist elements advocated economic planning, favored government ownership of basic enterprises and the subordination of individual economic activity to the decisions of centralized authority. They did not have a far-reaching ideology nor did they favor a widespread social revolution. Among their leaders some courageously stood up against the party oligarchs, spoke without timidity against abuses, and exhibited a high degree of social responsibility. However, they had a minimum of influence in party councils. Their appeal was limited. They were too cautious and came too late to attract the peasants, and they left business interests uncertain about the future of private enterprise. In short, the liberals lacked a political base.

The two strongest factions in the Kuomintang were the C-C Clique and the Whampoa military group. Both opposed reforms and control of government by the people. Secondly, they opposed the Communists and wholly rejected permitting them any voice in a possible coalition. The C-C Clique gained its support from the upperclass landed gentry who profited by the neofeudalistic economic order. The second was led by graduates of the Whampoa military academy and could count on the support of military officers who were indebted to them for their positions. Chiang sought to balance one group against the other but he was never free to override their basic interests. At the end of the war the Kuomintang enjoyed one great advantage. It was militarily much stronger than the Communists.

The Communists entered upon the postwar era having captured the imagination of the peasantry and a sufficient number of intellectuals to provide leadership. In the areas under their control they had mobilized social opinion against the more conservative elements and largely driven them from the scene. They had lowered rents and interest rates and their army, half political and half military, had lent a helping hand to the peasant. Having won mass support, the Communist Party leadership then let the masses do their political work. The party presented itself as the avant guarde of democracy and the voice of the people, but the democracy it represented viewed Western democratic practices and institutions as devices for perpetuating control by the elite. It substituted a new elite that spoke for the masses and claimed to understand their needs. The outcome was a new Geneva, a kind of secular monastery. It rejected, as Calvin had, the rights of individuals and placed in its stead the doctrine of justification by faith in a classless and egalitarian society.

A Chinese Communist guide told a group of Americans traveling through northern Shansi and Shensi in the summer of 1945 that democracy was "for the good of the majority, and not for the individual to do as he pleases." He informed his guests that in the Communist territory the people had the right to criticize in the press and to hold meetings for the discussion of public issues providing their thoughts were constructive. The main effort, now that the foreign war was over, was to win the war against the Kuomintang. The Communist Party would be in the vanguard of reshaping Chinese society. In this task the people must be made to feel that it was their struggle. The Communist guide told the Americans that Mao always urged his leaders: " . . . go to the people, learn from them. Obey their wishes. Let nothing come from above except that it answers the wishes of those below."[1]

The American representatives of the O.S.S., like most Westerners who visited the Communist areas, responded to the moral fervor and the determination to bring about a new order. "The Communists as a whole are a very serious people, polite, and quite kind," they wrote. "It seemed to us," they observed "that they took themselves and their life very sternly, much like we would imagine St. Francis did." The O.S.S. report explained, "They are a people apart from the average Chinese in that they have a mission, and one in which they have the utmost confidence." In comparing the people in the Communist area with those in southern Shensi, they concluded that "those differences we saw are big, very big, and that the Reds in China are expending every effort to bring the people in their area out of feudalism and trying to correct the habits of daily life as much as they can. The people are moving; they are not steeped in ignorance and poverty that we saw elsewhere, and this is the important fact to us that we carry away from our observations of a farmer's life in China."[2]

The Communists aimed to convert the Japanese defeat into a take-over of North China and Manchuria. If they could arrange to have the Japanese in the north surrender to Communist forces, they would be in control of the richest and most industrialized sections of the country. Fearful that the United States would intervene, their hostility toward the United States mounted and they moved ahead to establish their own governments. Michael Lindsay, a Britisher residing in Yenan, stated that the people "will certainly not accept any scheme which puts them at the mercy of the present Kuomintang government." They had been fighting for eighteen years, and Lindsay found that "most people seem to feel that if worst comes to worst they will go on fighting on their own." He wrote, "From what I saw of the front I think they could go on for a very long time."[3] Lindsay's estimate of Communist strength was shared by others. Yet, the Communists, although confident, did not at this time nor for many months to come, foresee the success they were to have. Their troops, although possessed of excellent morale, were ill-equipped and sometimes lacked an adequate diet. The Communists, too, did not discount either American direct involvement nor the assistance the Nationalists might receive from the United States in the form of artillery, munitions, and aircraft. Consequently, they continued to favor negotiations, looking toward a coalition government and in the months ahead they strove to nourish among Americans the idea that they were ready to support a political solution.

*   *   *   *

The American Joint Chiefs had given close attention to the question of the strategy to be employed in China, but their concern was with the large Japanese forces which might continue to resist after the government in Tokyo had surrendered. The problems involved were fully discussed at a session on July 26. The minutes of that session contain no reference to the Chinese Communists. The Joint Chiefs accepted the fact that the forces of the Soviet Union would occupy Manchuria, but they did draft plans for the occupation of Dairen. It was also decided that American forces would move into the Peking-Tientsin area and into Tsingtao so that the United States would achieve control of the Yellow Sea region and be in a position to shut off any sending of supplies to the strong Japanese forces around Shanghai.[4] In drafting these plans the Joint Chiefs had explicitly stated what the priorities were to be. The occupation of Japan ranked first. Korea ranked second in importance. China was declared a low third.

One day prior to Japan's surrender General Wedemeyer cabled the War Department giving dire warning of the portentous possibilities due to the strength of the Communists. He expressed doubt about the necessity of giving Japan the highest priority and urged that prompt action be taken with respect to China. Wedemeyer called attention to the fact that the geographical objectives of the Communists were "the very same key and strategic points and areas recognized as vital by the U.S. Joint Chiefs of Staff" and included Shanghai, Nanking, Taku, Tientsin, Peking, Tsingtao, and Canton. He assured the Chief of Staff in Washington, General Marshall, "We will do utmost to redispose and employ Chinese forces in strength to preclude widespread uprising and disorder, and to localize Chinese Communist efforts." He specified the number of divisions he would need and stated that he would need them immediately. He also urged that General MacArthur stipulate that the Japanese commanders in China be instructed to surrender to Chinese Central Government commanding officers.[5]

The initiative taken by Wedemeyer set the course for the months ahead. His approach received almost immediate strengthening by the haste of President Truman in seeking to place the United States in a position where it could influence the outcome of Chinese developments. On August 14, only one day after Japan's surrender, the President informed the Joint Chiefs who, in turn, instructed the commanders in the Pacific area that in addition to a port in Korea and Dairen, occupation of which had already been ordered, the President "now considered it wise from a political point of view to occupy also as soon as possible after the Japanese surrender some other mainland ports that definitely are not in the area of Soviet operations." The Joint Chiefs, in their instructions to the theater commanders, added that the State Department thought that the occupation of Tsingtao or Taku should take priority over Shanghai.[6]

But it was Wedemeyer in Chungking who sounded the warning of a Communist takeover. The strength of the Chinese Communists, in spite of scores of reports from China, including a well-balanced and factual assessment in an Army Intelligence Report of July, apparently had not penetrated to the higher echelons in Washington, but the Commanding General of the China theater did recognize their strength. During the first hours of peace he sent a series of cables warning that the Chinese Communists were capable of taking control of North China and Manchuria. In a message of August 14 Wedemeyer pointed to what was likely to happen if the general order to be issued by the Japanese directing all Japanese forces in China to surrender to the Generalissimo did not also include Japanese troops in Manchuria. Soviet presence in that area presented "extreme danger that Japanese equipment will become available surreptitiously or openly to the Chinese Communists in Manchuria." Because United States policy was full support of the Generalissimo and also because he was "the strongest leader and the only one capable of possibly accomplishing a modicum of stability," Wedemeyer believed his government should be strengthened. He viewed "Asia as an enormous pot, seething and boiling, the fumes of which may snuff out the advancement gained by Allied sacrifices. . . ."[7]

The following day Wedemeyer cabled Marshall calling for more support. Fighting between Nationalists and Communists, he noted, was already underway. "Each day's delay in placing a major force in the critical areas," he warned "increases the probability of widespread civil conflict. . . ."

The only restraints on taking immediate action had their source in concern over possible Japanese uprisings, the limited number of forces that could be deployed in China immediately, and the preference for avoiding military engagements with the Soviets. General Douglas MacArthur adhered to the original priorities, ranking Japan first, Korea second, and China third and also advised that the United States forces should be deployed in China "only to an extent that would ensure . . . [their] not becoming involved in a major land campaign in any part of the China Theater."[8] On August 18 the Joint Chiefs canceled plans for the occupation of Dairen because Soviet forces were already far advanced on the Liaotung peninsula and within easy reach of that highly important city.[9]

The urgent cables of Wedemeyer also led the State-War-Navy Coordinating Committee, at a meeting on August 22, to issue an order stating that the Potsdam Declaration providing for the surrender of Japan was an agreement between governments and that this meant that the Japanese were to surrender to the Central Government.[10] The Japanese accepted this interpretation and, because they were strong enough to resist the Communists, they simply continued to occupy the territories where they were until the forces of the Central Government arrived.

These difficulties were not unforeseen. On August 10 the Joint Chiefs of Staff had directed General Wedemeyer to transport troops of the Central Government to the Japanese-occupied areas and to restore control of China to the Central Government. However, the Joint Chiefs laid down the major stipulation that in carrying out this order General Wedemeyer was to avoid involvement in fratricidal strife.[11] The United States defended these actions on the ground that it was doing no more than continuing its military mission to defeat Japan and restore control to the government of China. By August 19 General Wedemeyer called Washington's attention to the incompatability of the directive to assist the Nationalists and to the proviso calling on him to avoid involvement in the fratricidal war. Wedemeyer warned that further assistance in transporting troops and prolonging the stay of the Marines would almost inevitably involve the United States in the internal struggle.[12] A decision on which of the two courses was to be followed awaited further developments.

The measures taken increased Yenan's distrust of the United States. In the months preceding the Japanese surrender, the Communist leaders had already cooled in their relations with Americans. On May 21 a message from the Dixie mission reported that during the previous ten days the situation had "almost completely deteriorated." The Communists had indicated to the American officer in charge of liaison that they were "unwilling to play along with us any longer without official recognition from our government." Their feelings against Hurley were bitter. They charged that he was opposed to them, that he, in turn, dominated the United States Army, and, finally, that he was dominated by the K.M.T.[13]

The close of the hostilities raised questions as to what the United States would do and, when the United States acted as it did, the Communists protested vigorously. Two issues stood out, the transportation by the United States of Nationalist troops and the order that Japanese troops were to surrender only to the Generalissimo. On August 15, General Chu Teh sent Colonel Ivan O. Yeaton, in command of the American Observer Mission, a lengthy letter outlining Communist military achievements in various provinces and then presented a set of demands. These called for the right of Communist forces to accept the surrender of the Japanese in the liberated areas and an end of lend-lease to the Kuomintang. Communist enmity rose to new heights after American Marines were landed in North China and took up positions in areas dominated by the Communists. On October 26 General Yeh Chien-ying, Chief of Staff of the 18th Army Group, sent word to Wedemeyer that American interference in the internal affairs of China caused deep concern and if these activities continued "then full responsibility for all grave consequences that may result in the future from this situation will rest entirely with the American side."

* * * *

In the intervening months of September and October the Nationalists and the Communists resumed their negotiations. Once again

Hurley flew to Yenan and then made the return flight with Mao assuring the latter of a safe passage. The Communists had long since lost faith in Hurley and they distrusted him as a mediator. This distrust now extended to the American government.[15] Two American officers who had traveled to Kalgan told of the deep animosity toward the United States and stated that it was based upon Communist resentment over the American deployment of Nationalist troops, the supplies provided to the Nationalists, and the Communists' expectations that American troops would occupy Peking, Tientsin, and cities on the coast. [16] Michael Lindsay likewise reported that Hurley was an object of particular distrust.

Chou En-lai opened the negotiations with a series of proposals, including the now well-established demands for a thorough government reorganization. However, the talks focused largely on the more immediate questions of surrender and the establishment of new governments in the occupied territories. Chou called for the surrender of Japanese armies to Communist authorities in those regions where the Communists were in control, the punishment and disbanding of puppet troops, and the recognition by the Central Government of Communist governors in those provinces where the party held the upper hand. Nationalist assent to the Communist demands would have been tantamount to fatalistic acceptance of a separate Communist state.

The series of agreements on high-sounding principles could not gloss over the basic cleavage. Hurley, prior to his departure for Washington on September 23, cabled that great progress had been made and that there was agreement by both sides on several major points. Both parties were agreed that Chiang's leadership should continue, both agreed that the Kuomintang Party was to be the dominant one, both affirmed that there should be a release of political prisoners and that there should be freedom of the press.[17] These accords, however, were only to take effect when agreement had been reached on a series of other issues. The other issues included who was to control local governments and the size of the Communist armies.

Early in October the negotiations turned to the reorganization of the Central Government. The most significant achievement was agreement to organize a Political Council to prepare the plans for the new government. The Council was to have nine representatives of the Kuomintang, nine from the Communists, nine from the other parties, and nine independents. On October 8 Chou En-lai informed the American Embassy "that only one point remained on which some sort of agreement had not been reached, namely, question of government of liberated areas now under Communist control . . ."[18] The areas named by Chou included Shantung, Hopei, Suiyan, and Chahar. Quite rightly, the American Chargé remained pessimistic. The Nationalists adamantly opposed any concession on this final point. Nationalist representatives in the negotiations argued that China's administrative integrity should be respected and that consideration of appointments to provincial posts must await Communist willingness to place their armies under the control of the Central Government.

On October 30 the Nationalists presented six proposals. These stipulated that both sides should order their troops to remain where they were, that the Communists were to withdraw their troops from the railways, that the People's Political Council should set up supervisory committees to make inspections along the railways, that the Government would not move troops over railroads in the Peking area without first consulting the Communists and that both sides would seek to reach an agreement about reorganization of Communist troops and the places where they were to be stationed.[19] The Communists made no response to these proposals but submitted a series of their own. Nothing further took place in the negotiations for two months. Both sides had carried on the talks, having as their primary aim a settlement that would leave them in a strong position to govern the country; both viewed the possible triumph of the other as worse than the evils of a civil war.

The futile negotiations took place at a time when Nationalist and Communist troops clashed in various areas. The first fighting took place in Honan and Hopei. Fighting also occurred along the railroad south of Peking. When American naval vessels approached Chefoo early in October, they found it occupied by the Communists, and the Communists warned them not to land. On October 30 the American consul at Tientsin reported that the Japanese in Tientsin had surrendered on October 6 and in Peking on October 10 but that in the open country and along the railway between the two cities the Communists were active. The American marines, he stated, were dependent upon former puppet troops and the Japanese to prevent the Communists from taking control.[20] On November 11 the American Chargé observed; "With large areas of China already in a state of civil war, it is questionable how much longer these two inflexible and determined political forces can continue to discuss peace."[21]

*   *   *   *

The United States confronted the China situation unable to pursue any one course. Different considerations and viewpoints pulled in different directions. Each of the options posed problems. If the United States gave all-out military assistance to the Nationalists, there was still no certainty of victory. The successful training and equipping of a few Chinese armies during the war suggested that this could be done on a larger scale and thereby China could be made stronger; but there was likewise a lack of faith in the Central Government, and this rested on quite overwhelming evidence of the inability of the Kuomintang to transform itself into a unified entity free of paralyzing rivalry among factions. At best, the change would be slow and the struggle in China of long duration. This posed the question of how long the war-weary American public would support the effort. Such a program likewise ran counter to the long-cherished ideal of not intervening in the internal affairs of another nation. The danger of eventual involvement and possible conflict with the Soviet Union inhibited bold decision making.

A policy of strict impartiality presented itself as a second option. Given the speech of Walter Judd in the House of Representatives in March 1945, it was certain that there would be strong political opposition to letting the Nationalists fend for themselves. Other considerations carried even greater weight. Given the superfluity of incompetence among officials of the Central Government and the Kuomintang's inability to gird itself for an effort to win public support, a completely neutral policy on the part of the United States would almost certainly end in a Communist victory. In fact, simply evidence that the United States had withdrawn its support would result in a tremendous setback to the Kuomintang. As contemporaries saw it a Communist victory meant that the Soviet Union would dominate China and reign supreme from western Europe to the Pacific. This was what Averill Harriman was warning against, and there is strong evidence that his warnings made a profound impression on the White House and in the upper echelons of the administration.[22] Those who believed that the entire balance of power in the world was at stake were not prepared to accept fatalistically such an outcome.

Those occupying the highest positions in the Truman administration had become conditioned during the war to viewing themselves as the architects of victory. They did not propose to see the fruits of that victory slip through their hands. At the time no one among them contended that a Communist China could be independent of the Soviet Union. A year earlier there were those who had argued that the proper course was to break relations with the Central Government. Some had then believed that the Communists would follow an independent course if they were not reduced to dependence on the Soviet Union and that they could be won over to a policy of cooperation. Great Britain's decision to recognize Tito had been cited as the precedent to follow. Indeed, that development had caused Chiang deep concern. In the summer and fall of 1945 no one within the circle of decision makers argued for that course or suggested that Mao could be induced to align himself with the United States.

The prevailing climate of opinion narrowed the vision and dictated the course eventually followed. Victory in the war over the Nazis vindicated the argument that the United States must concern itself with the balance of power and fend off the aggressors before they could challenge the United States. Compromise and an attitude of philosophical tranquility in the face of threats to the existing system of international relations were now identified with the perjorative term "appeasement." Experience in the recent past was reinforced by the long-standing tradition of seeing international issues in moral terms. Nationalism, from James Madison to Woodrow Wilson had been a close ally of moralism, and Americans almost instinctively reduced complex questions of international relations to questions of right and wrong and readily labeled nations as aggressive or peace loving. Faced with a challenge from Communism, old habits of thought and a deep-seated hostility toward radicalism prevailed. It was almost inevitable that Americans should find themselves at Armageddon and battling for the Lord of the Kuomintang. Given the strangeness of Communist ideology, it was easier to dismiss it with moral judgments than to grapple with its tenets, easier to interpret its dynamism as conspiracy than to understand its own peculiar claims to a monopoly of social redemption, and less confusing to condemn it than to try to distinguish between its violent nationalism and the fervor of its denunciations of capitalist society. The determination of the Russians to establish Communist regimes in eastern Europe was, at the time, explained as part of an effort at world revolution rather than the Soviets' way of establishing a *cordon sanitaire*. However real the threats Communism presented, the challenge of the Soviet Union was primarily rooted in security considerations rather than in the fervor of its ideology.

The prospect of a Communist victory in China might have been less frightening if it had not been linked to fear of Soviet domination in world affairs. However, that link was taken for granted in the United States. In reality, while ideology did create ties between the Chinese Communists and the Soviet Union, distrust was also on both sides. This received no attention in meetings of American government officials.

However, there was no one American response to the revolution in China. In the agony of reappraisal, old ideas and attitudes competed with new assessments. Traditional paternalism bred by the missionary enterprise influenced public attitudes toward China. This did not always work to the advantage of the Central Government but it did contribute to Americans taking a great interest in China's internal problems and great numbers of Americans identified friendship for China with friendship for the Kuomintang. Former missionaries generally called for support of the Kuomintang, but there were likewise those who were critical. Important religious journals such as the *Christian Century* took a neutral position. There was also the economic factor. American business concerns who had been engaged in the China trade actively sought a trade treaty with the Kuomintang governent that would facilitate American enterprise in China. Some of these became outspoken advocates of all-out aid for the Central Government. However, within the executive branch of government there was no great expectation of significant commercial expansion. An interdepartmental committee on postwar economic policy toward China met irregularly for about two hours less than once a month during 1945 and failed to develop anything more than a series of innocuous observations.

The major concern in American government circles was political. The United States had entered the Pacific war to prevent Japanese domination of Asia and, as was repeated innumerable times, had as its goal a strong and friendly China that would serve as a stabilizing force and contribute to lasting peace. It now seemed that this goal was about to fall victim to Soviet expansionism. Almost all assumed that Communism was a monolithic structure and that the Kremlin was playing a game of cosmic puppetry.

The policy that emerged ranged from caution to boldness. A few days prior to the Japanese surrender the Joint Chiefs of Staff instructed General Wedemeyer that the United States would "continue to support Chinese military operations essential to re-occupation by Central Government forces of all areas in the China theater now held by the Japanese." The same directive called for Wedemeyer to assist the Central Government "in the rapid transport of Chinese Central Government forces to key areas in China."[23] During the same weeks the United States stationed 53,000 Marines in North China. Yet these orders were accompanied by the instruction that no action was to be taken that would involve American forces in the civil war.

The American decision to repatriate four million Japanese was based on the importance of freeing the wartime ally of the presence of well-armed enemy forces. Because the deployment of Nationalist armies to strategic areas aided one side in the internal struggle and worked to the serious disadvantage of the other, this mission was subject to criticism. There is no evidence that at the outset the aim was to assist the Nationalists against the Communists, but before many months had passed there were those in Washington who viewed repatriation of the Japanese as a convenient excuse for strengthening the Nationalists in the domestic struggle.

It was General Wedemeyer who first questioned his orders. On August 19 the general cabled Washington pointing out that it was impossible to carry out the repatriation without coming into conflict with the stipulation that American forces were not to become involved in the fratricidal war. Incidents in which American soldiers and marines would become involved in skirmishes with the Chinese Communists were likely to occur. Wedemeyer's inquiry brought no response.

The developments taking place obviously suited the Nationalists who were most anxious to involve the United States. Continued American support gave prestige to the regime. It also desperately needed American supplies and equipment for the war ahead. The best guarantee, and possibly the only one, for a Nationalist victory in the internal struggle was a considerable degree of American involvement. It was with this in mind that the Chiang government had insisted that the United States was under obligation by an earlier agreement between Roosevelt and Chiang to train and furnish ninety divisions even if this could not be done until the Japanese had been defeated. And for the same reason Chiang had been urging the sending of a large American military mission. By early September T.V. Soong was back in Washington. Soong had boasted that he could always get what he wanted. He did not confine his efforts to the State Department, where he lacked close friends. He had consistently circumvented that department, soliciting support in a variety of other departments and agencies and calling on his close friends, including Thomas Corcoran and Harry Hopkins, to open doors for him. On September 14 Soong reached the White House, where he informed President Truman that President Roosevelt had promised to equip ninety army divisions. Truman scaled the request down to thirty-nine but agreed to do what he could.

The request for an American military mission, already discussed during the preceding spring, had the support of the armed services. In April the Department of State had raised serious questions about the political aspects and had succeeded in postponing a commitment. In a paper drafted by John Carter Vincent, the State Department called in question the wisdom of entering upon a fixed policy of supporting Chiang's Nationalist regime permanently. That government, the paper noted, was a one-party government, and it suffered from both corruption and incompetence. These weaknesses had greatly undermined its public support, and various dissident elements were challenging its continuation in power. The uncertainty of what would happen, Vincent argued, dictated that the United States should maintain a position of flexibility. Secondly, Vincent questioned the advisability of assisting China to build a modern air force. China was an underdeveloped country, desperately poor, and urgently in need of using her resources to build an economy that could raise living standards. A modern air force could only be maintained by extensive imports, and this would be an unwise use of the country's limited resources.[24]

The close of hostilities gave new life to the proposed mission. T.V. Soong arrived in Washington in late August and immediately took steps to have the United States send a military advisory group. On August 27 Secretary of the Navy Forrestal, after talks with Soong, informed Secretary of State Byrnes that he had already sent to the President a proposal for legislation.[25] Some days later Soong called on the Secretary of State conveying China's desire that the United States send a military mission. Byrnes informed President Truman that he approved of the proposal and then pointed out some of the legal barriers.[26] The Far East Committee of S.W.N.C.C., under directions from the President, was already preparing a paper which included proposals for furnishing military supplies to China and for sending a military mission.[27] John Carter Vincent did not, at this stage, object to an American advisory group but he advised that officers serving in the group should not be on the active list of the United States Army, should be paid by China, and that the group should have no official connection with the United States government.[28] On September 7 Soong saw the President and was assured by him that S.W.N.C.C. was already at work on a proposal. On September 13 Acting Secretary of State Acheson sent a message from Truman to Chiang assuring him that American military personnel "could and would be furnished in an advisory capacity."[29]

Thus, less than thirty days after Japan's surrender, the United States was prepared to lend the Central Government a helping hand. The sending of a Military Group—Chiang objected to the term mission—would lead to a permanent American influence and cause China to buy American equipment in the years ahead, thereby helping the American economy. These considerations, however, were less important than the desire to see China unified under the Central Government.

On September 23 Hurley and Wedemeyer left Chungking for Washington, and one of their aims was to promote a program of military assistance and the sending of an advisory group. On October 17 Wedemeyer appeared before the Joint War Plans Committee and testified in favor of sending an advisory group. He explained that the mission would assist and advise in the training of Chinese forces, participate in planning and operations, and "should render such assistance and advice as is practicable to help the Chinese prepare for any situation that may be created to the North." He expressed the view that the American officers should be regular officers of the American armed forces who were on active duty. When questioned about the Generalissimo and the nature of the regime, Wedemeyer expressed confidence in Chiang's integrity but he also acknowledged that Chiang had only loose control and that he was surrounded by unscrupulous people and his authority was circumscribed by independent warlords who were the heads of feudal dynasties. When asked about possible Soviet reactions to the establishment of a Military Advisory Group, he responded that the Russians would not look on it with favor. He added that the Soviets were determined "to penetrate North China and to set up a buffer area there similar to what they have done in Europe, . . ."[30] At this same session Wedemeyer expressed a view that was at variance with his earlier reports. He stated "that the strength of the Communists in China has been overrated in this country and there is no need to fear them unless the Russians give them support beyond the present scale."

When the proposal came before the State-War-Navy Coordinating Committee in November 1945, it called for sending a mission of more than 4,000 men and officers. China was to make a series of concessions in return for the assistance rendered. Members of the group were to pay no import duties or other taxes on goods for their own consumption and they were to be exempt from Chinese legal jurisdiction. In addition, China was to agree not to buy any foreign military equipment without first consulting the United States. The proposal included a list of concessions considered desirable but not essential. These provided for the development of China's commercial aviation under United States supervision, freedom for operation of American airlines in China, and preferential treatment for the United States government, citizens, and commercial organizations in respect to pipelines, roads, airbases, and other installations in China constructed by or at the expense of the United States.[31]

If the members of the Joint Chiefs had any knowledge of the one hundred years of Chinese humiliation and the powerful feelings against foreign intrusion, the proposal failed to reveal it. John Carter Vincent, well aware of the explosion of Chinese national feelings in the years before Japan attacked, vigorously opposed the proposal. The mission, he said, was so large, in fact greater than the number of British officers in the peacetime Indian colonial army, that it raised serious questions. "The size and character of the Group, the statement of concessions desired, and the general tenor of the Joint Chiefs of Staff papers," Vincent told Secretary of State Byrnes, "raise a question as to whether we are not moving toward establishment of a relationship with China which has some of the characteristics of a *de facto* protectorate with a semi-colonial Chinese army under our direction." Vincent asked what effect would such a move have on "international political relations?" Would not military assistance on this scale and manner make Chiang even more intransigent in his opposition to a political solution? Would adoption of the plan not constitute interference in the internal affairs of China? He was, he said, not opposed to giving military assistance and advice, but he asked if the plan would not have the effect "of carrying the Group, and us, into the field of intervention and involvement in China's internal and political and military affairs."[32] Byrnes endorsed the Vincent paper and set it before the Coordinating Committee on January 5. Once again the views of the State Department delayed action, but in February President Truman issued an order establishing a smaller military mission.

The debate over the sending of a military mission had reached a crucial stage in November 1945. At the same time the continued American participation in the repatriation of Japanese raised questions of fundamental importance. Ambassador Hurley's cables in September may well have contributed to delaying recognition of the fact that the United States was treading dangerously close to involvement in China's civil war. He had informed Washington that the conflict between the troops of the two Chinese camps had been greatly exaggerated by those who wished to make trouble.[33] Not until Hurley had returned home and repeated reports of fighting reached Washington did the problem receive full-scale attention.

On October 22 the State-War-Navy Coordinating Committee had outlined the aims of the United States in China and recommended a program for their realization. The goals of American policy, affirmed many times in the past, were again set forth. To achieve these goals China was to be assisted in maintaining internal peace and security, and this was to be done in Manchuria and Taiwan as well as in China proper. Having committed itself to this dangerous mission, the Committee also took note of relations with the Soviet Union. It was judged important to avoid giving the Soviets cause for departing from their present policy of cooperation, and the Committee expressed the view that it was probably desirable to seek a cooperative solution. Finally, as a gesture to the State Department, the Committee included in its report a statement referring to the weaknesses and deficiencies of the Nationalist Government.[34]

Viewed in perspective the State-War-Navy Coordinating Committee had established no new policy. It had done no more than to reaffirm its faith in the approaches taken in the recent past. The United States had been assisting China on a large scale during the war and the momentum now carried over into the postwar period. The United States, it was said, was doing no more than it had been doing all during the war. The attention paid to the Soviet Union was likewise a continuation of the effort to cooperate with that government. Ever since the Cairo Conference the legitimate interests of the Soviet Union in Asia had been recognized repeatedly, and the Coordinating Committee took note of the Soviet Union again. The report stated:

> The Russian intention to withdraw all Soviet forces from Manchuria and recent informal but authoritative expressions of Russian opinion indicate that the USSR is for the present at least prepared to deal with us on a partnership basis in the Far East. It is to our interest to encourage and support this position on the part of the USSR. It is likewise the general policy of the United States to consider common problems on a consultative basis.[35]

The action of the Coordinating Committee also continued the pattern of past decision making by reiterating with firmness that the United States was not handing Chiang a blank check. Hurley's policy, strongly opposed by many members of the government since the preceding January, was rejected. Assistance, said the report, would be discontinued "if at any time it is established to the satisfaction of the United States Government that the Chinese forces are being used in support of an administration not in conformity with the general policies of the United States, to engage in fratricidal war, or to afford a threat of aggression."[36]

The wide spectrum of recommendations represented an effort at combining reasonableness with firmness, but events in China had already passed the stage in which the United States could reestablish control by the Central Government in all parts of China and yet not face the danger of involvement in a civil war. On November 5 Wedemeyer cabled the Chief of Staff that he had refused the Nationalist request to transport two more armies to North China and that he was prepared to withdraw the marines from North China on November 15 and all the armed forces of the United States by January 1, 1946. He based these decisions on the instruction that he was not to permit his forces to become involved in the civil war, and on the fact that the Chinese armies were now in a position to accept the surrender of Japanese forces if these Chinese armies were not deployed elsewhere.

At first glance it would appear that Wedemeyer was anxious to avoid involvement in fratricidal war. Whatever reluctance he entertained on this score, he did favor transporting more Nationalist troops. In this respect Wedemeyer's later account in which he stated that he viewed the orders of the Joint Chiefs instructing him to avoid involvement in China's internal struggle as a burdensome and unwise restriction was accurate.[37] Wedemeyer enthusiastically supported the proposal to establish the Advisory Group and to furnish China with military equipment. His cable of November 5 was designed to have the Joint Chiefs issue new orders that would give him greater latitude in employing American forces and to assist the Central Government directly in its struggle against the Communists. However, he did not recommend a change in policy until two weeks later; he merely called attention to the situation he faced and what he proposed to do to carry out his existing orders.

Wedemeyer's cable marked the beginning of a period of searching reanalysis. Those who participated in these deliberations now had to face the question as to how American goals were to be achieved short of involvement. No one was prepared to argue that the two goals were reconcilable. As the days passed, new cables from Wedemeyer made it abundantly clear that the choices were both dangerous and difficult. On November 9 Wedemeyer informed Marshall that he had followed the policy of transporting troops to the border of Manchuria but had refused to transport them into Manchuria on the ground that China and the Soviet Union had reached an agreement on the sur-

render of the Japanese there.[38] On November 14 he reported to
Marshall that he advised the Central Government not to try to take
control of Manchuria. He noted also the popular support of the Communists in the major cities of North China "due to dissatisfaction of
local populace with corruption and inefficiency of Kuomintang administration in those areas."[39] In a cable to Eisenhower, who replaced Marshall as Chief of Staff, Wedemeyer expressed confidence
in Chiang's good intentions, but he also noted that Chiang lacked
competent advisers and administrators and that he was surrounded
by unscrupulous men "who are interested in their self-aggrandize-
ment." Chiang was loyal to them and appointed them to positions of
responsibility. However, if China went Communist it would be a
mere puppet of the USSR. Controlling both Europe and Asia, the
Communists would have a preponderant influence in the world. The
United States, said Wedemeyer, should assist China economically
and provide supplies but withdraw all military forces. He proposed
that he be issued new directives.[40]

Some days later, on November 23, Wedemeyer warned that it
would be "absolutely impossible to avoid involvement in fratricidal
warfare" unless American forces were withdrawn. If the United
States chose to carry out repatriation and, "we are to assume control
of Manchuria by Central Government, this means war and possibly
war with the Soviet Union."[41]

Wedemeyer's alarm was seconded by Admiral Barbey. He urged
that an agreement between the Nationalists and Communists was of
utmost importance "even if such an agreement involves giving Mao
Tse-tung the complete political and military control he demands of
Communists-dominated provinces." It might, he said, result in nothing more than a loose federation, but it would provide a breathing
spell in which to attempt to work out a solution with Russia.[42] John
Carter Vincent advised Secretary of State Byrnes that this proposal
deserved close study.[43]

The realistic appraisals from China immediately gave rise to an
exchange of views in Washington. At an early meeting representatives of the defense department speculated on the strengths and
weaknesses of several possible courses. Assistant Secretary of War
John McCloy observed that the problem of transporting four million
Japanese was staggering and beyond the capacity of the Chinese.

McCloy also stated that continued America presence would strengthen Chiang's prestige but a withdrawal would have disastrous effects on his standing.[44] McCloy doubted that the Nationalists would be able to absorb and administer Manchuria and feared that the chaos that was likely to develop there would give the Soviets an excuse to remain. He concluded that it was necessary to assist the Nationalists, but he likewise observed that if the Russians then gave support to the Communists we would be "in a real mess." Secretary of War Robert Patterson spoke only briefly but he was inclined to favor withdrawal.[45]

After further discussions in the Joint Chiefs of Staff, H. Freeman Matthews, Chairman of the interdepartment Coordinating Committee, recorded the views that had been expressed. The Joint Chiefs concluded that if the threat of civil war in North China and Manchuria had not been eliminated by the time American forces were withdrawn, then it might be necessary for some outside party to intervene. This intervention might be carried out by the Soviets or possibly by Japanese forces under orders from the Central Government. The alternative would be full-fledged civil war. No one of these three possibilities gave any promise of security for American objectives. After this desultory discussion, the Joint Chiefs asked the State Department for its point of view on political aspects.[46]

Everett Drumright, only recently returned from a long tour of duty in China, where he had differed with foreign service colleagues but had also shared in their disillusion with the Central Government, now injected himself into the position of speaking for the State Department. It is highly doubtful that his recommendations accurately represented the Department's views, but the Department did not disavow them. Drumright advised that the United States should help the Central Government regain control of North China and Manchuria. "Considering the character, the ideology, and the past attitude of the Chinese Communists," Drumright found it difficult to perceive "how American interest of any kind could flourish in such a Communist state." He argued that the United States should be guided primarily by considerations of its own security interests. A Communist controlled Manchuria meant that there would be two Chinas, who would be antagonistic to each other. It would also mean that the Communist state in Manchuria would be dominated by the

Soviet Union. Such a situation would not promote the security or the interest of the United States. Drumright feared that the result would be quite the reverse. He wrote:

> It is rather a situation that will produce a continuation of internal strife in China and the possibility of a clash between the United States and the U.S.S.R. As the Japanese absorption of Manchuria contributed to the exacerbation of American-Japanese relations, so would Soviet control of Manchuria seem to sow the seeds for a fundamental cleavage between the United States and the U.S.S.R.[47]

Drumright's memorandum came before the Coordinating Committee along with an equally lengthy statement prepared by Assistant Secretary of War McCloy. He asserted that if China was to constitute a stabilizing force it must include North China and Manchuria. These were the richest areas in China, and China's future economic development depended upon having the industry and resources available. McCloy went on to point out what it would mean if the Central Government were not to gain control of these areas. Not only would the great numbers of Japanese not be disarmed but the United States would not have lived up to its international commitments to support the establishment of a unified China. Even more dangerous was the possibility that failure to bring about unification would lead to Soviet intervention. After this presentation McCloy added almost as an afterthought, "under what circumstances is the United States willing to see Manchuria become a Chinese Communist state in somewhat the same category as Outer Mongolia?"[48]

Four days later the Coordinating Committee met once again, and now the anguish of indecision gave way to a renewed faith in American power. Secretary of the Navy Forrestal led the way, not with a further analysis but with the report that Henry Luce had informed him that a recent editorial in *Life* advocating support of Chiang Kai-shek had brought a favorable public response.[49] Secretary of the Army Patterson, who only some days before had been inclined to support withdrawal, now proclaimed with bounce that the "Marines who are there could walk from one end of China to the other without serious hindrance." Patterson said, "Such incidents as there have been are merely comic opera fighting." In conclusion Patterson, who was wholly new to the China question having been involved in procurement during the war, jauntily observed that the marines were there to effectuate the repatriation of the Japanese and "if the incidental effect of their presence is to support the Government of Chiang Kai-shek so much the better."[50] At this late stage, on November 25, Vincent of the State Department, sought to call the attention of Byrnes and Acheson to the merits of Admiral Barbey's proposal. Vincent was of the opinion that if both the Nationalists and Communists were approached with firmness and with explicit proposals, they could be induced to agree to a truce.[51] Two days later, on November 26, Forrestal and Patterson sent a memorandum to the Secretary of State recommending continued aid and support for the Nationalist Government on the ground that China should be unified and that only that government, with American assistance, could bring that about. Failing to bring about unification, Manchuria and North China would probably pass under Soviet control or dissolve into separate states under Soviet domination. But Forrestal and Patterson also advised consultation with other powers.[52]

At a session of the Coordinating Committee on the following day Secretary of State Byrnes and Assistant Secretary of State Acheson raised some questions but they did not take sharp issue with the recommendations of Forrestal and Patterson. Byrnes thought it might be wise to try to force the Nationalists and the Communists to get together and to line up Soviet support in this effort.[53] This was the beginning of the Marshall Mission.

At this point Patrick Hurley dramatically entered upon the scene. Upon his return from China he had told Secretary of State Byrnes that he would resign due to ill health. Later he had changed his mind and decided to return to China, but just prior to his scheduled departure he had come to the Secretary's office and presented a letter of resignation addressed to the President. Byrnes urged him not to resign and on the afternoon of the same day Hurley returned and said he had decided to retain his post. However, he wished to remain in Washington for a few more days since he was scheduled to address the National Press Club two days hence. In his speech before the representatives of the press he announced his resignation and charged that his policy and that of the United States had been undermined by foreign service officers and members of the State Department. These individuals, he alleged, had supported both the European imperialist and Communist blocs. It was time, he contended, that American foreign policy serve American economic interests.[52] Presumably Hurley saw in the practices of both these blocs barriers to American economic interests. This received little attention, but Hurley's charges that there were pro-Communists in the State Department elicited widespread news coverage.

Notes to Chapter IX

1. O.S.S. Report on North Shansi and North Shensi, File XL 22188, National Archives.

2. Ibid.

3. Michael Lindsay to Sir Horace, August 24, 1945, copy in the Hurley Papers.

4. Examination of the Practicability of Concurrent Occupation of Tokyo, Dairen and Keijo, and Early Occupation of North China port, July 26, 1945. C.C.S. 386.2 Japan Section 4, Military Records Branch, National Archives.

5. Wedemeyer to War Department, August 12, 1945. C.C.S. 386.2 Japan Section 4, Military Records Branch, National Archives.

6. Joint Chiefs of Staff to Wedemeyer, August 14, 1945. C.C.S. 386.2 Japan Section 4, Military Records Branch, National Archives.

7. Wedemeyer to War Department, August 14, 1945. Military Records Branch C.C.S. 386.2, National Archives.

8. MacArthur to War Department, August 14, 1945. C.C.S. 386.2 Japan Section 4, Military Records Branch, National Archives.

9. Joint Chiefs of Staff to Wedemeyer, August 18, 1945. C.C.S. 386.2 Japan Section 4, Military Records Branch, National Archives.

10. Memorandum by the Secretary of the State-War-Navy Coordinating Committee to the Secretary of the Joint Chiefs of Staff, August 22, 1945, *U.S.F.R. 1945*, p. 521.

11. Joint Chiefs of Staff to Wedemeyer, August 10, 1945, *U.S.F.R. 1945*, pp. 527–28.

12. Wedemeyer to Marshall, August 19, 1945, *U.S.F.R. 1945*, pp. 532–33.

13. General Chu Teh to Colonel Ivan O. Yeaton, August 16, 1945. Dixie Mission File, Federal Records Center, Suitland, Maryland.

14. General Yeh Chien-ying to Colonel Yeaton, October 26, 1945. Dixie Mission File.

15. Lindsay to Sir Horace, August 24, 1945, Hurley Papers.

16. Chargé in China, Robertson, to the Secretary of State, October 6, 1945, *U.S.F.R. 1945*, p. 576.

17. Hurley to the Secretary of State, September 23, 1945, *U.S.F.R. 1945*, p. 467.

18. Chargé Robertson to the Secretary of State, October 2, 1945, *U.S.F.R. 1945*, p. 470.

19. Ibid., November 10, 1945, pp. 483–85.

20. Consul at Tientsin, Meyer, to the Secretary of State, October 30, 1945, *U.S.F.R. 1945*, p. 599.

21. Chargé Robertson to the Secretary of State, November 11, 1945, *U.S.F.R. 1945*, p. 613.

22. The White House, by September, took the lead in supporting a policy of support of the Kuomintang and opposition to possible Soviet dominance in Manchuria. This is most strongly indicated by the White House directive to the U.S. Navy to hold a port in China. The possible sources of influence and pressure on the White House are, of course, several, but insofar as the documents permit speculation it would appear that Harriman and Forrestal may have been most influential. Forrestal's cold war views are well known. Regarding China, he had long been troubled by the prospect of a shift in the balance of power. Late in August he had recommended to the President the establishment of a naval mission to China. Harriman, it is likely, had equal influence. He had met Truman at Potsdam, where he had taken the lead in organizing American support for Soong, who was engaged in negotiations with Stalin. Throughout August, Harriman expressed great concern over Soviet designs in Manchuria. During the spring of 1945 Forrestal was greatly influenced by Harriman's cables warning of Soviet ambitions, and the Secretary of Navy was also very much influenced by Harriman during the latter's visit in Washington early in May 1945.

23. Joint Chiefs of Staff to Wedemeyer, August 10, 1945, *U.S.F.R. 1945*, pp. 532–33.

24. Memorandum concerning United States Post-War Military Policies with Respect to China, April 3, 1945. *U.S.F.R. 1945*, pp. 74–79.

25. Forrestal to Byrnes, August 27, 1945, *U.S.F.R. 1945*, pp. 538–39.

26. Byrnes to Truman, September 3, 1945, *U.S.F.R. 1945*, pp. 547–49.

27. Vincent to Acheson, September 6, 1945, *U.S.F.R. 1945*, pp. 550–51.

28. Ibid.

29. Acheson to Hurley, September 13, 1945, *U.S.F.R. 1945*, p. 557.

30. *Minutes of the Joint Chiefs of Staff*, October 17, 1945.

31. Report by the Joint Chiefs of Staff, October 22, 1945, *U.S.F.R. 1945*, pp. 590–98.

32. Memorandum by the Director of the Office of Far Eastern Affairs to the Secretary of State, November 12, 1945, *U.S.F.R. 1945*, pp. 614–17.

33. Hurley to the Secretary of State, September 4, 1945, *U.S.F.R. 1945*, pp. 549–50.

34.   Report by the State-War-Navy Coordinating Committee, October 22, 1945, *U.S.F.R. 1945,* pp. 583–90.

35.   Ibid., p. 588.

36.   Ibid., p. 584.

37.   Albert C. Wedemeyer, *Wedemeyer Reports!* (New York: Henry Holt and Company, 1958), pp. 359–60.

38.   Wedemeyer to Marshall, November 9, 1945, *U.S.F.R. 1945,* pp. 611–13.

39.   Ibid., November 14, 1945, pp. 627–28.

40.   Wedemeyer to Eisenhower, November 20, 1945, *U.S.F.R. 1945,* pp. 650–60.

41.   Ibid., November 23, 1945, pp. 662–65.

42.   Chargé Robertson to the Secretary of State, November 24, 1945, *U.S.F.R. 1945,* pp. 668–69.

43.   Vincent to Acheson, November 24, 1945, FW 893.00/11–24–45, Department of State, National Archives.

44.   Minutes of the Meeting of the Secretaries of State, War, and Navy, November 6, 1945, *U.S.F.R. 1945,* pp. 606–07.

45.   Ibid.

46.   Memorandum by the Acting Chairman of the State-War-Navy Coordinating Committee to the Secretary of State, November 13, 1945, *U.S.F.R. 1945,* pp. 619–21.

47.   Memorandum by the Chief of the Division of Chinese Affairs, November 16, 1945, *U.S.F.R. 1945,* pp. 629–34.

48.   Memorandum by the Assistant Secretary of War, November 16, 1945, Minutes of the Joint Chiefs of Staff, National Achives.

49.   Minutes of the Meeting of the Secretaries of State, War, and Navy November 20, 1945, *U.S.F.R. 1945,* pp. 646–47.

50.   Ibid.

51.   Vincent to Acheson, November 24, 1945, FW 893.00/11–24–45, Department of State, National Archives.

52.   Memorandum by the Secretaries of War and Navy to the Secretary of State, November 26, 1945, *U.S.F.R. 1945,* pp. 670–78.

53.   Minutes of the Meeting of the Secretaries of State, War, and Navy, November 27, 1945, *U.S.F.R. 1945,* pp. 684–86.

54.   *Congressional Record, 1945,* Appendix, p. 5539.

CHAPTER X

The Marshall Mission

The dramatic resignation of Patrick Hurley and his charges that members of the State Department and the foreign service were guilty of disloyalty and insubordination gained the headlines for a few days. Hurley's testimony before a Senate committee revealed the emptiness of his charges and largely discredited him. The Republicans would have liked to exploit Hurley's exodus from office, but their chances of doing so were removed by President Truman's prompt appointment of General George C. Marshall as his special emissary. The appointment of this highly respected wartime leader defied criticism. The troublesome China question, it seemed, was now in safe hands.

Agitation for support of Chiang Kai-shek was still in its early stages and lacked organization, but individual voices were already proclaiming that all-out support for China's leader was part of a benign tradition of friendship for China. As early as March 1945 Walter Judd, Congressman from Minnesota and a former medical missionary, delivered a lengthy speech in the House of Representatives calling for full support of the Kuomintang and charging the Communists with treachery. Judd was an effective speaker, symbolized the highly regarded missionary effort, and his long years in China added a note of authority to his pulpit-like oratory. In this first major speech Judd admitted the presence of corruption, acknowledged that the regime was not democratic, and did not deny its failures, but he contended with ardor that these weaknesses were the result of long years of war. Once peace was achieved, he argued, Chiang would bring about democracy and enlightened rule.[1]

In the fall of 1945, after Japan's surrender, Judd assumed the role of Congressional watchdog of Chiang's interests. Whenever an article appeared that accorded with his own interpretation of the China scene, Judd read it into the *Congressional Record*. He soon found an ally with infinite greater power to mold public opinion. Henry Luce, son of a prominent missionary and editor of the nation's two most influential magazines, *Time* and *Life*, promptly made support of Chiang Kai-shek one of his major causes. The new editorial policy of Luce appeared under the title "What Price Peace?".

This editorial masterpiece tapped the most commonly held public feelings and reduced them to a series of moralistic teachings. The reader's vision was unclouded by any realistic examination of the maze of Chinese internal politics. Readers were flattered with the reflection of their rescue of the world from Nazism, of their military might, of the great productive power of their country, and of the responsibilities that were inherent in the possession of both power and moral virtue. Support of China provided the test of whether Americans would shoulder the new burdens and prove that they were truly international. Luce called up the past to verify further the sanctity of the program to be followed. Chiang was now on the verge of establishing unity, the goal the United States had supported since Hay's Open Door Notes at the turn of the century. Friendship for Chiang was equivalent to friendship for China. Luce closed by summoning his readers to the exciting task:

> Now is the time to support the legitimate government with all our heart and soul. We need regret nothing if we stick by our friends in Asia, the best friends now and the greatest-friends-to-be a nation ever had.[2]

Within a week, Luce informed Secretary of the Navy Forrestal of an overwhelmingly favorable response.

Three days after the appearance of the *Life* article, on November 23, the editor of the *New York Times* pleaded earnestly against with-

drawing from China. The United States, he wrote, had extended aid
to the legal government prior to American entry into the war and
must do so now. "To extend aid to any other authority in China," he
maintained "would have been tantamount to fomenting rebellion
against our ally and a flagrant intervention in China's internal
affairs." The editorial closed with the advice, "The National Government of China is not as yet as democratic as we should like it to be,
but it offers more hope for liberty than the totalitarian regime of the
Chinese Communists."[3]

However, there were also those who wanted to bring the boys
home and who had no heart for fighting a war in China. Luce's
appeal to heroism and self-sacrifice could not triumph at once over
the desire to return to normal domestic pursuits. And some resisted
because they had come to view Chiang with great distrust and sympathized with the Chinese Communists. On November 3 three separate resolutions were introduced in the House of Representatives
calling for a withdrawal of all American forces from China. Even
earlier Mike Mansfield, a member of the House of Representatives,
had spoken for the recall of all soldiers, sailors, and marines. Mansfield's speech prompted Judd to ask if he objected to sending a military mission. Mansfield assured him that he did not.[4] Like many who
wanted to bring the boys home and who were against any involvement that might lead to war, Mansfield was not opposed to assistance
to Chiang. Criticism of the Chinese leader had not yet become com-
monplace. After a speech in Lowell, Massachusetts, Eleanor Roosevelt was asked about the future of democracy in China and her view
of Madame Chiang. She replied that Madame Chiang, like the Chinese people, talked about democracy but did not know how to live
it. The press criticized Mrs. Roosevelt severely, and John Rankin,
representative from Mississippi in the House, came to the defense of
China's first lady. Rankin asked, "Is Christianity her only crime? In
my opinion she is the greatest Christian leader that China has seen
in a thousand years."[5]

The underlying public admiration of the Generalissimo and aver-
sion toward anything named Communism provided politicians and
editors with an appeal, but the most decisively held view of the
public was that peace was to be preserved. Even Patrick Hurley's
dramatic charges that members of the State Department and of the

Foreign Service were guilty of disloyalty and insubordination received little credence after Hurley's testimony before a Senate committee revealed the lack of evidence to support his charges. When President Truman summoned General Marshall to undertake a special mission to China, public confidence in this wartime leader immediately removed the distrust Hurley had sought to promote.

During the week following his appointment, Marshall met with President Truman, Secretary of State James Byrnes, and others to formulate a program. The hard-pressed Secretary of State confronted a disturbing disarray in the international field. The Foreign Ministers Conference of the preceding September had ended in a stalemate over who was to have a determining voice in drafting the prospective peace treaties. More recently, distrust of the Soviet Union had increased because of the Soviet's use of her troops in Iran to prevent the Iranian government from putting down a popular revolt. There was likewise considerable uneasiness regarding Soviet intentions in Manchuria. The distrust originated in part in the continued occupation of Dairen by the Soviet military but even more in the fears based on speculation and unverified rumors. At the time of Marshall's appointment Byrnes was preparing to go to Moscow for another meeting of foreign ministers. Byrnes knew that the Soviets were suspicious of American policy toward China and he hoped to allay their fears.

At his first meeting with Marshall and Truman, Secretary of State Byrnes stressed the importance of the Chinese political parties reaching an accord, but he also took the position that Nationalist forces must be assisted in taking over in Manchuria. Marshall dwelt on the importance of repatriating the Japanese, stressing that should they be permitted to remain they might once again strive to dominate. But the conflict in China received the highest priority. A full-scale civil war posed dangers to the immediate and long-term interests of the United States. It was assumed that the Soviet Union would be tempted to give support to the Communists and in return would expect to acquire a dominant influence in Chinese affairs. These leaders also feared that the civil war would end in a division whereby the Communists would rule in the north and the Kuomintang in central and southern China. A major American aim during the war had been the establishment of a strong China, capable of stabilizing the situation in Asia and of promoting peace. A divided China would almost inevitably enhance Soviet influence and perhaps make Russia the dominant power. Considerations of this order lay at the heart of the formulation of the program Marshall was to promote.

The President made public his new policy on December 15. The civil war in China, he said, constituted a threat to world peace, and therefore the United States was prepared to assist in resolving the conflict. To achieve this it would be necessary for the Chinese to break with the one-party rule of the past and to establish a broad-based government in which all parties in China had an effective voice. Truman declared that the United States continued to adhere to the tradition which forbade interference in the internal affairs of other nations. The United States did not propose to dictate the form of government; it only meant to assist the parties in China in reaching an agreement.

In the first meeting of Truman, Byrnes, and Marshall, the new emissary wanted to know what bargaining power was to be available to him to bring about the desired goal. A large-scale program of assistance to China was already in the planning stage. Byrnes stated that if the Communists proved cooperative and the Nationalists did not, then aid to the Nationalist Government should be withheld and the United States would be forced to deal directly with the Communists insofar as the evacuation of the Japanese from North China was concerned. If, on the other hand, the Nationalists showed themselves to be reasonable and the Communists stood in the way, then, said Byrnes, "our full support would be given the National Government and we would move her armies into North China as required." However, at the final meeting this decision was modified. Truman and Byrnes stated that the United States would have to back Chiang in North China even if he were not conciliatory because the repatriation of the Japanese must be completed.[6]

In the discussions that took place from the time of Marshall's appointment to the time he departed for China, there was no discussion of the internal situation in China or assessment of the chances of success. The complete readiness to undertake the stupendous task of unifying China after thirty years of fratricidal strife and the recent failure of the Hurley mission contrasted sharply with the gloomy forebodings of those who knew China firsthand. The chances of success were slim, but the options were also limited. A hands-off policy would only postpone decisions and add to the difficulties. Given American domestic politics, the pressure to give assistance to Chiang might easily become irresistible but at the same time create sharp internal divisions, which the opposition party would inevitably exploit. An effort to bring about unification, even though it failed, would give the administration a freer hand.

However, confidence in eventual success rather than doubts ruled in the highest circles in Washington. A program of nonmilitary aid would bring about greatly improved economic conditions in China and restore public confidence in the Central Government if that government at the same time siphoned off political discontent by adopting a liberal course.

Readiness to undertake the mission also owed much to distrust of the Soviet Union. It was acknowledged that up to this time there was considerable evidence of restraint upon the part of the Soviets in Manchuria, but this did not quiet fears about the future. The important Russian strategic and economic interests in Manchuria meant that they were unlikely to sit idly by in the face of continued disorder in that area. Moreover, although the American leaders admitted that there was no evidence of collusion between the Russians and the Chinese Communists, many of them believed that the temptation to affiliate with their ideological brethren, if the Russians could be assured of the Chinese being relegated to a dependent position, would be irresistible. The way to avoid such a development was to restore unity and promote a strong China.

President Truman tailored his news release to avoid the appearance of partisanship and at the same time to place the United States in the position of assuming responsibility. The original draft of his release stated that the United States "will continue to furnish military supplies and to assist the Chinese National Government in the further transportation of Chinese troops so that it can reestablish control over the liberated areas of China including Manchuria." Also omitted from the news release was a statement expressing the desire to have the British and the Soviets participate in establishing the peace.[7]

On December 14, a day prior to Truman's policy announcement, an important agreement was reached between the Soviet commander in Manchuria, Marshal Rodian Y. Malinovsky and General Hsiung Shih-hui.[8] At the request of the Chinese the Russians agreed to delay their departure from Manchuria until Chinese Nationalist forces were ready to move in and they also agreed to protect airfields near the major cities so that planes carrying Nationalist officials and troops could land.

At the time Marshall arrived in China the Nationalists held the upper hand. They employed both Japanese and puppet troops to protect the railways and to hold off the Communists. The Japanese general, Okamura, reported that his forces had fought about 1,000 skirmishes each month in the period from August 15 to November 10, and 1,306 Japanese soldiers had been killed.[9] The assistance provided by the Japanese caused the Central Government to oppose, however quietly, the American program of repatriation. Puppet troops were also fighting on the side of the Nationalists. This use of enemy forces, expedient from a strictly military point of view, was extremely unpopular with the Chinese people in the formerly occupied areas who had eagerly looked forward to being liberated from the hated enemy.

The Nationalists also enjoyed a five to one advantage in the number of troops and were likewise better equipped. Some American-trained Nationalist troops who were deployed in Manchuria made a favorable impression. However, both Nationalist and Communist troops were more often in no condition to fight. In some areas of North China the Communists faced starvation.[10] Nationalist troops were often undernourished, ragged, and poorly equipped. An American medical doctor serving on a transport carrying Nationalist troops from southern China told of the wide prevalence of disease, the poor physical condition of the troops and reported that many died on board ship. Some were mere boys not more than ten years old. On arriving at the landing area the doctor was directed to visit each transport to ascertain whether the sick had disembarked. The ill were removed on stretchers carried by the Chinese. The doctor, Emmett D. Hightower, described what he saw: "I noted, to my amazement, that when the patient hit the beach the stretcher was overturned, rolling him on the sand. He was then beaten with sticks, and if he got up and fell into ranks, O.K. If not he was either left there or perhaps tossed into the water. On one such occasion, upon remonstrating at this treatment, we were told. 'He no fight—he seek'."[11]

The military advantages of the Nationalists caused the Communists to take a serious interest in the continuation of the negotiations in Chungking. In October the Political Consultative Council was established by joint agreement with the Communists. The Council was to find a way of establishing a multi-party democratic system. Its meetings were to begin in January 1946. By December Chou En-lai seized the initiative by making two new proposals, a cease-fire order and an agreement that reorganization of the government and reorganization of the Army proceed simultaneously.[12] Both proposals conveyed the impression that it was the Communists who were prepared to be reasonable.

Communist spokesman alternated between policies of charging the United States with promoting civil war and welcoming American cooperation. The exceedingly frank Army leader, General Chu Teh, contended that it was the United States that precipitated the conflict in North China by transporting Nationalist troops. Chu maintained that without American support the Chinese government could not afford to continue the struggle.[13] The notes of reprimand, however, were drowned out by repeated words of assurance that the United States had nothing to fear from the Communists. At a conference attended by Tillman Durdin, *New York Times* correspondent, Liu Shao-chi, a member of the highest echelon of Communist party officials, explained the major points of the Communist program. The program, said Liu, "for the present is one of democratic capitalist development, based on state, private and cooperative enterprise." For the present, he explained, Russian communism was not the model. "The program of the Chinese Communists," Liu stated, "is comparable to the political and economic concepts in the United States at the time of Jefferson and Lincoln." And, he added, "The Chinese Communist party maintains no liaison with the Russian Communist party or any other foreign Communist party."[14]

A few days after Liu's conciliatory pronouncements General Peng Teh-Huei, vice commander of the Communist armies, asserted that the Communists stood for a wholly independent China free of foreign privileges or interference. Directing his comments to Americans, Peng dismissed the American's fear that the Communists would affiliate with the Russians. "The position of the Chinese Communists," said Peng, "remains still for a free, independent and democratic China."[15]

These friendly gestures toward the Americans mounted in anticipation of General Marshall's arrival. Every effort was made to impress Marshall with the readiness of the Communists to negotiate.

The Kuomintang leaders put forth an equal effort. On his arrival in Chungking Marshall was met at the airport by the Generalissimo and then elaborately entertained.

The Communist gestures brought no response from the United States. Instead, American interest focused on evidence of the strengthening of the Nationalist position and on the apparent parallel support of the Chungking government by both the Soviet Union and the United States. Nationalist troops were now well on their way into Manchuria and were about to occupy such major centers as Mukden and Harbin. On December 14 a *New York Times* editorial hailed the rapid progress Chiang Kai-shek was making, welcomed the cooperation of the Russians, and strongly defended the aid extended to the Chinese government.[16] That editorial scarcely accorded with the reports of its able correspondent, Tillman Durdin, who was exceedingly cautious in his observations and who held out little hope for the success of Marshall's mission.

The absence of response to Communist gestures, while to be explained in part as stemming from the traditional distrust of radicalism, owed even more to uncertainty as to the Soviet Union's intentions in Manchuria. In November the Soviets had refused to permit the landing of Chinese forces on board American transports in Dairen, informed the Chinese that they could land at Hulutao and Yingkow; but when American transports approached these two ports, Chinese Communists denied them liberty to land.[17] Communist forces moved into Manchuria without the Soviets opposing them, but Nationalists were barred from many areas. Toward the close of September an advance party of Nationalists entered the capital city of Changchun with Soviet approval, but on November 12 more than 2,000 Chinese Communist troops took over the city and General Hsiung Shih-hui withdrew.[18]

Yet the Soviet Union representatives in Manchuria did not openly range themselves against the establishment of Chinese Nationalist authority. During the first months of occupation the Russians took over one hundred and fifty locomotives, many railroad cars, and some factories and shipped them to Soviet territory.[19] The Russian officials justified the looting as nothing more than the taking of reparations, but in this case, unlike the Soviet zone in Germany, the action was taken at the expense of a friendly power. At the same time the Soviets gave promise of evacuating Manchuria in accordance with an announced schedule and did withdraw troops from the southern section.

Distrust of Soviet intentions was widespread. In late October the American Ambassador in London, John Winant, cabled that the British Foreign Office "believes it possible that Soviet policy is to build up Communist strength in Manchuria as check on Chungking and for use as lever in any difficulties which may arise over railways, bases and other matters considered in the treaty without giving Communists exclusive authority which would expose Soviets to charge of breaking the treaty and might also make Chinese Communists too independent of Soviet support."[20]

Edmund Clubb, American consul at Vladivostok and a frequent critic of the Kuomintang during his previous assignments in China, warned against anticipated sharp practices on the part of the Soviets. On December 6 Clubb gave the Secretary of State a gloomy analysis of developments. He termed the agreement reached by Marshal Malinovski, commander of Soviet forces in Manchuria, and General Hsiung, representing the Chinese Nationalists, "only superficially a Soviet move of cooperation." The agreement to postpone evacuating Soviet troops until the Chinese Nationalists were ready to occupy certain Manchurian cities, Clubb pointed out, would be of greater advantage to the Chinese Communists, who were in even greater need of time to prepare than were the Nationalists. He saw the agreement as part of a larger Soviet plan whereby Soviet "partisans" would rise up to help the Chinese Communists take over control and the Chinese Communists would, in turn, be dependent upon the Soviets. Clubb saw a parallel between Soviet actions in Manchuria and in Iran where they were preventing the estabished government from putting down a revolt in Azerbaijan.[21]

On his arrival in Moscow on December 15 Secretary of State James Byrnes hoped to give the Soviets a satisfactory explanation of American involvement in North China and to elicit from Molotov, Soviet

Minister of Foreign Affairs, assurance that his government would not stand in the way of Chinese control of Manchuria. Byrnes was quickly put on the defensive. When he explained that United States forces were present to prevent civil war and to facilitate the repatriation of the Japanese, Stalin responded that the Chinese Nationalists should long since have learned how to handle the Japs. The Soviet Union had made the Japanese prisoners of war, and they were now in Russia. Molotov chided Byrnes about the presence of American marines in China and proposed that they set a fixed date for the removal of all American and Soviet forces. Byrnes favored an agreement to withdraw but took the position that he could not fix a date because he did not know when the repatriation of the Japanese would be completed. Molotov and Byrnes did announce at the conclusion of the Big Three Ministers meeting that they agreed on "the need for a unified and democratic China under the National Government and for a cessation of civil strife."[22]

General Marshall spent his first days in China listening to Chiang Kai-shek, Madam Chiang, and representatives of the Communists and of the Democratic League. Chiang said little about the Chinese Communists but spoke bitterly of the Russian looting in Manchuria and charged the Chinese Communists with contriving to prevent establishment of Nationalist control. Marshall questioned him closely. The Russians, Marshall observed, had followed the same policy in Germany of removing property but, while he deplored this, he was less concerned about this than he was in the long-term aims of the Russians.[23] He plied the representatives of the Democratic League with questions on this same point and then cabled Washington for evidence on this question.[24] Marshall, however, refrained from expressing his views, protested that he was there to learn, and he proved himself a good listener. During these early meetings no one received even a clue as to his thinking.

Yet he spoke forthrightly when the occasion called for it. On December 20, Dean Acheson, Acting Secretary of State, cabled him that the communcations from the public "are practically unanimous in opposing U.S. participation in the Chinese civil war." Acheson informed him that the messages from C.I.O. labor unions constituted the largest group, but there were also appeals from A. F. of L. and Communist unions. He concluded with the statement, "Other communications are so varied and the geographical spread so great as to suggest that the protests represent a strong feeling among people who are acting, for the most part, spontaneously."[25]

Marshall promptly conveyed with emphasis to those Chinese with whom he was conferring that there "was extreme reluctance on the part of the people in the United States to take any action that could be interpreted as interference in the local affairs of any other country." He reported, "The feeling in this regard is intensely strong at this time and whatever the President may desire to do he is definitely affected by this public reaction." When he made this point to the Generalissimo and his wife, Madame Chiang burst forth, "You mean the American people favor a Communist victory?" Marshall said it only meant that the American people were determined not to take sides.[26] The question told much about Nationalist expectations.

Shortly after Marshall left for China, President Truman issued an order to all government departments and agencies who might be approached by China for assistance that they were not to engage in negotiations and informed them that any plans for assistance underway were subject to Marshall's approval. In a cable of December 24 Acheson spelled out in detail how this was to be implemented. He noted that China had ample credits abroad to finance imports necessary for the immediate future. In addition the Export-Import Bank would probably approve a loan for purchase of American cotton and transportation and telecommunications equipment. China, Acheson stated, would require greater credits for long-term reconstruction and industrial development.[27]

Before Marshall approved projects in this latter category, China should be required to give assurance of political improvements, to take a positive approach toward the negotiation of the proposed American trade treaty, to adopt a realistic exchange rate, take measures to stabilize her currency, and to take steps that would encourage American trade and investment.[28] These latter requirements reflected Assistant Secretary Will Clayton's economic foreign policy, a policy aimed at opening foreign markets to American goods, creating opportunities for the investment of American capital, and providing access to those materials needed by the American industrial machine.

At the moment, as Edwin A. Locke, Jr., the President's representative, had made clear, there was only a very remote prospect of any significant market in China.[29] The immediate problem was to avoid civil war in China. The problem in terms of the total world situation was to bring about rehabilitation in the devastated countries around the world. There was no need to worry about markets for American goods, for it was abundantly clear that world markets would absorb all and more than the United States could produce.[30]

On his arrival in China, Marshall concluded that only if hostilities could be terminated would there be a favorable opportunity to bring about a political agreement. With this in mind, he directed his staff to prepare two documents, the first a cease-fire order and the second a plan for the establishment of an organization which was to police the cease fire. Drafts of these were ready by January 1, and Marshall then discussed them in separate meetings with General Chou En-lai, who represented the Communists in Chungking, and with Governor Chang Chun, the representative of the National Government. On January 7 he began a series of meetings attended by both.

A major obstacle immediately emerged. Chang Chun insisted that the cease fire should not apply to Chihfeng in Jehol and Tolun in Chahar. Communists had moved into both cities, but Nationalist troops were now within striking distance. The two cities were railway centers and were of considerable strategic importance in relation to the future of Manchuria. Chang, on instructions from the Generalissimo, maintained that an agreement had been reached with the Soviets who had occupied the cities that the Nationalists were to take over upon Soviet withdrawal.[31] Any cease fire that would bar the carrying out of this agreement, Chang vehemently affirmed, would be wholly unacceptable. Chou En-lai said he had no knowledge of such an agreement and that his party could not possibly agree to the Nationalist demand. The present conflict, said Chou, was a direct product of the Nationalists denying the Communists the right to exercise control over areas they had liberated. If the Nationalists insisted on the right to seek to take the two cities by force, then, said Chou, they must bear the responsibility for continuing the conflict.[32] Only an appeal by Marshall to the Generalissimo removed this barrier to the issuing of a cease-fire order.[33]

On January 10 both sides, after long and tedious debate, reached agreement on the cessation of hostilities and the establishment of the

Executive Headquarters in Peking to implement it. Marshall had reason to be pleased. Both parties, except on the issue of Chihfeng and Tolun, had been cooperative.

The cease fire went into effect on January 13. It stipulated that hostilities were to cease, that communications were to be restored, and that all troop movements, with specific exceptions, were to halt. The Nationalists were to be free to move armed forces into Manchuria for the purpose of reestablishing Chinese sovereignty in accordance with the Sino-Soviet Treaty of the preceding August. They were likewise to be free to move troops south of the Yangtze River either to ports for transfer to Manchuria or for the purpose of the reorganization of the armed forces. In the course of the discussions the Communists freely concurred in the Nationalist contention that they were under obligation by treaty with the Soviets to take over sovereignty in Manchuria.

The second agreement, providing for the establishment of the Executive Headquarters in Peking, called for the naming of three commissioners, one representing each of the two major parties and one American. Colonel Henry A. Byroade was named chief executive. The agreement called for a staff of 465 men and the establishment of truce teams to investigate places where there was conflict or danger of conflict. Each of these truce teams would have one American and one representative of the Nationalists and one of the Communists. Their decisions required a unanimous vote. The three commissioners were Walter S. Robertson of the United States, General Chen Kai-min of the National Government, and General Yeh Chien-ying of the Communists. Executive Headquarters reported to the Committee of Three in Chungking, namely Marshall, Chou En-lai, and Chang Chun. The truce teams were soon off to a promising start, hostilities diminished sharply; but Manchuria, an area covered only in part by the cease-fire order, soon posed difficulties of a serious nature.

On February 9 the Committee of Three in Chungking reached another important agreement on a proposal for the protection and reconstruction of railways. One of the most serious barriers to economic recovery had been the destruction of railways by Communist forces. The unorthodox guerrilla tactics of the Communists focused on making it impossible to transport Nationalist troops and on preventing the shipment of materials from the interior to the industrial centers. Guerrillas made a particular point of attacking important mining centers and the railways leading from these to the cities. The Communists were strikingly successful and so crippled industry that there was widespread unemployment. Marshall was intent on restoring the economy and instructed Executive Headquarters to draft a plan.

The plan as approved provided for the establishment of a Railway Control Section at Executive Headquarters and for control teams of three to deal with questions of destruction and reconstruction of the railways. Military commanders were assigned responsibility of protecting the lines in areas under their control and of protecting crews working on repairs. The agreement specified that the commissioners at Executive Headquarters were to implement the plan so that no military advantage was to be gained by either side and that no movement of troops or armaments was to be allowed over reopened lines except as authorized by Executive Headquarters.[34]

January 10, the day of the agreement on the cessation of hostilities, also saw the first meeting of the Political Consultative Council. Marshall took no part in its deliberations but he did seek to influence the Generalissimo to accept liberal reforms. The Political Consultative Council included representatives of all parties. The Democratic League took the lead in advocating the establishment of a broadly based government, an executive directly responsible to a popularly elected legislature, and guarantees of civil rights. The Communist members of the Council supported these reforms. By the close of January the Council completed its work.

At the time the Council was meeting, Marshall pressured the Generalissimo to consider similar proposals. On January 22 he handed Chiang a copy of a proposed charter for an interim government that would carry on the functions of government until a new government could be established.[35] This representative body was also to be charged with appointing a commission to draft a new constitution. Marshall's proposal provided for guarantees of civil rights during the interim period and specified that during this interim period local governments should continue to be under the control of whatever party exercised power when the interim charter went into effect.

The C-C and Whampoa cliques in the Kuomintang strongly opposed the reforms. When the Nationalists made public a draft of a proposed constitution, the structure was designed to prevent popular control. The executive was granted full control over taxes and fiscal matters, the National Assembly was to meet only every three years and for one month only, and there was no guarantee of civil rights.[36] The determination of the Kuomintang to sidetrack the popular demand for liberal reforms was further confirmed by Chiang's announcement in mid-January that the National Assembly would meet on May 5. That body had been elected in 1936, and its makeup provided assurance that it would adhere to the old order.

Marshall, however, remained hopeful and on February 4 reported to President Truman that the Political Consultative Conference "did their job well and included enough of the details of the interim constitution I had most confidentially given the Generalissimo to provide a fairly definite basis for a democratic coalition government."[37] The Communists, too, were pleased. After a trip to Yenan for consultation with Mao, Chou En-lai conveyed Mao's deep appreciation to Marshall for his work in putting through the truce agreement. Both Mao and Chou, while stating that the recommendations of the Political Consultative Council did not meet all their wishes, welcomed the proposals as opening the door to democracy.[38] In the months ahead the Communists insisted on adherence to the Council's recommendations, while the Nationalists refused to accept them.

The efforts to promote political reform ran parallel to negotiations on a plan submitted by Marshall for military reorganization. The Nationalists and the Communists invited him to serve on a committee with Governor Chang Chun and Chou En-lai to study the problem. Marshall met with the two throughout a large part of January and February, and they completed their work on February 23. The plan presented by Marshall was based on the principle of separation of the military from politics and subordination of the army to civilian control. It specified a sharp reduction in the number of divisions, provided that Nationalist and Communist divisions should be integrated into armies at the close of twelve months and likewise called for the integration of staffs.

Even when good intentions prevailed, and the two Chinese members of the committee worked together in considerable harmony, the military reorganization problem posed great difficulties. How were armed forces that had been fighting each other for many years to be conditioned to a new point of view? Marshall was realistic and he believed it would only be possible over a long period and as older officers were replaced with younger men. There was also the difficulty growing out of the great differences in training, equipment, and political orientation of the two armed forces. Marshall proposed that it would be useful for the Americans to establish a training school for soldiers at Kalgan to provide a period of retraining for Communist soldiers. This school was to be equipped and staffed by the United States. Mao welcomed this proposal with great enthusiasm.

At the signing of the agreement on military reorganization, Governor Chang praised Marshall for his contributions. The agreement, said Chang, put an end to the long struggle between the Government and the Communists.[39] Chou praised Marshall and exuberantly declared that along with the resolutions of the Political Consultative Conference, the truce agreement, and now approved military reorganization, China had made "a big step toward the democratization of politics, the nationalization of the armies and the equality of the parties."[40]

On the surface it appeared that China was moving toward peace and unity. Indeed, more had been accomplished than could have been anticipated by a most optimistic observer, but these very achievements stiffened the determination of the reactionary cliques in the Kuomintang. Members of the American embassy staff recognized that dislodging the Kuomintang monopoly remained to be achieved. On February 7 Robert L. Smyth, Counselor of the Embassy, cabled the Secretary of State that the general optimism was tempered "by scepticism [sic] with regard to purposes of both sides faithfully to carry out agreements." Smyth reported that the minor disturbances that had taken place at some political rallies, and police interference with minor party delegates to the Political Consultative Conference indicated the "possibility that reactionary Kuomintang elements may get out of control as agreed measures to limit the power of the Kuomintang are put into effect." For the first time there were indications of resentment against American interference. Smyth observed, "Aside from disgruntled Rightist elements within the party, even some liberal Kuomintang members, although pleased by cessation of hostilities and basic agreement on major issues, are reported to believe that United States has forced government into agreement which may lead to eventual Communist domination of China."[41]

The more immediate barrier to progress was the difficulty encountered by Executive Headquarters in implementing the cease-fire order. Success in bringing hostilities to a halt depended upon the cooperation of local military commanders. Their inclination was to move with speed to achieve the best possible position before the truce went into effect at midnight on January13. Truce teams soon found themselves trying to determine exactly which forces had been where at midnight on the 13th. These moves led to minor military engagements during the opening days of the truce period. In some instances local commanders had not yet received word of the order until it had gone into effect, and during the first few days fifteen American planes dropped leaflets in the hope of getting the information to all concerned. Another difficulty stemmed from the reluctance of Chinese members of the truce teams to take action that was unfavorable to their own side. This soon led one or the other party representative to absent himself from an investigation.

The most serious threat to the establishment of peace arose in Chifeng in Jehol province. This strategic railway center, a point of sharp debate during the discussions preceding the issuance of the cease-fire order, had been under occupation by Soviet troops and local Communist militia. Contrary to the agreement, Nationalist Commander General Tu Li Ming, whose forces had been approaching the city, continued the advance. Chiang and the National Ministry of War supported him. They maintained that under the agreement entered into with the Soviets they were under obligation to occupy Chifeng when the Soviet troops withdrew.[42] Chou En-lai protested vigorously, and Executive Headquarters then sent a truce team to Chifeng to investigate. The truce team under Colonel R. R. Tourtillot immediately ran into difficulty with the Communist troop commander, who denied that he was subject to the orders of Executive Headquarters.[43] When the investigation revealed that a large part of the Communist forces in Chifeng had moved into the city after midnight on January 13, the truce team ordered their withdrawal, permitting only the local militia who had been there since the previous August to remain.[44] Orders were also issued to Tu Li Ming not to advance beyond his present position some twenty miles southeast of the city, and a similar order was given to the Communist 8th Army force ten miles southwest of the city.

An equally troublesome situation arose at Canton when the Nationalist commander, General Chang Fa-kwei, launched campaigns against Communist forces under General Tsen Sheng. The Nationalist general ignored the cease-fire order, holding that it did not apply to bandits.[45] Only after weeks of pressure by General Marshall was the situation at Canton brought under control.

Within a month of January 13 the situation in Manchuria became the center of attention. The Nationalists showed great fear of the Soviets, who remained in Manchuria in considerable numbers. When Chinese authorities questioned Russian officials, they were told that withdrawal could be hastened by further economic concession.[46] There were also reports, although unverified, that small groups of Russian soldiers fought alongside Chinese Communist forces against Nationalist troops. American officials, although suspicious of the Soviets, also believed that the right wing of the Kuomintang promoted fear of the Russians in the hope of discrediting reform measures.

Greater distrust was aroused by an announcement from Yenan on February 14 announcing that a force of 300,000, carrying the designation Manchurian Joint Democratic Army had been organized. The existence of this large force in Manchuria, where there had been almost none at the time of the Japanese surrender gave rise to new fear among Nationalists of collusion between the Soviets and Chinese Communists. Robertson, American Chargé in Chungking, did not share this alarm. He found reason to believe "that the present obscure Manchurian situation, coupled with the Communist release, had been made use of by disgruntled rightist elements of the Kuomintang, opposed to full implementation of the resolutions adopted by the People's Consultative Conference . . . and to drastic military reorganization, to inject into the scene a national security issue in order to divert attention from the urgent necessity for immediate internal reforms." Robertson informed Secretary Byrnes that Chou En-lai and other Communists in Chungking appeared genuinely anxious that the Russians withdraw.[47]

The American Chargé did not at this time explain in full the more deep-rooted cause of the Manchurian crisis. What had provoked the crisis was Communist determination to prevent the Kuomintang from gaining monopoly control over Manchuria. Therefore, they were doing everything possible to gain control of as many places as possible. Chou repeatedly emphasized that while his party would not interfere with the Central Government's conduct of foreign affairs and was quite willing to leave negotiations with the Russians concerning Manchuria to the Nationalists, it was wholly free to establish its own local governments in Manchuria. The Nationalists had interpreted their acknowledged right to move troops into Manchuria as the right to establish full Kuomintang control.

During these early months, relations between Communist leaders and the members of the Marshall mission were generally cordial. The cordiality arose out of the fact that the Marshall mission and the Communists were in agreement on the immediate goals. President Truman, in his announcement of December 15, committed the United States to opposing one-party government in China. Marshall was having almost spectacular success in Chungking in bringing this about, and the Communists had as their first aim the breakdown of the Kuomintang political monopoly. In a message to Byrnes on February 28 Robertson closed by noting, "in fairness to the Communists it must be pointed out that during the past few months their willingness to cooperate with all parties and groups and their evident trust in American efforts to advise and assist in the solution of Chinese administrative and military problems leaves little to be desired."[48]

The continued tensions in Manchuria caused the Committee of Three to undertake inspection tours throughout northern China. They arrived in Peking on February 28 and received detailed reports summarizing the experiences of the field teams. These reports made clear that there were commanders on both sides who were not cooperating, that railway reconstruction was still remote, and that in Shantung and in some places in Manchuria the Communist forces continued to lay siege to cities in possession of the Nationalists and to prevent the sending in of desperately needed food supplies.[49] The Committee of Three then visited a number of cities and conferred with field teams. The three members, Marshall, Chang, and Chou, discussed the complications and more especially the difficulties that arose when a representative of one party on the team took a partisan view and refused to cooperate. At the close of the 3,000-mile trip Marshall explained to President Truman that he believed the Committee had been successful in helping the members of the truce teams to see the larger issues and that he was confident that the committee would now be free to give its attention to demobilization and reorganization of the armed forces.[50]

Marshall, though never given to jubilance, was clearly confident that a great start had been made. Hostilities had been sharply reduced, a plan for the reorganization of the armed forces had been agreed upon, and the Political Consultative Council had acted in a responsible and reasonable spirit in making recommendations for a new government. Consequently, Marshall prepared to make a trip to the United States for the purpose of securing economic assistance that would bring some measure of relief to the people of China. He had already given consideration to removing the American marines from China, and President Truman had responded that he was anxious to bring this about.[51] The unprecedented mission whereby a major power was to mediate a civil conflict in a second major country appeared to be headed for success.

Notes to Chapter X

1.   *Congressional Record,* 79th Congress, 1st Session, pp. 2294–2302.

2.   Ibid., Appendix, p. 10863

3.   Ibid., pp. A5071–72.

4.   Ibid., p. 9629

5.   Ibid., p. A5348

6.   China Theater Policy Book P10. Memo by Marshall of meeting with President Truman, Admiral Leahy, and Secretary of State James Byrnes, December 11, 1945. Contemporary Military Records, National Archives.

7.   Ibid.

8.   Notes on Conference of Three (Meeting No. 2)—General Marshall, Governor Chang Chun, Central Government Representative, and General Chou En-lai, Communist Party Representative—at General Marshall's Residence, Chungking, January 8, 1946, 10 A.M. *Foreign Relations of the United States,* Vol. IX, *The Far East:* China, p. 62. Hereafter in this chapter this volume will be cited simply as *U.S.F.R.,* Vol. IX, and minutes of meetings of the Committee of Three will be so cited without including names of the participants.

9.   Major General Clayton Bissell to General Marshall, December 19, 1945. Subject: Situation in China, G-2 Intelligence Report, File OPD 350.05, Contemporary Military Records, National Archives.

10.   Meeting of Military Sub-Committee, March 9, 1946. *USFR,* Vol. IX pp. 517–18.

11.   Emmett D. Hightower to Admiral Barbey, Barbey Papers, China File, Office of Naval History, Navy Yard, Washington, D.C.

12.   Bissell to Marshall, December 19, 1945, G-2 Intelligence Report, File OPD 350.05, Contemporary Military Records, National Archives.

13.   "Manchurian Exit Put Off to Jan. 3," *New York Times,* December 2, 1945, p. 35.

14.   Tillman Durdin, "Chinese Reds Deny Aim of Rival Rule," *New York Times,* December 5, 1945, p. 5.

15.   "Reds for 'Free China'," *New York Times,* December 11, 1945, p. 4.

16.   "Progress in China," ed. *New York Times,* December 14, 1945, p. 26.

17. Walter S. Robertson, Chargé to the Secretary of State, November 16, 1945. *USFR China 1945*, pp. 1040–42.

18. Robertson to Secretary of State, November 16, 1945. *USFR China 1945*, pp. 1040–42.

19. Edwin W. Pauley to Secretary of State, December 11, 1945, ibid., p. 1050.

20. John Winant, U.S. Ambassador in London, to the Secretary of State, October 31, 1945. *USFR China 1945*, pp. 1036–37.

21. Clubb to the Secretary of State, December 6, 1945. *USFR China 1945*, pp. 1048–50.

22. The Acting Secretary of State to General Marshall, December 29, 1945, *USFR 1945*, Vol. VII, p. 824. f.n. 65.

23. Marshall to the Secretary of State, December 26, 1945. *USFR China 1945*, p. 813.

24. Notes on General Marshall's first conference with the Democratic League, December 26, 1945. *USFR*, 1945, Vol. VII, pp. 816–24.

25. Dean Acheson to Robertson, December 20, 1945. *USFR China 1945*, p. 786.

26. Minutes of Meeting Held at Nanking, China, December 21, 1945, attended by Chiang, Madame Chiang, Marshall, Wang Shih-chieh, Robertson, and Wedemeyer. *USFR China 1945*, p. 794–800.

27. Dean Acheson to Robertson, December 24, 1945. *USFR China 1945*, pp. 1194–97.

28. Ibid.

29. Edwin A. Locke, to President Harry Truman, December 18, 1945. China Theater Policy Book (P &O), Contemporary Military Records, National Archives.

30. The semiannual reports of the Export-Import Bank show that at the close of the war and for at least a year thereafter officers of that institution were not worried about markets for American goods. The third Semi-Annual Report of January 1, 1947, noted that operations throughout 1946 were carried out "under conditions of heavy demand for United States exports limited only by the ability of the United States to supply and the ability of foreign countries to pay." The major concern was political, namely rehabilitation of the countries that had suffered devastation during the war so as to bring about stability in world affairs.

31. Meeting of Committee of Three, January 10, 1946. *USFR*, Vol. IX, p. 102.

32. Ibid., p. 103.

33. Meeting of Committee of Three, January 9, 1946. *USFR*, Vol. IX, p. 104.

34. Agreement on Restoration of Communications, February 9, 1946, *USFR*, Vol. IX, pp. 422–23.

35. Charter for the Interim Government of the Republic of China. *USFR*, Vol. IX, pp. 139–41.

36. Memorandum by the Second Secretary of Embassy in China (Sprouse) Subject: The May 5th Draft Constitution. *USFR*, Vol. IX, pp. 137–38.

37. Marshall to President Truman, February 4, 1946. *USFR*, Vol. IX, pp. 206–207.

38. Marshall to President Truman, January 31, 1946. *USFR*, Vol. IX, pp. 148–51.

39. Meeting of Committee of Three, February 25, 1946. *USFR*, Vol. IX, p. 293.

40. Ibid., p. 295.

41. Smyth to the Secretary of State, February 7, 1946. *USFR*, Vol. IX, pp. 152–53.

42. Robertson to Marshall, January 25, 1946. *USFR*, Vol. IX, pp. 380–81.

43. Ibid., p. 382.

44. Ibid., p. 389.

45. Chou En-lai to Marshall, February 8, 1946. *USFR*, Vol. IX, pp. 396–97.

46. Marshall to President Truman, February 9, 1946. *USFR*, Vol. IX, pp. 426–29.

47. Robertson to the Secretary of State, February 28, 1946. *USFR*, Vol. IX, pp. 448–50.

48. Ibid.

49. *Briefing of Committee of Three and Commissioners,* Thursday, February 28, 1946. *USFR*, Vol. IX, pp. 453–62.

50. Marshall to President Truman, March 6, 1946. *USFR*, Vol. IX, pp. 510–11.

51. Ibid., February 9, 1946. *USFR*, Vol. IX, pp. 426–29.

CHAPTER XI

The Final Breakdown

General Marshall received warm applause from the people in each city on his trip throughout the north during the last days of February and early March 1946. At Yenan there was the same warm reception as there had been in Peking. In many instances crowds greeted the truce teams with enthusiasm and the authorities of whichever of the two parties in control of the city or town arranged social functions in their honor.

Not all difficulties had been overcome. There were instances where team representatives met with hostility and a lack of cooperation, but the prevailing tone during the first two months of Marshall's mission was one of the public welcoming the restoration of peace. A news release by Executive Headquarters on February 1, 1946, ebulliently reported, "There is a feeling of genuine optimism prevailing among the personnel of all three branches of Executive Headquarters." The "sincere determination of leaders and senior commanders of both forces to keep the peace" received commendation. "There is no longer any doubt," the spokesman said, "that both parties want peace and will do everything in their power to attain it."[1]

Before Marshall left on March 12 for a brief visit in the United States, he wrote of the situation in Manchuria, described it as festering and expressed regret that the Generalissimo had opposed the dispatch of truce teams.[2] Manchuria was the striking exception to the greatly improved situation.

That area, so important strategically and in terms of mineral resources and industry, fell in a separate category in the arrangements for the cease fire of January 13. The National Government was free to move troops into Manchuria to establish Chinese sovereignty as the Russians withdrew. The exception rested upon the Sino-Soviet Treaty of August 1945 which specified that the legal government of China was to be sovereign in Manchuria. Prior to December the United States avoided transporting Chinese Nationalist troops to Manchuria out of recognition that this was in the Soviet theater, but at the time Marshall was appointed the decision was reversed and the American Navy and Air Force were ordered to assist in the transport of Chinese government troops to Manchuria.

The Chinese Communists gave their assent to the government's movement of troops into the area but with the understanding that the additional government forces would be there only to establish Chinese sovereignty. Their approval did not forfeit their right to extend their own program of people's liberation into Manchuria. In fact, they did so with success. While National troops took over major cities, Communist armies moved through the countryside, installed new local governments overnight, conducted people's courts where the former leaders of the community were subjected to kangaroo trials while, at the time of the irregular proceedings, other groups ransacked their homes.[3] The victorious local Communists, encouraged by their successes, did not halt their activities after the cease-fire orders. They saw their liberation campaign as an effort to rescue downtrodden peasants from the imposition of reactionary rulers. The literally millions of refugees from the upper classes who sought to escape the vindictive hands of the revolutionaries were merely part of the price to be paid.

The Nationalists, in turn, were no less intent on preventing a Communist take-over of local governments. They were quite as determined to block the Communists as they were to have the Russians relinquish control. They showed no willingness to allow the Communists any voice in the local government, undoubtedly recognizing that they could not match the political and propaganda techniques of the Communists. Before Marshall's return to China in April the conflict in Manchuria reached serious proportions. Marshall was more critical of the Nationalists' policy on Manchuria than he was on any other one aspect of their policy.

In presenting the Communist case on Manchuria, Chou En-lai displayed remarkable talent as a diplomat. His willingness to allow that the Nationalists should rightfully assume sovereignty as the Soviets withdrew was no more than a recognition of a *fait accompli,* but it had the tone of sweet reasonableness and avoided an immediate confrontation with the mediator he was so anxious to win to his side.

Chou argued most persuasively that it meant no more than that the National government was symbolically taking over in behalf of the Chinese people. It did not mean that the Kuomintang Party was accorded the right to control the local government. Who was to govern in Manchuria, Chou argued, was wholly a domestic problem. Who was to take over from the Russians was a question in the realm of external affairs, and the Communists never questioned the propriety of the National Government acting in relation to foreign powers. In a memorandum delivered to Marshall on March 10 Chou stated:

> It means that we have conceded to an overwhelming military supremacy on part of the government in Manchuria, and laid no claim over the maintenance of a strong regular Communist force there which would have appeared rather well grounded, seeing that right now we are maintaining a huge force in that part of China, instead, we demand only for political democracy, the application of the PCC decisions to the Northeast, the reorganization of the Northeastern Political Council and the various provincial governments, and the implementation of the provisions of the Joint Platform with respect to local government.[4]

Chou went on to maintain that the opposition of the Nationalists to this contention was simply a part of the larger effort of the reactionaries to retain monopoly control, that their real object in Manchuria was to put down the forces of democracy and to set aside the decisions of the PCC. Chou then told how he had informed American correspondents that the Communists were anxious for the Russians to withdraw.[5] When they did, Chou's party was more than ready to establish governments throughout Manchuria. But, Chou explained, "we don't like to announce this publicly lest we might be giving others the wrong impression as if we want to monopolize the whole Northeast."[6]

In a meeting with Marshall on the following day, March 11, Chou spoke in irenic tones again of the importance of replacing the military government in Manchuria with civilian administration. To this Chou added, "General Marshall has repeatedly said that U.S. hopes for China's peace and stability which will make possible for the American loan to and investment in China. Then it will benefit both China and America. We are in favor of cooperation between China and America."[7]

Within a few days of this conciliatory presentation the Communists protested vigorously against the Nationalists moving more than five armies into Manchuria. Chou argued that it was clearly understood at the time the truce was negotiated that only five armies were to be admitted. His protest was overruled on the ground that the agreement had not placed a limit. It was acknowledged that the Nationalists had violated the cease-fire agreement in failing to inform Executive Headquarters of the number moved. The Nationalists countered the Communist charges with allegations that the Russians were delaying evacuation of some key cities until the Communists were in a position to move in. American foreign service officers shared in the Nationalists' concern. Russian removal of property from Manchuria suggested that they did not plan to take over Manchuria, but on the other hand they were blocking the Nationalists while at the same time they placed no obstacles in the way of the Communists.[8]

In response to the extensive fighting taking place, on March 27 the Committee of Three agreed to send field teams into Manchuria, and on March 30 four teams arrived in Mukden. This action bore no results. Members of the teams often refused to reach a decision except when the commanding officer of armed forces on their side gave consent to the decision. In the words of an American officer at Executive Headquarters truce team members were left standing by helplessly as observers.[9]

In mid-April the Soviet authorities announced that their forces would complete their withdrawal by April 30. The announcement let loose a chain of military actions. The Communists, with 30,000 troops, attacked Changchun, the capital of Manchuria, and on April 18 entered the city. The Nationalists, according to reports, suffered 7,000 casualties. Another large-scale battle took place near Sze-ping-kai, and still another thirty miles southeast of Mukden. On May 3 the

Nationalists captured Pen-hsi-hu, an important city in one of the best coal-mining areas. On May 6 the Communists captured Tsitsihar and Nung-chiang.

These hostilities spread into North China. Violent clashes took place in Hupei, Honan, Kiangsu, and Anhwei. In late April Chou charged that Nationalist forces, nine armies strong, in Honan were redeployed for an assault on a Communist army of 60,000. The Nationalists, said Chou, permitted no UNRRA food supplies to enter the Communist area. There were 1,200 aged, young, sick or wounded who could not be cared for, but the Nationalists would not allow their being evacuated.[10] General Marshall, who had returned to China on April 17, immediately made arrangements for Chou and General Byroade, of Executive Headquarters, to meet with the field team in Hankow. At the session in Hankow, Chou again presented his allegations. General Hsu, commander of Nationalist forces in the area, maintained that there was no plan to attack the Communists and that great efforts had been made to supply food.[11] The American representative accepted Hsu's detailed statement and left the meeting believing that Chou had greatly exaggerated the situation and had done so for reasons unrelated to any danger of an attack.

The following day the field team, Chou, and a representative made the trip to Hsuan Hwa Tian, where they met with Communist officials. Two Communist generals reported in detail on the recent movements of Nationalist military units. They asked that orders be issued and carried out permitting the Communist forces to move to another area where they would not be encircled.[12] The testimony revealed that there was no plot to annihilate the Communist troops, that the Communist forces were subject to understandable fear of being attacked, that the Nationalist commanders entertained equally understandable suspicion that the Communists were planning to move contrary to the cease-fire order, and that the real purpose of the exaggerated Communist charges was to promote an arrangement that would permit them to move so as to escape their present encirclement.[13]

The efforts of the truce team to restore peace and reduce tensions proved futile. Government troops did not launch any offensive in the area, and the government did make efforts to supply food. The Communists, rendered ineffective by the encirclement, however, continued to threaten escape and made the position of the truce team in Hsuan Hwa Tian so untenable it found it necessary to move.

The incident told much about the difficulties of maintaining peace. Marshall saw in such circumstances evidence of fear and distrust on both sides, creating tinderbox situations in which each party acted irrationally. The leaders of each party saw the struggle in terms of survival and sought to turn each situation, including the presence of the Marshall mission, to its own advantage.

While these developments took place in North China, practically full-scale war broke out in Manchuria. The Nationalists delayed approval of sending truce teams in the hope of capturing Changchun prior to their arrival.[14] The Communists, no less intent on gaining control, added greatly to their forces there notwithstanding the truce agreement. As early as late March the Communists protested vigorously against American transport of more National armies into Manchuria, but Lt. General Alvan C. Gillem, Jr., who took Marshall's place on the Committee of Three during his trip to the United States, overruled the Communists. Chou immediately protested, arguing strongly that he had been assured that no more than five Nationalist armies would enter Manchuria. Chou warned, "In case the U.S. Forces Headquarters shall continue to move Government troops into Manchuria, we would deem such action as a change of the U.S. policy toward China, and lack of faith on the part of the Government to implement a real truce in Manchuria."[15] These strong words expressed a deeply held conviction, and the American decision to continue the transport of Nationalist armies marked the first breach between the Marshall mission and the Communists. Gillem, who had said he would placate Chou with references to the basic agreement, responded to Chou's charges with peremptory language and without dealing with either the real issue or the question as to what agreement had been reached. Gillem's hostile retort was dictated by his conviction that the Communists had violated the original cease fire by introducing large forces into Manchuria.[16]

The arrival of the four truce teams in Mukden occasioned another unhappy incident. Communist members were held in custody for four hours and released only after a protest by General Byroade.[17] Further difficulty arose when General Yao, head of the Communists on the truce team, affirmed that the January 13 cease-fire order did not apply to Manchuria and that any movement of government forces must first be approved by a mutual agreement.[18] At the same time Chou in Chungking, informed of Marshall's effort in Washington to gain approval of a loan to the National Government, demanded that no loan be granted until the government had carried out in good faith the recommendations of the PCC. Marshall indicated concern and did not lightly dismiss Chou's protest but he believed that to refuse a loan "would be cutting the ground from under the Gimo who is having a struggle with the recalcitrant members of the Central Government."[19]

The role of mediator became almost infinitely difficult as the tensions mounted in March and April. During the last week of March and the first week of April the Nationalist commissioner was absent from Executive Headquarters and during the second week the Communist commissioner was likewise absent.[20] As a result, the Executive Headquarters was paralyzed at a critical time. Gillem reviewed the entire situation in a lengthy cable to Marshall on April 8, citing the lack of good faith on the part of the Nationalists, the firm opposition of the Kuomintang conservatives to the PCC recommendations, the lack of cooperation on the part of the Nationalist military regarding the troublesome situations at Canton and near Hankow. These, in turn, had "caused burning resentment on the part of General Chou who is accused by his party for failure to resolve Central and South China military problems while at same time making concessions to National Government in North China."[21]

The Manchurian question drove a wedge between the United States and Yenan. The Nationalists benefited in their bid for control by American transport of their troops. Chou, recalcitrant on this point, compared what was taking place to the assistance Hurley and Wedemeyer had provided the Nationalists. Except for that assistance the Communists would have taken control of the major cities in North China. "If now the Kuomintang government should attempt to reproduce that page of the history in Manchuria, then," said Chou, "I wish to state categorically, that that would never be approved by us."[22] That Chou had cause to protest appears clear today, but it did not so appear to the Americans at Executive Headquarters. They were convinced that the Communists violated the agreement of January 13. They were equally firm in their belief that there was collusion between the Communists and the Russians in Manchuria.

Neither the Communists nor the Nationalists constituted a monolithic bloc. The conservatives held the upper hand in the Central Executive Committee of the Kuomintang, but many members were outspoken in their criticism of party strategy. The same was true of the Communists in Manchuria. Edmund O. Clubb, who had been transferred to Mukden as Consul-General, named three factions. There were the Nationalistic group represented by Lin Piao and Peng Chen, the original Manchurian group who followed the Communists for convenience sake and who stood for Manchurian autonomy, and the New Fourth Army group closely allied to the Soviets. This division might have led to serious consequences, but the uncompromising attitude of Chiang, who dismissed all of them as illegal elements who must give way, provided a cohesive force. Clubb noted that Chiang's position gave the Communists little choice but to fight.[23]

It was against this background that the Communists captured the capital city of Manchuria on April 18. The momentous Communist victory led Marshall to lecture the Nationalist general, Yu Ta-wei, in bold language. The present situation, said Marshall, could have been avoided by the government. For weeks he had urged the sending of truce teams to Manchuria only to be blocked by the Generalissimo. "I do not know who the Generalissimo's advisors are," said Marshall, "but they are very poor ones." The Nationalists had consistently set up barriers and acted in ways that provided the Communists with excuses for doing what they had done. In conclusion Marshall stated that "no one has offered any alternative except a great war and you cannot support a great war." Marshall warned, "It [the war] is not going to be supported by Americans or the Seventh Fleet or Executive Headquarters."[24]

In a conference with Chou on April 23 Marshall asked for his views. Chou explained that at the outset of their negotiations he had not anticipated anything like the situation that exists today. "With the Russian withdrawal," said Chou, "it has become a race between the National and Communist troops to occupy the vacuum." He complained to Marshall of his own difficult situation. He and his party wanted a cease fire in Manchuria, but Chiang was insisting that he would only agree to this if the Communists turned over Changchun to the Nationalists while Yenan was now insisting on changes in the military reorganization plan allotting them a greater percentage of forces in Manchuria.[25]

Marshall withdrew from the negotiations on Manchuria early in May because his own proposal had been rejected by both sides and he did not wish to become involved in a stalemate. At this time Marshall took two positions worthy of note. Chou pressed vigorously to have the United States stop the transport of armies and supplies to Manchuria, but Marshall indicated he was not ready to recommend this step to Washington. He did refuse a request from the Nationalists to transport two more armies; on the other hand, when he called President Truman's attention to Chou's protest, he said he thought it would be unfair to cut off supplies to the greatly outnumbered Nationalist troops isolated in Manchuria.[26] At the same time he also strongly advised Chiang that it was most unwise to try to take northern Manchuria, that he must face the reality of Communist strength, and that he should concentrate his efforts on southern Manchuria. The experienced wartime strategist saw realities and urged the necessity of compromise. Marshall, critical of the Nationalists for their past errors, was likewise critical of the Communists for their complete lack of cooperation on the field teams in Manchuria.

A close and friendly relationship developed between Marshall and Chou. Both earnestly deplored the prospect of full-scale war. Each shared with the other, in a manner that betokened mutual confidence, the difficulties each faced in his particular role. Marshall spoke of the intransigence of the recalcitrants in the Kuomintang, how he would lose all credibility if he assumed the role of negotiator on the Manchurian question and then found himself facing a stalemate, and how the Nationalist leaders believed that he had given them poor advice and were now unresponsive to his recommendations. Chou continued to criticize the leaders of the Kuomintang for taking a course that was absolutely uncompromising, but he also made clear his own difficulties as a result of victorious Communist generals in Manchuria, who had now gained great influence in Yenan. Marshall and Chou—able, honest, and firm advocates of peace—found themselves facing the predicament of being buffetted by forces beyond their control.

By late May the Communists were on the verge of victory in

Manchuria. Their success caused them to nullify the efforts of Executive Headquarters to enforce the peace. Communist members of truce teams absented themselves and thereby rendered the teams inactive. On May 21, Walter Robertson at Executive Headquarters informed Marshall that the Communists in Jehol were trying to move across the supply line of the Government forces. Robertson noted that the move "would make their vicotry in Manchuria virtually complete."[27]

Marshall, although he had nominally withdrawn from negotiations on Manchuria, was in daily communication on this subject with Chou En-lai and Chiang Kai-shek. By May 22 both sides indicated a readiness to make concessions. Fearful that the Nationalist generals were about to undertake a campaign against Changchun, Chiang flew to Mukden on May 23 with the aim of dissuading them. Marshall urged haste on the ground that, in the course of a delay, developments would overtake efforts to restore peace and release forces that could no longer be controlled.[28] At this point Chou assured Marshall that his earlier proposals regarding Manchuria were acceptable. The day of the Generalissimo's arrival in Mukden Nationalist forces captured Changchun. Rather than issue a cease-fire order as he had indicated he would, he laid down a series of conditions the Communists must meet preceding a ceasefire.[29] He also peremptorily informed Marshall that he must guarantee that the Communists would abide by the agreements.[30] In spite of the crisis, a full week after his departure from Nanking, Chiang remained in Mukden. Marshall reacted with vigor, warning him:

> The continued advances of the Government troops in Manchuria in the absence of any action by you to terminate the fighting other than the terms you dictated via Madame Chiang's letter of May 24, are making my services as a possible mediator extremely difficult and may soon make them virtually impossible.[31]

Two days later, on May 31, Chiang was still in Mukden. Marshall repeated his message. Chiang did not return to Nanking until June 3. Chou charged that Chiang had postponed negotiations so that Nationalist forces could take Harbin.

On his return to Nanking the Generalissimo agreed to an immediate cease fire, to establish a branch of Executive Headquarters in Changchun, and to a fifteen-day truce. He made it clear that this would be his last effort to reach an agreement.[32] The continuation of half-war and half-peace, with the Communists destroying communications, was creating economic disaster and there was starvation in the cities.[33] War, said Chiang, was preferable to the present situation. The Communists accepted the fifteen-day truce, and it went into effect on June 7.

If the truce were to be the open door to peace, a whole series of agreements on both political and military matters would have to be reached in the limited time span. The questions of local government in Manchuria, of restoration of communications, and of demobilization and deployment of troops would have to be resolved. The complexity of each of these questions and the ambitions of many within both camps did not bode well. The leader of the C-C Clique, Chen Li-fu, who had at one time worked in the coal mines of Pennsylvania, told a member of the American Embassy he had left the mines because of Communist connivance and determined to return to China, where he had been fighting them for eighteen years. Chen said he was ready to fight them for another eighteen years.[34] In spite of the truce, local conflicts continued with each side protesting they were fighting in self-defense.

As the days of the truce passed, Marshall sought to negotiate agreements but he encountered only captious rebuttals and inflexible demands from the Nationalists. Chiang's terms were closer to demanding a Communist surrender than they were proposals looking toward accommodation. Between the hard line of Chiang and the realities of Nationalist power existed a chasm. The Nationalist demands exceeded their bargaining power. The Generalissimo called on the Communists to evacuate Chahar and Jehol and demanded that they withdraw from Chefoo and Wei Hei Wei. In a cable to President Truman, Marshall stated "that there was no chance, in my opinion, of the Communists accepting his [Chiang's] terms without considerable moderation." Marshall informed the President that the government officials were publicly calling for a policy of force.[35] He bluntly told two Nationalist generals that their plan would place the Communist troops under control of the government.[36]

At the time of this particular crisis the Communists exhibited a new distrust of American policy. In a six-hour interview on June 3 Chou questioned Marshall about the transport of additional Nationalist troops to Manchuria and stated that the United States appeared to be pursuing a double policy. The fact that Marshall provided a plane for the Generalissimo's trip to Mukden and then the Gimo appeared to be prolonging his stay for the purpose of delaying a truce until the Nationalist armies carried out new offensives gave rise to additional mistrust. And to add to Marshall's difficulties, new aid to China bills were being introduced in Congress. In his message to the President on June 26 Marshall stated that these moves were causing difficulty and embarrassment. "The Communists," he explained, "profess to regard measures and official statements in Washington as proving their contention that American economic and military support to the Kuomintang Government will continue to be given irrespective of whether the government offers the Communists a fair and reasonable basis for settlement of military and political differences." Marshall thought "it was a fact" that some die-hard Kuomintang elements "are utilizing recent American measures as a basis for pressing the Generalissimo to push forward with a campaign of determination against the Communists."[37] He also noted that while he did not wish to so inform Chou for fear of giving way to pressure, the United States was no longer transporting troops to Manchuria; this was now being done by the Chinese.

After fifteen days, when the truce was due to expire, it was agreed to extend it for eight days. In a meeting with Marshall on June 27 the Generalissimo was adamant in his demands that the Communists evacuate specific areas under their control and that government troops occupy the areas. Marshall told the Gimo he was presenting stiff terms. The Communists, said Marshall, believed that acceptance would place their lives and their party in jeopardy. In a meeting Marshall stated that the mass demonstrations and riots sponsored by the Nationalists indicated a deliberate effort to interrupt the negotiations. He further stated that he would not conduct negotiations under such circumstances.[38]

The Gimo now demanded that the Communists leave the province of Kiangsu and that government troops occupy it.[39] This was the point most objectionable to the Communists. But they, too, by aggressive actions in Shansi and Shantung were contributing to the impasse in negotiations. Marshall called this to the attention of Chou.

The central issue continued to be the control of local government in North China and Manchuria. Marshall found himself trapped in a debate on the question of sovereignty. Chiang made a new truce dependent upon Communist withdrawal of armed forces from large areas. Chou, in turn, made these withdrawals conditional upon Chiang's agreeing not to establish garrison forces in the areas evacuated.

Chou argued that the agreed-upon long-term aim of army reorganization was the subordination of the military to the civilian branch of the new government. Therefore, the Nationalists should not insist on establishing army garrisons in all areas. It was the aim of the Nationalists, said Chou, in their proposal for the distribution of troops to have Communist forces withdrawn into isolated areas, then station garrison troops in the areas then controlled by Communists and these forces would then overthrow the local Communist governments. To accept the government proposal, Chou maintained, "would deprive China of its prospect of democracy, because under such conditions there would be no democracy in China."[40]

Marshall was not ready to accept Chou's argument. He believed that both sides had engaged in military offensives for the purpose of establishing political control. He also believed that the whole purpose of a cease fire was to bring a halt to these military offensives and thereby diminish the sense of insecurity of both parties. Once this had been accomplished then progress could be made toward a political solution.[41]

Chou objected. He contended that the government was determined to gain every possible advantage by stationing troops in areas where Communists had established local democratic governments so as to hold the military balance and then when the time came to affect a political reorganization the government would use its military advantage to gain the political settlement it desired.

Chou held tenaciously to his position. This issue, he contended, was the crux of the whole argument. His statement to Marshall made clear what was at stake:

> The actual situation is that the Communists are protecting the rights and social gains of the peasants in particular. As soon as Government

troops enter those areas, those benefits will be withdrawn and the peasants put under immense exploitation and sufferings.[42]

Chou cited as an example what had taken place in Tingyuan after the government troops occupied it. Any concession that sacrificed the peasants would, he said, constitute a failure of the Communist Party.

The following day Marshall communicated Chou's argument to Chiang Kai-shek. The Gimo, in turn, asked Marshall to convey to Chou "that he knew of no instance where the inhabitants of a region occupied by the National government had fled to a region under the control of the Communists; that on the contrary over 5 million people had fled from Communist controlled areas principally to the large cities under National control. . . ."[43]

Marshall was never able, of course, to reconcile these fundamentally different views on social and economic problems and these, in turn, were closely intertwined with the struggle for power of the two very diverse groups.

During the preceding months Marshall had recommended the appointment of Wedemeyer as ambassador, but he finally advised against this appointment on the ground that Wedemeyer was a highly controversial figure. He then recommended Leighton Stuart, who was named ambassador on July 5, 1946. Dr. Stuart had fifty years' experience in China as an educator and enjoyed the confidence of both sides. Like Marshall, Stuart hoped to bring about peace; he and Marshall worked closely together, but Marshall continued in the role of chief negotiator.

The discord between Marshall and the Nationalists continued throughout the summer. He became convinced that the controlling group in the government was scuttling the negotiations and intent on war.[44] His distrust was strengthened in July when the Gimo refused to permit truce teams to enter the Hankow area, where it was clear hostilities were about to take place.[45] Marshall told General Yu Ta-wei that the only possible reason for the Generalissimo's stand was "to permit military action on the Nationalist side to proceed during the uncertain period of no negotiations." If such was the case, he warned Yu, "he feared he would be forced to withdraw from the negotiations."[46] Marshall was further discouraged when a series of assassinations of liberals took place in Kunming. To make matters worse at the height of the tensions, the Generalissimo took off for a vacation at Kuling, leaving Marshall with the conclusion that Chiang was content to let the current developments follow their course to all-out war.

The Communists also added to Marshall's troubles. Beginning in June, Yenan launched a strong anti-American propaganda effort, holding the United States responsible for the civil war and questioning Marshall's integrity. The public relations officer in Yenan skillfully appealed to antiforeign feelings. Whatever Yenan's intent, it appeared that the aim was to discredit the Kuomintang further by identifying it with a foreign power. Marshall protested to Chou but he found the attacks so devoid of substance that he deemed them unworthy of sober refutation. He did seek to remove Chou's apprehensions that the United States was pursuing a double policy of appearing to favor a policy of peace and democracy while at the same time conniving to assist the Kuomintang.

On July 29 came the Anping incident. An American marine patrol of fifty-five men enroute to Peking was ambushed by a Communist force of three hundred. Three Americans were killed and eleven were wounded. The Communists agreed to an investigation but then placed barriers in the way of the inquiry, at the same time charging that the incident took place only because the marines were accompanied by Nationalist troops. Later investigation showed that this was not true. The presence of the American marines had long been offensive not only to the Communists, but to the Chinese in general. The incident was in part a product of hostility promoted by the behavior of some American troops.

Chou and Marshall did not spare each other's feelings in their exchanges, but mutual respect prevailed. Both men spoke with great frankness. Chou exploited to the full every indication by the Nationalists of their determination to settle problems by force, while arguing persuasively that the Communists had worked for a peaceful solution. Marshall was equally persistent in pointing out actions of the Communists which made it difficult to achieve peace. At a meeting with Chou on August 9 Marshall made the significant statement that he could never be certain of the intentions of either side and therefore he found it difficult to take decisive action.[47] He was well aware that both sides were ready to use him and he was determined not to be used. He might on many occasions have brought decisive pressure to bear on either side but he could only do so at the risk of helping the one side to victory. His instructions called for a victory by neither side. Chou may not have believed that this was the most desirable outcome, but in all of his discussions with Marshall he sought to convey that he sincerely accepted Marshall's goal. Marshall never challenged Chou's sincerity but he was not loathe to let Chou know that he had reservations about the intentions of those for whom Chou spoke.

In late July, as full-scale war appeared imminent, Chou took the initiative in seeking to launch a reorganization of the government along the lines of the principles laid down by the Political Consultative Council. A start would, he reasoned, diminish the widespread feeling of futility. Marshall had been turning over a similar idea in his own mind and thought it might be possible to begin by setting up the proposed State Council. Within a few days Ambassador Stuart secured a tentative agreement from the Generalissimo to the appointment of a group of representatives of both parties to sit with Stuart serving as chairman to determine the first steps to be taken toward reorganization of the government.[48] But the Gimo laid down a set of demands the Communists must first meet . These demands added up to a large-scale withdrawal of Communist forces from territory which they occupied and the turning over of local governments in Kiangsu, long in the hands of the Communists, to the Nationalists. Chou termed the demands "high handed and dictatorial."[49]

After prolonged negotiations in which Marshall and Stuart took the lead, it was agreed to go ahead with the committee to be chaired by Stuart. Marshall's aim was to bring about the establishment of the State Council provided for by the draft constitution. Once established it should take over the negotiations. In the background the question of a cease fire persisted. It was the Communists who wished to see an end to the fighting. With this in mind Stuart proposed that Mao Tse-tung issue such an order to his commanders. Marshall and Stuart would then seek to have the Generalissimo do the same. If the Gimo declined, Marshall would then issue a news release stating the facts.

When Chou met with Marshall on August 29 he was prepared to

go along. Fearing that Chou might have been misled, Marshall endeavored to make fully clear to him that he would be taking certain risks. Marshall pointed out that his exchange with the Generalissimo offered no assurance as to how the Generalissimo would respond to the proposed cease-fire order by Mao.[50] This conversation represented the very epitome of Marshall's fair dealing. Marshall made clear his own assumptions regarding the thinking of both parties. The Communists, he assumed, "have practically reached the conclusion that the Government is intent on going ahead with military operations to gain at least more favorable positions and to proceed to use a general policy of force." Marshall explained, "So far as the Government is concerned I have assumed there are individuals, particularly military leaders in the Government who are firmly convinced that the policy of force is the only practical course, and they are also of the opinion that it is within their capability of carrying out such a policy."

Chou appeared as anxious as Marshall to take steps that gave promise of peace. Rarely have two representatives of two governments with so much at stake proceeded with such honest effort to find a peaceful solution.

Chou pursued his analysis of the possible effect on public opinion if the proposed steps ended in failure. Would the American government continue to support the Nationalists even though they must bear the responsibility for the breakdown of the negotiations? Marshall had devoted much time to relieving Chou's fears on previous occasions. He never pretended to speak for the future but he reiterated that the Truman administration had supported his efforts without reservation and had actually left the formulation of policy in his hands in spite of vigorous attacks within the United States. Now Marshall responded:

> The next point pertains to your reference to American support of the Government. In my opinion you are confusing propaganda with fact and Chinese propaganda is far from fact. It consists of any item that can be found, regardless of whether or not there is any actual support of hostilities involved. I have stopped, I think, almost every direct support of the Government in a military way and yet the propaganda would seem to indicate that the fight could not go on a week without the military supplies and support the U.S. Government is alleged to be giving the Kuomintang Party—otherwise the Government.[51]

Marshall then explained the recent transfer of American surplus property to the Central Government. Chou, in spite of fears that the government merely agreed to political discussions so as to prolong the war and evade agreement on a cease fire, consented to go ahead.

However, new difficulties soon led Chou to rescind his agreement. Public statements by government officials to the effect that Chiang would not issue a cease-fire order and that the cessation of hostilities would be left to the proposed State Council to discuss gave Chou some cause to reverse himself. Stuart and Marshall had previously agreed that the proposed discussion would make no progress unless hostilities ceased but they were not able to guarantee that Chiang would issue a cease-fire order. They saw no hope unless the committee to be chaired by Stuart met and made the effort. Chou, after another day of reflection, stated that there were three reasons why he could not agree: (1) failure to guarantee a cease-fire order; (2) the sale of surplus property by the United States to the National Government which would net that government revenue as the goods were sold; and (3) announcement by a Nationalist general that preparations were underway for an attack on Kalgan, a major Communist center.[52]

As the discussions continued the question of a cease fire was the most important, but before long most of the attention focused on the number of representatives the Communists were to have on the State Council. It had previously been specified by the PCC that one-third of the membership could veto a proposal. The communists lacked one of having the veto power and now insisted they must be given an additional vote. The negotiations ran into a final stumbling block when the Generalissimo said he would not agree to a cease fire until the Communists named their delegates to the National Assembly, which was now scheduled to meet in November.[53] The Communists had long been denouncing the calling of the National Assembly. It should meet, they maintained, in accordance with the recommendations of the PCC and not by the unilateral action of the Generalissimo. Marshall was as opposed as the Communists were to the Gimo's highhanded violation of the agreement reached by the PCC.

September came to a close with Chou remaining in Shanghai and refusing to consent to a meeting of the Stuart Committee. The Nationalists pushed ahead with a large-scale military offensive toward Kalgan. On September 30 Chou informed Marshall that if the government did not "instantly cease its military operations against Kalgan and the vicinity areas, the Chinese Communist Party feels itself forced to presume that the Government is thereby giving public announcement of a total national split, and that it has ultimately abandoned its pronounced policy of peaceful settlement."[54] Marshall and Stuart, bitter over the Nationalist offensive, felt they were being used as "stooges" by the government, which was only pretending to negotiate while in reality making war.[55] Marshall gave serious thought to requesting that his mission be terminated. On October 1 he sent a memorandum to the Generalissimo stating that unless a basis for agreement was found to terminate the fighting without further delay he would recommend to the President that he be recalled.[56] On October 5 Marshall sent a message recommending his recall.

Marshall's action so alarmed the Generalissimo that he immediately moved to give new life to the negotiations. He now proposed a ten-day truce and a compromise on membership in the State Council. The Communists rejected the truce, insisting that only if the government withdrew their troops to their original position and if there were no time limit on the truce would they agree. In a final effort, Marshall, on October 9, flew to Shanghai in the hope of committing Chou to a more moderate position. In a tense meeting, in which the cordiality of the two men in the past was missing, Chou insisted on an indefinite truce and then once again decried the assistance the National Government was receiving from the United States. Marshall, greatly discouraged by Chou's response, believed that Chou was now so much the victim of unjustified suspicions that there was no way to bring him about to see the facts. Chou had come to the conclusion that the proposal to establish a committee under the chairmanship of Stuart was simply another move on the part of the government to deceive the Communists into believing that the government was serious about negotiations when in fact it was determined to carry out a military offensive. Marshall's explanation that he was the originator of the proposal and that he had gained Chiang's acceptance only with the greatest of difficulty appeared to make no impression on Chou. The final blow came on October 12 when Nationalist forces captured Kalgan.

At this point communications between Marshall and Chou terminated temporarily, but members of China's third parties met with Chou in Shanghai. Marshall encouraged the minority parties in this effort and also urged them to unite into one effective organization capable of wielding significant influence. Chou returned to Nanking and again entered into discussions with Marshall and Stuart, but these meetings came to naught. The Communist spokesman saw in the meeting of the National Assembly the continued efforts of the reactionaries in the Kuomintang to stave off any meaningful participation in the government by Communists and by other parties. The National Assembly was meeting in violation of the procedures agreed upon by the Political Consultative Conference, and the Communists had consistently made adherence to the recommendations of the PCC the previous January a primary requisite for the establishment of a new government. Chou maintained that a military truce could not long survive the political split and was therefore a mere gesture put forth by the Nationalists as a screen to hide their scheme for perpetuating one-party control.

At their final meeting Marshall asked Chou whether Chou's return to Yenan meant that the Communist Party no longer wished to have Marshall participate as a mediator. Chou did not answer, whereupon Marshall asked him to ascertain the wishes of the authorities in Yenan and to give him an answer as soon as possible. No direct answer ever reached Marshall, but Communist demands made it clear that the Communists had reached a decision to terminate efforts at negotiation. On November 19 Chou returned to Yenan. While two representatives of the Communist Party remained in Nanking and met occasionally with Marshall and Stuart, the effort to bring about a peaceful settlement had come to an end.

The National Assembly met on November 12 and after a brief recess proceeded to deliberations on the draft constitution. The Democratic League did not officially participate but some members did take seats. The Youth Party and the Social Democratic Party did join the Assembly.[57] Before the close of the year agreement was reached on the new constitution. The debates were surprisingly free, and liberal representatives insisted on their right to be heard. Adherents of the C-C Clique threatened from time to time to revolt. Chiang Kai-shek attended the sessions, presided over many, and found himself unabashedly challenged.

The National Assembly did not represent China's masses. No one spoke for the peasants, more than eighty percent of the populace. The liberal document was a product of the efforts of the country's small middle class of professional people, businessmen, and educators. With some minor exceptions, the new constitution followed the draft of the PCC.

On December 1 Marshall, in anticipation of a meeting with the Generalissimo, met with leading members of the Embassy to discuss the new constitution. Present were W. Walton Butterworth, Minister-Counsellor, Raymond Ludden, Second Secretary, John F. Melby, Second Secretary, Philip D. Sprouse, Second Secretary, and Colonel J. Hart Caughey of Executive Headquarters. The Embassy representatives were men with a long experience in China and in the American foreign service. Marshall, unlike his predecessor Patrick Hurley, valued their judgment. Both Butterworth and Sprouse enjoyed Marshall's full confidence, and he had come to view them as invaluable assistants. They had never shared Marshall's cautious faith in the establishment of a coalition government as a solution to China's problem but, like Marshall, they sought faithfully to carry out their assignment. Butterworth contributed a sense of humor and wit plus an undeviating hardheaded analysis of the forces at work and from the beginning understood that the aims of the contesting parties dictated that they would use the American mediation effort to gain their own ends. Marshall was not unaware of this but, unlike Butterworth, he refused to become cynical and was determined to make selfish interests serve constructive ends.

At the meeting on December 1 the Embassy representatives agreed that the new constitution was based on the PCC resolutions, was democratic and adaptable to China's needs. But, like Marshall, they also believed that the new government, in spite of the merits of the constitution, would only be democratic if the people running the government were themselves democratic-minded and worked in the spirit of serving the people.[58] Marshall had prolonged his stay in the hope that the American presence during the sessions of the National Assembly would serve as a liberal influence. He, like his advisors, was fully aware that the political structure was less important than the character of the men who would make the structure serve their purposes.

Marshall had stayed away from the National Assembly sessions on the ground that his presence would be interpreted as sanctioning the unilateral way in which it had been convened.[59] He was wholly opposed to its meeting in a way that contravened the principles laid down by the PCC. Now that the Assembly was approaching its close he once again confronted the question of whether to ask for his own recall. He had no reason to believe that negotiations could be renewed. The Communists had laid down the conditions for renewal of mediation: (1) the dismissal of the National Assembly; (2) the convening of a new one; and (3) the return of armed forces to the positions they had occupied prior to January 13. The Nationalist military leaders were intent on crushing the Communists by force. Marshall believed that they could never achieve this goal and that the time had already arrived when economic catastrophe was about to overtake the government. Unlike Ambassador Stuart, who had great faith in Chiang Kai-shek, Marshall saw that the Gimo was as committed as the reactionaries were to the futile policy of a military solution. In moments of crisis Chiang always fell back on the advice of the most reactionary elements, the very ones Marshall held guilty of undermining his own efforts at mediation.

At the meeting with the leading members of the Embassy staff, Marshall raised the question of his own departure. Should he leave, he explained, Dr. Stuart would continue as Ambassador and Executive Headquarters would remain. In reply to Marshall's question as to what effect his leaving might have on the general situation, Butterworth stated that Marshall's presence in China was a desirable restraining influence on the government. Then he added, according to the minutes, "that he felt General Marshall's departure would be catastrophic, and in view of Dr. Stuart's inclinations, would cause the United States, as far as policy is concerned, to drift toward full support of the National Government."[60] Marshall took a different view. He believed that as long as he remained many, and particularly the reactionary group in the Kuomintang, would find it necessary to keep him in the picture but they would continue their undemocratic practices and military campaigns "under the guise of a willingness to negotiate." This, Marshall thought, placed him "in a position which could compromise the United States policy."[61]

For several months Marshall had been well informed about the campaign of Henry Luce and Roy Howard of the Scripps-Howard newspapers to change American policy to one of all-out support of the National Government. A cablegram stating Luce's position prompted Marshall's judgment that the argument was shallow and reflected Luce's bias in favor of the Gimo.[62] Aid to the government, he said, was likely to strength the hands of the reactionaries, thereby canceling out any chance of reform. On December 9, in a conference with Wei Tso-ming, Vice President of the Legislative Yuan, Marshall again referred to the efforts of Luce and Howard. That effort, he thought, would lead to a strong argument in the United States and only serve to expose "a lot of dirt to the disadvantage of both sides." The reactionaries, Marshall advised, would make a serious error "If they crippled the Constitution . . . on the hope of aid from the United States as a result of the Luce-Howard publicity campaign." The United States said Marshall, "was dead set against condoning the civil war in China." American public opinion, he asserted, "was affected by corruption within the Kuomintang more than by fear of Communist ideology."[63]

In a lengthy telegram to President Truman explaining the total situation and summarizing a discussion he had with the Generalissimo, Marshall closed with the statement:

> Now that the Constitution has been adopted there is no real place for me in the coming maneuvers to reopen negotiations and my continued presence will constitute an embarrassment to future adjustment, especially if I speak out frankly as I feel I must, which will generate bitter feelings among many on both sides.[64]

His decision came as no surprise. The President had long been aware that Marshall's resignation was only a matter of time. In the eyes of the President and Dean Acheson, Marshall had served well although futilely, and they had supported him unstintingly even to the unprecedented degree that it was Marshall who had formulated China policy in 1946.

Notes to Chapter XI

1. History—Executive Headquarters, Peiping, Vol. I. Marshall Mission Papers, 92–PG1–0.1 47330. Federal Records Center at Suitland, Maryland.

2. Marshall to President Truman, February 9, 1946. *USFR The Far East: China 1946*, Vol. IX, pp. 426–29.

3. History—Executive Headquarters, Section XIII, October-December 1946, pp. 25–27; 92–PG1–0.1. Marshall Mission Papers.

4. Statement made by General Chou En-lai to General Marshall Regarding Chinese Position Toward Manchuria, March 10, 1946. *USFR The Far East: China 1946*, Vol. IX, pp. 529–35.

5. Ibid.

6. Ibid.

7. Minutes of General Chou En-lai's Interview With General Marshall. *USFR The Far East: China 1946*, Vol. IX, pp. 535-38.

8. Robert L. Smyth, Counselor of Embassy, to the Secretary of State, March 11, 1946, ibid., pp. 538–40.

9. History—Executive Headquarters, Peiping Headquarters Group Section V, Operations D, Section I, Introduction.

10. Memorandum by Chou to Marshall, April 29, 1946, *USFR The Far East: China, 1946*, pp. 648–49.

11. Meeting of the Acting Committee of Three at Hankow, May 5, 1946, ibid., pp. 663–64.

12. Ibid., May 8, 1946, pp. 669–79.

13. Ibid., pp. 683–84.

14. Byroade to Gillem, March 28, 1946, ibid., pp. 714–15.

15. Memorandum by Chou to Gillem, March 31, 1946, ibid., pp. 719–20.

16. Memorandum by Gillem to Chou, April 1, 1946, ibid., pp. 720–21.

17. Memorandum by Gillem to Chou, April 5, 1946, ibid., p. 732.

18. Walter S. Robertson to Gillem, April 3, 1946, ibid., p. 728.

19. Marshall to Gillem, April 6, 1946, ibid., pp. 737–38.

20. Walter S. Robertson to Gillem, April 7, 1946, ibid., pp. 739–40.

21. C. Gillem to Marshall, April 8, 1946, ibid., pp. 742–44.

22. Memorandum by Chou to Gillem, April 10, 1946, ibid., pp. 752–53.

23. Clubb to the Secretary of State, April 11, 1946, ibid., pp. 755–57.

24. Minutes of Meeting Between General Marshall and General Yu Ta-wei, April 22, 1946, ibid., pp. 788–90.

25. Minutes of Meeting Between General Marshall and General Chou En-lai, April 23, 1946, ibid., pp. 790–92.

26. Marshall to President Truman, May 6, 1945, ibid., pp. 815–18.

27. Robertson to Marshall, May 21, 1946, ibid., pp. 866–68.

28. Notes by General Marshall of Meeting with Generalissimo Chiang Kai-shek at Nanking, May 22, 1946, ibid., pp. 880–81.

29. Madame Chiang Kai-shek to Marshall, May 24, 1946, ibid., pp. 891–92.

31. Memorandum by Marshall to T. V. Soong, President of the Executive Yuan, May 29, 1946, ibid., p. 912.

32. Marshall to President Truman, June 5, 1946, ibid., pp. 977–79.

33. Ibid.

34. John F. Melby, Second Secretary of the Embassy, Memorandum on Political Situation in China, June 13, 1946, ibid., pp. 1045–46.

35. Marshall to President Truman, June 17, 1946, ibid., pp. 1099–1101.

36. Minutes of Meeting Between General Marshall, General Hsu Yung-chang, and General Yu Ta-wei, June 18, 1946, ibid., p. 1093.

37. Marshall to President Truman, June 26, 1946, ibid., pp. 1201–1203.

38. Notes of Meeting Between General Marshall and Generalissimo Chiang Kai-shek, June 27, 1946, ibid., pp. 1215–18.

39. Ibid.

40. Minutes of Meeting Between General Marshall and General Chou En-lai, June 26, 1946, ibid., p. 1205.

41. Ibid., pp. 1210–11.

42. Ibid., p. 1214.

43. Notes of Meeting Between General Marshall and Generalissimo Chiang Kai-shek, June 27, 1946, ibid., p. 1216.

44. Notes on Meeting Between General Marshall and Generalissimo Chiang Kai-shek, June 30, 1946, ibid., pp. 1263–65.

45. Minutes of Meeting Between General Marshall and General Yu Ta-wei, July 13, 1946, ibid., pp. 1353–54.

46. Ibid.

47. Minutes of Meeting Between General Marshall and General Chou En-lai, August 9, 1946, ibid., p. 1489.

48. Marshall to President Truman, August 2, 1946, ibid., pp. 1439–40.

49. Stuart to the Secretary of State, August 7, 1946, ibid., pp. 1465–68.

50. Minutes of Meeting Between General Marshall and General Chou En-lai, August 29, 1946. *USFR The Far East: China*, Vol. X, pp. 96–107.

51. Ibid., p. 105.

52. Minutes of Meeting Between General Marshall, Dr. Stuart, and General Chou En-lai, September 6, 1946, ibid., p. 154.

53. Marshall to President Truman, September 6, 1946, ibid., pp. 160–62.

54. Memorandum by General Chou En-lai to General Marshall, September 30, 1946, ibid., pp. 258–59.

55. Notes on Meeting Between General Marshall and Dr. Stuart, October 1, 1946, ibid., pp. 260–62.

56. Memorandum by General Marshall to Generalissimo Chiang Kai-shek, October 1, 1946, ibid., pp. 267–68.

57. Ambassador Stuart to the Secretary of State, November 29, 1946, ibid., pp. 570–71.

58. Minutes of Meeting Between General Marshall and Mr. Butterworth, December 1, 1946, ibid., pp. 573–75.

59. Marshall to President Truman, November 16, 1946, ibid., pp. 547–48.

60. Minutes of Meeting Between General Marshall and Mr. Butterworth, December 1, 1946, ibid., pp. 573–75.

61. Ibid.

62. Minutes of Meeting Between General Marshall and Dr. Stuart, December 9, 1946, ibid., pp. 599–602.

63. Minutes of Meeting Between General Marshall and Dr. Wei Tao-ming, December 9, 1946, ibid., pp. 602–605.

64. Marshall to President Truman, December 28, 1946, ibid., pp. 661–65.

CHAPTER XII

Irreconcilable Differences

In the course of his stay in China, General Marshall encountered a varying response to his efforts. The Kuomintang militarists and reactionaries did not attack him directly but publicly advocated policies that revealed that in their estimate Marshall alone stood between them and their crushing of the Communists. Marshall knew only too well that the restraint of the Nationalists from personal attacks had its source in the continued hope that the United States might yet come to their aid. Chiang Kai-shek listened to Marshall even when the American general was blunt in his criticism and indicted his regime, a gracious virtue for which Marshall gladly gave him credit. His relations with Chiang were cordial; both were frank with each other; yet Chiang, although himself conciliatory, found it necessary or perhaps preferred to accept the advice of those in his regime who opposed compromise.

Of more enduring significance were the relations between the United States and the Communists. Marshall engaged Chou En-lai in closer and more frequent consultations than he did any other Chinese. In considerable part this came about on the initiative of Chou who worked with great energy to bring about a peaceful transition to a new order. Marshall and Chou worked together in a manner conducive to frankness, to compromise, and to mutual respect. Chou was not always fully cognizant of Marshall's firmness with Chiang and the Nationalists, for Marshall could not share with him how he opposed, sought to persuade, or warned that the United States was unalterably opposed to becoming involved in the fratricidal conflict. At the same time, Marshall appears to have respected Chou, although he believed that the extreme Communists were no less determined to win at all costs than were the extreme Nationalists.

This good working relationship did not prevent an ever-widening breach between the United States and the Communists. The persistency of the Communists in attacking the United States served as a measure of the growing division. The attacks on the United States and on Marshall slipped into high gear on June 14, 1946, when Mao denounced the American government as reactionary, as seeking to reduce China to colonial status and to an appendage of American capitalism and charged that it was the United States who was carrying on the civil war in China for the purpose of suppressing democracy. From that date on the anti-American campaign increased in intensity and in extremism.

In terms of Chinese domestic politics the Communists had much to gain by this propaganda campaign. The presence of the United States caused deep resentment far beyond Communist circles. American correspondents, among them Nathaniel Peffer, reported strong hostility, especially among the educated classes.[1] The Communists exploited this sentiment with success, identifying the Kuomintang as the party ready to serve foreign interests. A hundred years of humiliation at the hands of foreign nations had left a heritage of distrust, which made it easy to place the blame for domestic difficulties on the foreigner.

The vitriolic attack on Marshall and the United States was more than a propaganda device motivated by a desire to gain wider public support. It was the product of a genuine conviction that the United States continued to assist the Nationalists in spite of their failure to give Marshall support and to adhere to agreements he negotiated. That the Truman administration was sincerely seeking the establishment of a unified government and was convinced that this goal required a broadening of the political base in China and an end to the one-party dictatorship made no great difference. The Communists came to their conclusion by the actions of the United States, and these seemed to them to make lies out of Truman's and Marshall's professions.

In a statement issued at Yenan on December 28 Chou En-lai cited the facts as he saw them. The United States had transported nine Nationalist armies to Manchuria, supposedly to establish Chinese sovereignty but in reality to make war on the Communists. American marines had been stationed in North China under the pretext of carrying out repatriation of the Japanese but in actuality to prevent the Communist democratic governments from exercising sovereignty. In spite of the fact that it was the Nationalists who had violated the truce agreements, the United States had continued to extend aid to the Nationalist Government. Some forty-five Nationalist army divisions had been equipped by the United States. Chou cited the continuance of lend-lease aid to the extent of 1,500,000,000 U.S. dollars, the turning over of 271 war vessels, and the sale of 855 million U.S. dollars worth of surplus property, and loans totaling 66 million U.S. dollars. Chou then gave way to a cynical assessment:

> Aim of the barefaced policy of the United States Government aiding Chiang to wage civil war is to force Chinese people into suppression and transform China entirely into a dependency of the United States. From recently concluded Sino-American "treaty of friendship, commerce and navigation, Sino-American air agreement, the agreement on United States military advisory group and various kinds of military training it can be proved that the action of Chiang Kai-shek's Government in selling out the state sovereignty and national interests fits with the policy of the United States Government—assisting Chiang Kai-shek to wage the civil war.[2]

Chou's indictment told almost as much about the Communist fear of annihilation at the hands of the Kuomintang as it did about the facts, but his attack was not mere rhetoric inspired by imaginary grievances. In the less tense atmosphere of negotiating with Marshall, Chou leveled the same basic accusation.

Marshall recognized the bases for the charges but he did not permit criticism of his own role to influence him or to deflect his efforts to be impartial. He also firmly believed that the picture conjured up by the Communists was false and one generated by fear, distrust, and suspicion. He objected to it in large part because the propagandists eventually believed it themselves and were therefore less and less capable of objective analysis.

Marshall sought earnestly to remove the grounds for distrust and at the same time to put the facts in what he saw to be their proper setting to reduce Chou's apprehensions. He explained the assistance rendered to the National Government during the first several months of his mission as the honorable discharge of commitments made during the war and immediately following hostilities. The transport of troops to North China and Manchuria was no more than acting in good faith toward an ally assisting it to resume control over its territory and to repatriate the three million Japanese. He was concerned, too, about the presence of 53,000 American marines but he did not see them as participants in the civil war. They were there to protect the railroad that carried coal to Shanghai and enabled that city to carry on some degree of economic activity of direct benefit to the people of that city. Aside from that, the marines were present in Peking and along the route to the sea to provide security for the Americans in Executive Headquarters. Marshall worried about their presence, recognized that their presence was offensive to native pride and lent itself to unfortunate incidents; and before he left, the number had been reduced to 5,000.

Marshall saw no reason to apologize for an Export-Import Bank loan financing the shipment of cotton to enable the Shanghai textile industry to relieve serious unemployment. And he took pride in the sale of surplus war material which contained nothing of direct use to the government in fighting the Communists but did provide consumer goods plus earth-moving machinery and trucks to a country desperately in need of transportation.[3] After June he could rightfully say that the United States was transporting no troops and supplying nothing in the way of military assistance. He acknowledged that this assistance had proved troublesome to his negotiations. At the same time Marshall was deeply aware that a termination of past commitments and an almost complete withdrawal at once of American forces would constitute such a repudiation of the Chiang regime as to topple it or at least make the action less than impartial. In short, Marshall's understanding of impartiality included reluctance to withdraw all forms of assistance to the established government in such an abrupt manner as to discredit it. As Marshall saw it, to do so would have been partiality in favor of the government's enemies.

Essentially the same viewpoint prevailed in the Department of State, whose approval was necessary to the granting of any kind of assistance. Dean Acheson played the role of judge, and he and Marshall did not differ in their viewpoints. Both enjoyed the confidence of President Truman who subscribed to the dictum that no assistance should be given which would contribute to the civil war.

In the eyes of the Communists this did not add up to neutrality. Whatever contributed in any way to the possible improvement of economic conditions in China constituted intervention. It mattered not that the aim of the United States in transporting armies to Manchuria was to establish Chinese sovereignty when Nationalist military leaders then employed the troops against the Communists. The Communists, as Marshall stated, lived in extreme fear of their extinction as a party and they saw the assistance rendered in terms of the dire consequences for themselves.

A part of the difficulty arose from the United States role as mediator. This imposed obligations of impartiality beyond what is required in more normal circumstances. Communist protests, ironically, did not become significant until June and did not explode into a full blown anti-United States campaign until September. By that time the American military presence had been sharply reduced and the United States had terminated transport of Nationalist troops. The United States government was also rejecting many kinds of Nationalist appeals for assistance and denying export licenses for any goods useful in fighting. The rigid adherence to a neutral policy shocked the Nationalists, and in the years ahead they attributed their defeat to the rulings of Marshall on aid.

However, American interests in China both strategically and economically stood in the way of adopting a hands-off policy. The effort to create a unified government was in itself dictated by these interests. Given the near economic collapse in China, unemployment, inflation, destruction of transportation facilities, and the woefully weak state of its armed forces, these interests appeared threatened. The most immediate of these interests was the balance of power. In a significant note on policy Dean Acheson, on November 23, 1946, telegraphed Marshall:

> As you know, one of our principal concerns, if not our principal concern, in endeavoring to bring about peace and unity in China, has been to forestall China's becoming a serious irritant in our relations with

Russia. There has been much loose talk about China's becoming the stabilizing influence in the Far East. We have never felt that this was a possibility in the reasonably near future but we have hoped that China would not become an unstabilizing influence—which is an entirely different thing. There is also loose talk about China's inability to fill the "power vacuum" in the Far East created by the defeat of Japan. . . . From our point of view there is no power vacuum in the Far East. It seems to have been filled by Russia and ourselves. Therefore, the principal problem is adjustment of our relations there with the Russians without prejudice to our legitimate interests.[4]

Other powers would be welcome to participate, said Acheson, but he also affirmed "we do not intend to relinquish our leadership."

From the beginning of the postwar period the United States had viewed China as weak and incapable of achieving significant strength. Old habits of thought and traditional attitudes toward China made for paternalism. The United States aimed to take the lead in creating a stable situation conducive to peace and also favorable to economic interests. At the outset of the Marshall mission, on December 15, 1945, President Truman stated that the United States would not intervene in China's internal affairs. This pronouncement was followed by an injunction to all departments and agencies that no negotiations with the Chinese for assistance were to be entered into without the approval of the Department of State. There was also the clear understanding that Marshall was to withhold assistance to the Central Government until that government took steps to meet the requirement of a broadly based democratic government. Marshall had the power to veto any aid that would undermine his bargaining powers.

There were important exceptions. It was already decided at the time of Marshall's departure for China that the United States would transport Nationalist armies to Manchuria and likewise furnish these armies with the military equipment required. It was likewise decided that various types of naval transport vessels were to be transferred to the Chinese for taking over this transport responsibility. There were also important exceptions in the form of commitments already entered into, the equipment of thirty-nine Chinese army divisions and the training within the United States of air force pilots. In addition, there were already present in North China 53,000

American marines allegedly deployed to assist in Japanese repatriation. These commitments would clearly favor the recognized legal government even though not entered into with the aim of helping the government crush the Communists.

Further development of the aid program, after the President's policy statements of December 15, added to the problems. Lend-lease was to expire in June 1946 and this fact immediately prompted the War and Navy Departments to seek to meet Chinese requirements within the time limit. Every effort was made to determine what these requirements were. Secretary of War Robert Patterson informed the Secretary of State on February 18 that the total dollar value of lend-lease aid from the end of the war and what could be expected to be furnished by the following October would be approximately $839,950,223. Some $66,658,917 was for ammunition.[5]

Aid beyond what could be provided under lend-lease up to June 30 would have to be made under separate agreements with China. During the war China had paid for the maintenance of American forces in China and the resulting American debt to the National Government could be liquidated at least in part by the transfer of goods. Shipments could also be financed through loans from the Export-Import Bank and through UNRRA. The first aid extended after the establishment of the Marshall Mission was a $22,657,485 loan from the Export-Import Bank whereby China was enabled to buy American cotton for the Shanghai textile industry.[6] In 1946, the Export-Import Bank approved a loan of $26,300,000 for cargo vessels, railroad equipment, coal mining machinery and equipment, and power plants. In June the State-War-Navy Coordinating Committee presented a report emphasizing the importance of Manchuria and the danger of the Soviet Union achieving a predominant influence, but again the Committee gave major stress to encouraging social and political reform in China. There was no departure from the earlier enunciation of policy on assistance. All assistance to China should be contingent upon the reform of China's government.[7]

In July the Chinese Supply Commission requested an export license for 40,000 steel castings for machine gun barrels and was also negotiating large orders for ammunition. Marshall placed no barrier to the orders but with the understanding that when those supplies were ready for shipment they would be withheld should that course be dictated by continuing conflict in China. In granting approval of the orders the State Department added that a proviso be appended to the agreement stating that they would only be shipped if "destined for an integrated and representative National Army under a coalition government."[8]

In July the Chinese also sought to buy from the Foreign Liquidation Commission a number of planes for use by the Chinese Air Force. The Chinese government had purchased a large number of surplus transport planes for commercial use. The new order included trainer planes convertible to military use. Because of this the State Department refused to approve the purchase. This decision was adhered to in spite of the fact that the planes were intended to complete the earlier commitment to assist China in establishing an air force of 8 1/3 Groups. The completion of that program was placed under temporary suspension.[9]

China desperately needed ships for transport of troops and supplies and also for the transport of goods to be used in meeting the needs of her economy. Early in 1946 China was permitted to lease several American liberty ships, and these carried troops and military supplies to Manchuria. The Communists protested vigorously and gave this practice wide publicity. Marshall then urged that the ships be sold to the Chinese. After prolonged debate the Maritime Commission and the National Advisory Council on August 22 approved the sale of 159 war-built commercial vessels valued at approximately $76 million; but in approving this transaction Marshall stipulated that the United States should be free to terminate the program whenever transfers appeared to violate American interests.[10]

One of the most highlighted transactions was the Surplus Property Agreement signed on August 30. This involved the transfer of civilian goods accumulated during the war in China and in other parts of the Pacific. It did not include any military equipment, but Chou En-lai protested that the revenue from the sale of the goods would strengthen the hands of the Central Government. Marshall had sought to promote the transfer to China during his visit in Washington in March, viewing the availability of these goods to the Chinese people as an asset. There was a delay of several months due to the Chinese haggling over the price and to decisions to turn some of the goods over to the Philippines and to return some to the United States.

The lapse of time was a matter of importance because most of the goods were in open storage and subject to rapid deterioration. Marshall bluntly told Chou, "It was a question of either completing this negotiation with China or immediately disposing of the 'cream' of the property to other governments in the Far East and dumping the remainder into the ocean." Marshall observed, "If your, and the Communist Party, recommendations and propaganda had been accepted, the people of China would have been denied the whole for the future."[11] The Communists rejected the explanation and denounced the transaction as deliberate interference in China's civil conflict.

Rightly or wrongly, depending upon the position of the observer, the aid program of the United States—in spite of the restrictions placed upon it, in spite of good intentions to render aid to the people of China, and in spite of the legitimate interest in both repatriation of the Japanese and the establishment of China's sovereignty in Manchuria—did strengthen the Central Government and that government diverted every ounce of assistance possible into crushing the Communists. However, the assistance was only a minor element, only one factor in the fratricidal war, but from a Communist viewpoint a matter of major concern. Even more it bred suspicion and gave rise to charges that the United States was following a double-faced policy of promoting peace under the label of mediation and civil conflict through its assistance program.

The aim of that program, nevertheless, was to counteract possible Soviet efforts to gain a dominating position in Manchuria and perhaps North China. The suspicions entertained made their way into the formulation of American policy. Distrust of Russian intentions was a primary factor in the establishment of the Marshall mission and in the decision of December 1945 to aid in the transportation of Nationalist troops into Manchuria.

The fear was reaffirmed by the State-War-Navy Coordinating Committee in early June 1946[12] and again in an estimate of Soviet aims in August. The War Department summary, which included this estimate, warned of the danger of withdrawing from China in the event of failure to establish a coalition government. "Our exclusion from China," the summary stated, "would probably result, within the next generation, in an expansion of Soviet influence over the manpower, raw materials and industrial production of Manchuria and China." It continued, "The U.S. and the world might then be faced in the China Sea and southward with a Soviet power analogous to the Japanese in 1941, but with the difference that the Soviets could be perhaps overwhelming[ly] strong in Europe and the Middle East as well."[13] The commitment of the United States to a policy aimed at forestalling a showdown with the Soviet Union over the question of Manchuria explains in considerable part why actions were taken that were inconsistent with the neutral role of the United States as mediator.

Twenty years later China was to share these fears, but the Communists in 1945 were concerned with the more immediate dangers from the Kuomintang and the possibility that the limited aid program of the United States in 1946 would drift into an all-out program of military assistance. Their distrust was nourished by other developments aside from American aid. The Communists embodied the frenzied determination to exclude foreigners that had prevailed in China during the Nationalist revolution of the 1920s. However, they did not have a monopoly of the feeling that China must no longer be dominated by foreign powers. The feeling was widespread and it militated against both the Russians who met with violent hostility in Manchuria and against Americans in the cities of central China.

American policy in 1946 underestimated the strength of Chinese nationalism. Consequently, the Navy made an effort to buy and also to lease land for the establishment of a naval station in North China and were only dissuaded by Ambassador Stuart who had lived through the Nationalist revolution of the 1920s and had some realization of their strong feelings.[14] The Army was equally determined to send a large military mission and specified conditions which were offensive to Chinese nationalism. Americans were aggressive in seeking rights for commercial airlines, and the Air Force proposed to acquire landing fields. Finally, in November 1946, a commercial treaty was negotiated. The hard-pressed National Government conceded privileges it would not have granted under other circumstances. The Communists seized upon these, charged that the United States aimed at reducing China to a colonial dependency. It was politically useful to the Communists to do so, but their nationalistic feelings assured a sense of injury. The fears of the Chinese were

exaggerated, but the general reaction of the Chinese was understandable.

*   *   *   *

The Marshall mission shortly became the center of one of the most
heated political controversies in the history of American foreign
relations. This came to a culmination in the Senate Judiciary subcommittee hearings on the Institute of Pacific Relations in 1951 and the
subsequent efforts of Senator Joseph McCarthy to impeach the loyalty of those who had been participants in relations with China during and immediately following World War II. The nature of the
charges, the star chamber nature of the proceedings before the Senate subcommittee, and the readiness to engage in character assassi-
nation were inconsistent with an objective inquiry into the question
of the strengths and weaknesses of America's China policy and consequently diverted attention from the forces operating in China. Those
forces determined the final outcome.

The aim of the United States, the reform of China's government
so as to include all parties and to substitute peaceful political decision
making for fratricidal strife, was in accord with American national
interests but beyond attainment. The effort was based on a serious
underestimate of the wide divergence in the aims of the contestants
and the irreconcilability of their dogmatically held convictions. The
effort proved to be futile. More unfortunate was the fact that it
involved the United States in China's internal affairs and created
lasting ill will and distrust on the part of Nationalists, Communists,
and a considerable part of the Chinese people.

Notes to Chapter XII

1. Minutes of Meeting Between General Marshall and Dr. Stuart, December 18, 1946, *USFR The Far East: China*, Vol. X, p. 638.

2. Ambassador Stuart to the Secretary of State, January 1, 1947, ibid., pp. 672–79.
   Chou En-lai was misleading in his charge. The figure of $1.5 billion included lend-lease from early 1941 until it was terminated in 1946. At the end of the war China had procured approximately $50 million worth of goods in the United States that remained to be shipped. By September 30, 1946 $40,117,000 had been shipped to China. *Twenty-Third Report to Congress on Lend-Lease Operation: for the Period Ended September 30, 1946*, Department of State Publications 2707.

3. Minutes of Meeting Between General Marshall and General Chou En-lai, September 4, 1946, ibid., pp. 121–22.

4. Colonel Marshall S. Carter to General Marshall, November 23, 1946, ibid., pp. 559–60.

5. Patterson to the Secretary of State, February 18, 1946, ibid., pp. 728–29.

6. James Byrnes, Secretary of State, to the Embassy in China, February 21, 1946, ibid., pp. 947–48.

7. Memorandum by the State-War-Navy Coordinating Committee to the Secretary of State, ibid., Vol. IX, pp. 933–45.

8. Acheson to the Administrator of the War Assets Administration, August 6, 1946, ibid., Vol. X, pp. 755–56.

9. Acheson to the Foreign Liquidation Commission, August 13, 1946, ibid., p. 783.

10. Colonel Marshall S. Carter to General Marshall, August 22, 1946 and General Marshall to Colonel Carter, September 4, 1946, ibid., pp. 800–801.

11. Minutes of Meeting Between Marshall and Chou En-lai, September 4, 1946, ibid., p. 122.

12. In its report the State-War-Navy Coordinating Committee concluded that there was a possibility that the Soviet Union would seek to control the Communist movement in China through small groups of Nationals "who will seek to turn legitimate indigenous liberal programs to Soviet ends." The report stated: "In Manchuria especially the USSR is expected to seek to foster the establishment of an autonomous state dominated by the Soviet Union. Such a state

would be receptive to Soviet requests for economic concessions, would eliminate any potential threat to Siberia, and might eventually be absorbed in the Soviet Union. With or without such physical incorporation into the U.S.S.R., a Manchuria integrated into the Russian economy would prove a grave threat to the United States as well as to China. The resulting self-sufficiency of the U.S.S.R. in the Far East would, taken together with her western industries, place under the control of the Soviet Union the greatest agglomeration of power in the history of the world. China without Manchuria would be no effective counter-poise to maintain the balance of power in the Far East." The committee thought trade with Manchuria would "not for decades assume real importance to our economic structure except as Manchurian resources can be utilized to strengthen China, improve her standard of living, and make of her a better customer for our products. While such an eventuality would be of considerable importance, it is the benefit to China itself which is of most importance to the United States in terms of our present policy toward China and in terms of our basic interests, which appear to require an Asiatic counter-poise to Russia." Memorandum by the State-War-Navy Coordinating Committee to the Secretary of State, June 1, 1946. Subject: Security Implications in Manchurian Situation, ibid., Vol IX, pp. 933–45.

13.   Colonel Carter to General Marshall, August 14, 1946, ibid., Vol. X, pp. 27–28.

14.   Ambassador Stuart to the Secretary of State, December 30, 1946, ibid., pp. 808–10.

Index